# The Great Recoil

# The Great Recoil

## Politics after Populism and Pandemic

Paolo Gerbaudo

**VERSO**
London • New York

First published by Verso 2021

1 3 5 7 9 10 8 6 4 2

**Verso**
UK: 6 Meard Street, London W1F 0EG

US: 20 Jay Street, Suite 1010, Brooklyn, NY 11201
versobooks.com

Verso is the imprint of New Left Books

ISBN-13: 978-1-78873-050-1
ISBN-13: 978-1-78873-053-2 (US EBK)
ISBN-13: 978-1-78873-052-5 (UK EBK)

**British Library Cataloguing in Publication Data**
A catalogue record for this book is available from the British Library

**Library of Congress Cataloging-in-Publication Data**

Names: Gerbaudo, Paolo, author.
Title: The great recoil : politics after populism and pandemic / Paolo
    Gerbaudo.
Description: First edition hardback. | Brooklyn : Verso Books, 2021. |
    Includes bibliographical references and index. | Summary: "In these
    times of pandemic, economic collapse, populist anger and ecological
    threat, societies are turning inward in search of protection.
    Neoliberalism, which has presided over decades of market globalisation,
    is on trial, while state intervention is making a spectacular comeback
    amid lockdowns, mass vaccination programmes, deficit spending and
    environmental planning. This is the Great Recoil, the era when the
    politics of national sovereignty, economic protection and democratic
    control overrides the neoliberal ideology of free markets, labour
    flexibility and business opportunity"— Provided by publisher.
Identifiers: LCCN 2021015707 (print) | LCCN 2021015708 (ebook) | ISBN
    9781788730501 (hardback) | ISBN 9781788730532 (ebk)
Subjects: LCSH: Neoliberalism—Economic aspects. | Populism. |
    Globalization.
Classification: LCC HB95 .G448 2021  (print) | LCC HB95  (ebook) | DDC
    330.15—dc23
LC record available at https://lccn.loc.gov/2021015707
LC ebook record available at https://lccn.loc.gov/2021015708

Typeset in Minion by Hewer Text UK Ltd, Edinburgh
Printed and bound by CPI Group (UK) Ltd, Croydon CR0 4YY

# Contents

*Acknowledgements*                                    vii

Introduction                                            1
1 The Post-neoliberal Horizon                          18
2 Global Blowback                                       43
3 Sovereignty                                           68
4 Protection                                            96
5 Control                                              120
6 The New Social Blocs                                 144
7 Enemies of the People                                169
8 The Post-pandemic State                              196
9 Democratic Patriotism                                224
  Conclusion                                           249

*Index*                                                265

# Acknowledgements

I am grateful to all the colleagues, friends and comrades that made this book possible. First and foremost, I would like to thank my editors at Verso for guiding and supporting me throughout the four long years it took me to finalise the volume, to the readers who provided useful advice, and to my personal editor Alex Foti for his constant advice and inspiration. The invitations to give talks on contemporary ideology by Yannis Stavrakakis and the Populismus research group at the University of Thessaloniki; Ege Moritz and Johannes Springer at the Department for Cultural Anthropology and European Ethnology at the University of Göttingen; Jan-Werner Müller and the Project in the History of Political Thought at the Center for Human Values at Princeton University; Marcos Nobre and the Mecila Research Centre in São Paulo in Brazil; and Josep Ramoneda and the Escola Europea d'Humanitats in Barcelona provided invaluable occasions to discuss some of the ideas that inform the book.

I am strongly indebted to the people who reviewed a first draft of the manuscript: Mirko Canevaro, Nadia Urbinati, Gaetano Inglese, Anton Jäger, Jacopo Custodi, Carlo Mongini, George Venizelos, Caspar Below, Brenda Vázquez Uribe, Louis Bayman, Darren Loucaides, Cesar Jimenez Martinez, Sabrina Provenzani, Jeffrey Broxmeyer, Patricia Ferreira, Ed Hadfield, Mariana Galvão Lyra, Roy Cobby Avaria, Adam Bull, Matteo Santarelli, Francesco Marchesi, Angelo Boccato, Natalia Miranda and Giuseppe Nardiello. I would also like to thank my colleagues and comrades for the fruitful conversations that offered insights for this book, and in particular Breno Bringel, Geoffrey Pleyers, Mark Coté, James Butler, Aaron Bastani, Jeremy Gilbert, Jennifer Pybus, Benjamin Fogel, Jodi Dean, Emanuele Ferragina, Lucia Rubinelli, Richard Barbrook, Jan Blommaert, Fabio Malini, Joan Subirats, Guendalina Anzolin, Simone Gasperin, Stathis Kouvelakis, Samuele Mazzolini, Tommaso Nencioni, James Meadway, Antonio Calleja and Javier Toret.

Last but foremost, I am grateful to my partner, Lara Pelaez, and my family and friends, for their inspiration and their constant support.

# Introduction

A number of traumatic events, starting with the 2008 economic recession and culminating with the coronavirus crisis, all combined with the impending ecological disaster of climate change, have shaken all political certainties and plunged Western capitalism into political chaos, causing societies to be dominated by anxiety and fear. This is the Great Recoil – a period when the coordinates of history seem to have been reversed. Things that have been taken for granted for a generation – globalisation; freedom of movement; economic growth; the clear demarcation of geopolitical friends, rivals and enemies – all seem to have been thrown into question, creating much disorientation and consternation in polities around the world. The Great Recoil is the moment when societies turn backward and inward: when globalisation goes into retreat, the economy contracts and is barely propped up by massive injections of money by central banks; when people have to withdraw to their homes due to lockdowns, quarantines and confinement measures, and must shrink from contact with others. It is the time when society 'returns to itself', when the shock vis-à-vis the negativity of the world leads to a desperate yearning for interiority and autonomy, and we have to collectively address foundational questions concerning society's basic conditions of existence and self-reproduction.

The Great Recoil is a Hegelian metaphor that captures the process of profound ideological transformation at a moment of organic crisis in democratic capitalist societies. Neoliberalism, the economic and political philosophy that shelved the post-war social-democratic consensus and remade the world in the name of freedom by boosting private initiative and social inequality over the last forty years, seems incapable of providing responses to emerging historical dilemmas. The old dogmas of free market economics that have held sway since the 1980s on both the left and the right now look like the rusty remains of a gullible era; meanwhile the pandemic has demonstrated the folly of cuts to the public budget in the name of fiscal austerity, which have left health and education systems in tatters.

As the neoliberal worldview started to falter with the post-2008 Great Recession, new movements emerged on the right and the left, often jointly described as manifestations of a 'populist moment'. From the 2011 protest movements to the Brexit referendum, from Trump's election to the rise of a new socialist left and leaders such as Corbyn, Iglesias and Sanders, recent years have witnessed extreme polarisation. Forces at opposite ends of the political spectrum have appealed to the people and against the elites and waged war against the central tenets of neoliberal dogma, with the left attacking its socio-economic premises, and the right demolishing its cultural tolerance. The populism of the 2010s was the dialectical negation of neoliberalism.

After the Covid-19 pandemic, it is time to look beyond the populist moment and assess the new landscape of post-neoliberal politics. Contemporary politics is not just a negative moment, a phase in which the 'old is dying and the new cannot be born', to cite a famous Gramsci quote obsessively repeated in recent years.[1] Out of the brutal fight between neoliberalism and populism and the shock and panic provoked by coronavirus, something new is emerging: a neo-statism that calls for stronger state intervention in the economy in order to protect society. In an embryonic form, statism was already present in the populist discourse of the 2010s – on the nationalist right, in the defence of hard borders; on the radical left, in the call for a 'twenty-first century socialism' and the rehabilitation of Keynesian interventionism.[2] The coronavirus emergency has made 'big government' a necessity, overturning the liberal mistrust of a strong state. From massive social transfers to address mounting unemployment and business failure, to proposals for the

---

1   Antonio Gramsci, *Selections from the Prison Notebooks*, ed. and transl. Quintin Hoare and Geoffrey Nowell Smith (London: Lawrence & Wishart, 1971), p. 276.

2   Jeremy Gilbert, *Twenty-first Century Socialism* (Medford: Polity, 2020).

nationalisation of strategic infrastructure and investment programmes to decarbonise the economy and address the climate crisis such as those put forward by President Biden, the interventionist state – that traditional bugbear of neoliberalism – is back. With the pandemic, neo-statism has become the political new normal, a meta-ideology that inflects virtually all political actors', but also a new battlefield where radically different visions of our political future are butting heads.

This book explores the post-neoliberal ideological horizon emerging in the aftermath of the coronavirus crisis. It charts the rise of government protectivism as the key ideological trend in understanding the contemporary reshuffling of political discourse and practice in Europe and the United States. *The Great Recoil* develops a 'diagnostic of the present', drawing links between emerging ideological motives and the socioeconomic demands that inform them.[3] The new statism of the 2020s and its relationship with the populism of the 2010s and with a fading neoliberalism are examined from a structural and content-oriented perspective, in order to overcome the formalism that has dominated much of recent analysis. The crisis of neoliberal globalisation is identified as the key motivation for the present ideological shift, because of the immense social anxieties it has created. To examine this political realignment, I draw from a wealth of key insights coming from the history of political philosophy at the crossroads between republican theory and Marxist theory. The reflections on the state found in Plato and Aristotle; the social contract described in Hobbes and Rousseau; the socialist view of the state in Marx, Gramsci and Poulantzas; and the critique of free market liberalism in Karl Polanyi's economic sociology are mobilised to explore the motives and implications of the current revival of the visible hand of the state, at a time when social uncertainty is met with a demand for political order.

My focus is on the new discourse of neo-statist politics and the political practices of the post-neoliberal era. On the one hand, the volume examines the new slogans, keywords, declarations and political imaginaries of contemporary politics. In so doing, it documents the seismic shifts in political discourse after worn-out free market dogmas have

---

3   'Diagnostic of the present' is a term used by the Frankfurt School to express the need to understand the relationship between historical circumstances and political agency.

been abandoned. On the other hand, my intention is to reveal how this change in political discourse concretely affects policy-making and electoral competition. I examine how the inward-focused orientation of the neo-statist politics of protection and control illuminates the nature of the social blocs which support the left and the right; the role played by different enemies, among the elites and the underclass, in cementing these blocs; the way in which the state is conceived by nationalist and socialist forces; and, finally, the different responses given to the resurgent question of nationhood. My hope is to provide some sense of political orientation amid a landscape marked by extreme uncertainty, so that we can locate the key challenges and the necessary strategy to address the collapse of the neoliberal order.

## Backward, Inward, Onward

'Recoil' describes a reaction of fear or disgust – the moment of flinching, cowering, quailing or pulling back before a threat. In ballistics it describes the kick of a gun when discharged. In the animal world, the pangolin, suspected to be the zoonotic origin of Covid-19, recoils in the face of attack from a predator by curling up into a ball. The rise of a new statism in contemporary politics needs to be read in light of this negative feedback response, and the way it redefines the topology of political action and the dialectic between inside and outside that is constitutive of all political communities. The Great Recoil revolves around a subjective shift from the centrifugal *exopolitics* of neoliberalism, oriented to the outside, towards the centripetal *endopolitics* of the present post-neoliberal era, with its concern for the 'inside', the re-establishment of a sense of interiority and stability.[4]

*Recoil* is the customary English translation of the Hegelian term *Gegenstöß* used in the dialectic to express the counter-push swinging back and forth between different poles, such as Being and Nothing.[5] In

---

4    The terms 'endopolitics' and 'exopolitics' do not have a storied pedigree, but they have been used by some classical scholars to discuss Plato. See Paris Arnopoulos, *Exopolitics: Polis, Ethnos, Cosmos: Classical Theories and Praxis of Foreign Affairs* (Commack, NY: Nova Science, 1999).

5    The notion of 'recoil' (*Gegenstöß*) is discussed by Slavoj Žižek as the moment of 'negating negativity' central to Hegel's dialectic. In my use of the term what matters is

Hegel's dialectical monism, history is constantly bouncing back: every action produces its own reaction, and every step of the movement of Spirit is caught in the side effects of the step that came before. This image helps to capture the nature of our times. In the first months of the coronavirus crisis, the World Economic Forum launched the idea of a 'Great Reset', as if the pandemic offered capitalism the opportunity to start anew. But history never begins from scratch; rather each era has to respond to the contradictions the previous era has thrown up. More than a Great Reset, we live in a Great Recoil, a time in which society is forced to address the strains and agoraphobia unleashed by neoliberal globalisation. We are traversing a new 'counter-movement' like the one which, according to Karl Polanyi, engulfed Europe and the United States in the aftermath of the 1929 crash. However, this is not simply a moment of regression or backlash, a purely negative retreat. More positively, it is also a moment of re-internalisation, or what Hegel himself described as *Erinnerung*.[6] The term literally means remembrance, but Hegel also uses it figuratively to signify the act of recollection and internalisation, or 'inwardisation'. *Erinnerung* is opposed to *Äußerung*, or externalisation, which both Hegel and Marx associated with objectification and reification, and today could be equated with the centrifugal logic of global capitalism. *Erinnerung* is the moment when the Spirit withdraws into itself and becomes self-absorbed, after recoiling at its outer existence. But, as Herbert Marcuse suggested, it is also a moment of 'recapitulation' which signals the end of a historical era and prefigures the opening of a new one.[7]

This combination of regression, introversion and internal reorganisation, expressed by the notion of *Erinnerung*, seems to pervade much of contemporary politics. Our time looks backward to previous historical eras for solutions that cannot be found in the present; it pushes back against the market and private actors, whose incapacity to meet basic

---

the moment of 'turning back to itself', which the notion of recoil shares with the Hegelian concept of *Erinnerung*. Slavoj Žižek, *Absolute Recoil: Towards a New Foundation of Dialectical Materialism* (London: Verso, 2015).

6 The term *Erinnerung* is discussed in Hegel's *Science of Logic* and in *The Phenomenology of the Spirit*. G. W. F. Hegel, *Hegel's Science of Logic* (Amherst, NY: Humanity Books, 2004), pp. 337–8. G. W.F. Hegel, *Phenomenology of Spirit*, transl. A. V. Miller (Oxford: Oxford University Press, 1977), p. 492.

7 Herbert Marcuse, *Hegel's Ontology and the Theory of Historicity* (Cambridge, MA: MIT Press, 1987).

needs has been brutally revealed by the pandemic and, finally, turns inward to seek a new centre of gravity promising a minimum of stability. The so-called 'populist moment' of the 2010s has been strongly marked by a backward and inward orientation, which many observers interpreted as a sign of regression after years of triumphant neoliberalism bent on rapid modernisation. The national-populist right has often appealed to people 'left behind' by the train of neoliberal globalisation. It has promised to reclaim what was taken away by 'global elites', as expressed in slogans such as 'Take Back Control' and 'Make America Great Again'. Furthermore, national-populists are the flagbearers of a conservative cultural backlash, a reactionary retrocession after decades marked by steady advance in terms of civil rights and cultural tolerance. Finally, they stand accused of isolationism, of peddling fantasies of an imaginary exit from the international economy in a narrow-minded attempt to turn back the clock of history. Similar criticisms of backward-looking attitudes have been directed at the emerging socialist-populist left, often attributed with a nostalgia for cradle-to-grave Keynesianism and fondness for the anti-imperialist enemies of the West. The British press repeatedly branded Corbyn as an old Marxist who wanted to send the country back to the 1970s. The leader of left-populist party La France Insoumise, Jean-Luc Mélenchon was accused of wanting societies 'withdrawn into themselves' (*repli sur soi*), because of his departure from the openness preached by neoliberal ideologues. Mass movements such as the Gilets Jaunes have often been presented by liberal commentators as parochial, vulgar and unreasonable.

The new 'corona statism' that is emerging in the early 2020s, with its orientation to foundational political issues, appears to be an even more pronounced embodiment of Hegel's *Erinnerung*. The emergency has forced citizens the world over to 'self-isolate', wear protective equipment such as masks and gloves, shelter at home, and shield themselves from contagion through family- and friend-based 'support bubbles'. Furthermore, it has led countries to turn their backs on the rest of the world in order to focus on their internal safety, closing borders and implementing strict control measures, while pushing millions of expats, tourists and international students to move back to their home countries. In response to this crisis, politicians had to search historical precedents for guidance in the present and adopt economic policies long considered anachronistic. Leaders such as Boris Johnson and Joe Biden have adopted the slogan 'build *back* better', to express the need for a *reconstruction* of their countries, in ways reminiscent of what happened after World War II. They have, at least partly, abandoned the neoliberal dogmas of inflation-targeting, deregulation and a non-interventionist state that prevailed for over thirty years, resurrecting ideas of Keynesian interventionism, deficit-spending, state subsidies, industrial policy, public ownership, and even economic planning.

From discussions about the need to reinforce domestic demand and the local economy rather than export sectors, to the concern about the basic needs of society for public services, health, education and employment that have long languished as political priorities, and calls for 'in-sourcing' to reverse out-sourcing practices, this logic of re-internalisation is painted all over post-neoliberal statism.[8] To follow Hegel's famous description in the preface to the *Phenomenology of Spirit*, the coronavirus crisis has heralded the moment in which '[t]he gradual crumbling that left unaltered the face of the whole is cut short by a sunburst which, in one flash, illuminates the features of the new world.'[9] The pandemic is for neoliberal elites akin to what the fall of the Berlin Wall in 1989 was for communists; a moment of shock and disorientation, which opens a space in which to redefine prevailing assumptions. After the obsession with the external and constant expansion embodied by neoliberal *exopolitics* – evident in practices of out-sourcing, offshoring and the prioritisation of exports – the pendulum is now swinging towards the inwardness of statist *endopolitics*.

This reorientation of contemporary politics towards interiority is best understood as a counterthrust of the crisis of neoliberal globalisation. The Great Recoil is neoliberal globalisation's 'second movement', to use the terms of Karl Polanyi – a reaction against the rapacity of capitalism's desperate hunt for profit.[10] It is the moment when neoliberal globalisation is driven back, having reached the limits of its ecological, social and political sustainability. Through its ineluctable expansion, engulfing ever

---

8   'Re-internalisation' – probably a reference to Hegel's discussion of inwardisation – is the term used by Austrian–Hungarian economist Karl Polanyi in *The Great Transformation* to describe society's response to capitalist disembedding of the economy from society. Karl Polanyi, *The Great Transformation: The Political and Economic Origins of Our Time* (Boston: Beacon, 2014).

9   G. W. F. Hegel, *Phenomenology of Spirit*, p. 8.

10   Karl Polanyi, *The Great Transformation*.

more countries, global capital has progressively saturated the entire planetary space. Having integrated ever more countries into its logic, from China and India starting in the 1980s and 1990s, to South and Southeast Asian countries like Bangladesh, Vietnam and Indonesia in the 2000s, transforming them into labour-intensive manufacturing centres, US-led capitalist globalisation is now caught in a state of asphyxia, marked by stagnation, overcapacity and overaccumulation, unable to find new profitable investment opportunities. No lasting growth seems possible under the present regime of capitalist accumulation.

The neoliberal drive for externalisation has pushed many citizens beyond the protections of collective bargaining and labour rights, creating a growing gap between insiders and outsiders.[11] Western societies have come to be dominated by a sense of agoraphobia – a fear of the open spaces of neoliberal globalisation and the risks presented by its multiple flows. With the Covid crisis, the wounds left open by globalisation over the course of the last three decades have become intolerable and untenable, while its social inefficiency and the health risks it has fostered have come to the surface. The current drive towards the re-internalisation or 'inwardisation' traversing contemporary societies has to be read as a reaction against this upsetting of social and economic coordinates, and the attempt to re-embed economic processes in social and political institutions.

## The New Statist Lexicon

The Great Recoil is the moment when neoliberal thesis and populist antithesis engenders a statist synthesis, eclipsing many of the central ideological tenets of the phase of neoliberal expansion. The key notions emerging in this neo-statist discourse – sovereignty, protection, control and security – adumbrate a radically different agenda from the one that was hegemonic in the 1990s and 2000s. The outward-focused neoliberal language of opportunity, flexibility, openness, aspiration and entrepreneurialism now gives way to a neo-statist reassertion of state authority, territorial domination and political power, and to a concern with the

---

11   Assar Lindbeck and Dennis J. Snower, *The Insider–Outsider Theory of Employment and Unemployment* (Cambridge, MA: MIT Press, 1989), p. 1.

essential conditions of existence of political communities: autonomy self-defence, survival and reproduction. Whereas neoliberal politics targeted people's desires, and in particular possessive consumerism and individual freedoms, post-neoliberal statism is concerned with addressing collective fears and lessening social risks. It speaks not of aspiration but of desperation; not of hope of upward mobility, but of status anxiety and economic precariousness. It does not promise tremendous growth, but rather to respond to urgent calls for social safety, environmental repair and public consolidation.

The term sovereignty, usually understood as the supremacy of the state, expresses the primacy of political power and territorial democracy over the space of flows of neoliberal globalisation. Globalisation was largely predicated on a subjugation of national economies to the interests of global finance and world trade in order to ensure the free movement of capital, goods and people. Now that this project seems to have failed, it is not surprising that its arch-enemy, namely 'national sovereignty', has been given a new lease of life. Sovereignty has become the object of inordinate attention in recent years and has been adopted by *sovereigntyists*, politicians like Brexiters who see the reassertion of national sovereignty as an end in itself, whatever the cost. But, interestingly, the term has also been claimed by activists on the left to reaffirm the democratic right of local communities to control crucial resources, such as energy, food supply and technology, and to fend off the rapacity of international corporations, digital oligopolists and investment funds.

Protection is an imperative that has been widely mobilised during the coronavirus emergency in pushing people to wear face masks and professional protective equipment such as isolation gowns. More generally, contemporary politics has become a politics of protection, in what has sometimes been described as the 'return of Hobbes', given the famous description by the English political philosopher of the fundamental role of the state as a purveyor of security and provider of protection offered in *The Leviathan*.[12] In our society, we see the emergence of demands for protection against all sorts of dangers created by capitalist interconnectedness. While the 'risk society' envisaged by Ulrich Beck in the 1980s already highlighted the emergence of previously overlooked

---

12    David Runciman, 'Coronavirus Has Not Suspended Politics – It Has Revealed the Nature of Power', *Guardian*, 27 March 2020.

environmental risks, we now live in a world in which 'risks' have turned into existential threats, and affect not only the natural environment but also the fundamentals of society's existence.[13] The driving motive behind current political discourse is not the expansive and aspirational notion of acquisitive individualism, but rather the survival instinct of social strata crucial for social reproduction, yet vulnerable to economic uncertainty, unable to find a modicum of stability in a hyper-connected world on the brink of collapse. Nationalists promise to protect us from migrants, who are seen as harbingers of crime and disease, and purveyors of alien culture, posing a demographic threat to the national community. The left instead advocates social protection, demanding measures against tax havens, the regulation of international trade to protect the local economy from the depredations of either digital or rentier capitalism, and major investment in public services to re-establish basic systems of social support. These days, even some centrists politicians appear inclined to admit the importance of reasserting state protection to address ballooning social inequality, and to prepare for the catastrophic scenarios unleashed by climate change, biodiversity collapse and the inevitable pandemics of the future.

Control is another term that frequently crops up in contemporary political discourse. The Brexit Leave campaign promised to 'take back control' over borders and over the economy, and the likes of Trump, Le Pen and Salvini reiterate the mantra of putting Americans, French and Italians first. But 'control' has also been adopted on the left to express the objective of re-establishing the 'steering capacity' of the state – its ability to mobilise macroeconomic, industrial and planning policy to deal with mass unemployment and global warming. Control is an object of great contention in contemporary political debates. For some people, more state control over the economy, society and environment is necessary to overcome the condition of a world out of joint, in which the warping of sovereignty deprives political communities of any sense of autonomy. But the return of strong state control is resented by large numbers of people, as we have seen in the protests against the wearing of masks, the opposition to Covid-19 vaccinations and the denunciation of lockdowns from the business community. While increased state protection is often

---

13    Ulrich Beck and Mark Ritter, *Risk Society: Towards a New Modernity*, transl. Mark Ritter (London: Sage, 2013).

welcome, the enhanced state control powers it carries in tow are frequently resented. Finally, the politics of control also raises the ultimate question of democracy, of what kind of influence citizens have over the state. After years in which democratic decision-making has been appropriated by technocrats and businessmen, the present organic crisis of capitalist democracies calls for the establishment of new democratic institutions by means of which political communities might recover some control over their destiny and overcome their perception of impotence and despair.

## A Strategy for the Post-pandemic Left

The Great Recoil is best conceived as a moment of bifurcation, a crossroads where alternative paths towards the future diverge. It is a realm of extreme polarisation that pits the progressive left and the extremist right against one another, and against the neoliberal centre, with more moderate forces also looking for an adaptive response to the collapse of neoliberalism. The right's version of neo-statism is what I will describe as 'proprietarian protectionism', which combines authoritarian law-and-order policies, mercantilistic state intervention to defend 'national champions' in foreign trade and Darwinian economic individualism.[14] The left's response, what I term 'social protectivism', develops in a radically different direction, approaching the neo-statist moment as an opportunity to reaffirm principles of social equality and democracy and prepare society for the devastating effects of climate change.

Social protectivism – a progressive narrative of sovereignty, protection and control – provides a way forward amid the present troubles. This vision could allay people's fears in an era of catastrophic risk, while attending to the popular desire for inclusion in political decisions. Protectivism encompasses a number of protective functions that have become particularly relevant in this phase of crisis and retrenchment: from health and welfare protection, ravaged by years of austerity and privatisation, to the restoration of the environment threatened by carbon

---

14  'National champions' is a phrase used to describe powerful companies, often leading internationally in a given industry, that governments intend to protect from international competition.

emissions; from the defence of local economic ecosystems vis-à-vis the 'extractivist' tendencies of digital capitalism to the protection of all citizens from illness, economic insecurity, isolation and exclusion.[15] It suggests the need to pursue fiscal expansion and redistribution but also to give a new lease of life to socialist notions such as nationalisations, indicative planning and workers' participation in the governance of companies, all of which the left abandoned after the 1980s' defeat. Progressives need to learn the lessons offered by the pandemic on the need to mend and reinforce key support structures that guarantee social protection and reproduction. In particular, the essential contribution made by healthcare, delivery and sanitation workers to society requires a policy to increase wages and redress salary inequality. More power to unions and a pattern of economic organisation structured around domestic demand rather than foreign exports could also allow the left to win back sections of the electorate that have turned to the nationalist right, and in particular the bulk of the working and lower-middle classes living in rural and declining areas.

To reconnect with these voters concerned about exposure to international competition, socialists also need to question the vapid cosmopolitanism adopted during the era of neoliberal globalisation and come to terms with the persistence of local and national identities. Progressive forces must break out of the urban redoubts in which the left has confined itself. This will require organisational investment in provincial areas and an effort to prioritise bread-and-butter issues that are high on the agenda of manufacturing and low-skilled workers living outside of metropolitan hubs. By denouncing the contradiction between the right's communitarian appeal to workers and its defence of capitalist interests, and boosting economic development projects that can assuage the anxieties of blue-collar workers, the left has some prospect of disrupting the social bloc of the nationalist right.

The promise of a 'socialism that protects' does not entail renouncing the left's values of cultural tolerance and social inclusion in the name of

---

15   'Extractivism' is a term used to described the similarity between the extraction of natural resources in mining and agribusiness and the mode of accumulation of new industries, and of digital companies in particular, which revolves around extracting value from social interactions and personal data. See Sandro Mezzadra and Brett Neilson, 'On the Multiple Frontiers of Extraction: Excavating Contemporary Capitalism', *Cultural Studies* 31: 2–3, 2017, 185–204.

a 'conservative socialism' – the shortcut proposed by some renegade leftists who have become full-on nationalists. On the contrary, it means foregrounding economic conflicts over cultural conflicts, while uniting voters of various backgrounds and creeds around a shared goal and against shared enemies – a unifying, non-sectarian mission that socialist movements have traditionally performed in moments of strength. Furthermore, recognising the power of location and national identity in contemporary politics does not mean abandoning the left's traditional commitment to internationalism and universalism; rather, it reflects the acceptance that any real universalism can only be achieved by acknowledging the peculiarities of people's identities and attending to their fear of dislocation and exposure. Only by walking this fine line – refocusing attention on essential socioeconomic issues to broaden electoral support among workers, while fighting for popular sovereignty, social protection and democratic control – can the left hope to emerge galvanised from the Great Recoil and start looking not only backward and inward, but also forward.

Chapter 1 discusses the ideological landscape of the Great Recoil, marked by the decline of neoliberalism, the challenge of populism and the rise of a post-pandemic statism. It begins by discussing the populist wave of the 2010s and some of the theoretical and practical dilemmas it has raised. It continues by delineating the various actors that are defining contemporary political conflicts: the nationalist right of Trump, Salvini and Bolsonaro; the socialist left of Sanders, Corbyn and Podemos; and the way liberal centrism is attempting to defend free markets and capitalist innovation from the anti-neoliberal onslaught. It concludes by introducing the triad of sovereignty-protection-control which lies at the heart of neo-statist ideology.

Chapter 2 considers the crisis of globalisation, and the way it is causing a return to statism. It reconstructs how globalisation was associated with an outward push – an emphasis on openness and externalisation, underpinning practices of outsourcing, offshoring and the emphasis on exports. The consequence has been a trend towards dislocation, the disembedding of the economy and political power from locality and the opening of rifts between global cities and impoverished peripheries. Following the outward movement of capitalist globalisation, we now see an inward moment of re-internalisation taking hold – concerned with addressing the perception of exposure and agoraphobia that digital and financial interconnectedness has produced.

Chapter 3 examines the question of sovereignty – the central notion of contemporary neo-statism. It highlights that the resurgence of contention around sovereignty is a return of the repressed, since sovereignty had become the privileged target of attack by the neoliberal theorists who envisaged a different global order from the one that emerged after World War II. Neoclassical economists such as Friedrich Hayek and Ludwig von Mises imagined a world in which all forms of sovereignty and territorial power would be lifted, facilitating the unhindered flow of capital and goods in a world united under capitalism and private enterprise. They preached openness against what they saw as the tribal solidarity of national communities. However, rather than leading to an expansion of opportunity and choice, the neoliberal project has resulted in extreme inequality and insecurity. Appeals for sovereignty seek to rebalance this situation, giving a new lease of life to state power, which is seen as the only counterbalancing mechanism that can stand between people and the economic and geopolitical chaos unleashed by global capital.

Chapter 4 addresses the range of concerns about protection that are taking centre stage in neo-statist political discourse – from measures against epidemic contagion to demands for trade protectionism, new forms of social welfare and a heightened concern for law and order. Protection is a term that lies at the core of state theory, given that, as political philosophy has made clear with Plato, Machiavelli and Hobbes, the prime function of politics is guaranteeing the survival and reproduction of the demos, defending it against both external and internal threats. Today, the renewed attention received by issues of protection reflects the change of social priorities with respect to the heyday of neoliberalism. Now, protecting one's own living and working conditions is an issue of greater urgency than pushing for upward social mobility in a world of shrinking economic opportunity. Rival ideologies attach different meanings to the term protection. The right's focus is on protecting property and the identity of the national community; the left instead concentrates on protecting workers' rights and attending to the health and social needs of citizens.

Chapter 5 explores the question of control as a key corollary of the notion of state sovereignty. The notion of control originates with the development of statecraft in the Middle Ages and denotes the means through which government concretely asserts its authority over population and territory. The language of control has come to be widely adopted in both the political and economic spheres, within debates concerned variously with mass testing, fear of surveillance, democratic accountability and growing demands for the strengthening of the state's ability to control the economy. For Trump and others on the populist right, control chiefly takes the form of border control, and of a reassertion of the power of the propertied classes; the focus of the left, on the other hand, is to re-establish the state's ability to face up to large firms and banks, and to the oligarchic class that controls the flow of capital and innovation in general, for example through the rehabilitation of planning as a tool for democratic decision-making.

Chapter 6 explores the class conflicts and class alliances of the Great Recoil. It argues that it is necessary to move beyond the problematic contemporary understanding that class does not matter. On the contrary, in order to understand the interests at stake in contemporary political conflict, we need to pay attention to the ways in which the socialist left and nationalist right strive to construct new social blocs, while competing with a neoliberal centre that maintains its influence over sections of the middle and upper classes. The right's alliance brings together the managerial class, the provincial middle class and large numbers of blue-collar workers. The left, by contrast, allies the urban middle class of so-called sociocultural professionals with service workers – both largely concentrated in cities. The strategic aim for socialists should be to explode the class contradictions within the right's social bloc, pulling away the blue-collar working class from the grip of national-populists.

Chapter 7 turns to the question of the enemies that are targeted by different political forces. Given the social diversity of contemporary social blocs and the presence of diverging interests in the coalitions mobilised by the left and the right, the construction of the enemy is especially important in the present conjuncture. The chosen enemies of the nationalist right are immigrants, who are presented as an alien element that threatens the cohesion and survival of the body politic. For the socialist left, the main culprits are instead the wealthy, seen as agents responsible for mass impoverishment, whose economic power also confers on them de facto oligarchic political power. Other enemies that have emerged in the populist moment include the cultural elites and the political class, accused of pursuing interests distant from those of ordinary people. The chapter concludes by questioning why, to date, anti-immigrant rhetoric has proven more effective than attacking the rich and powerful.

Chapter 8 discusses new state interventionism as a defining trend of the Great Recoil, as the perception of political and economic chaos bred by catastrophic crisis has induced citizens to call for state protection and control. Breaking with neoliberal orthodoxy, an economic statist imaginary is emerging that once again sees the state as a fundamental tool for channelling the general will for the improvement of society. Various fields of economic intervention are examined, from trade policies to taxation, from the nationalisation of strategic corporations to the provision of social welfare. While the right has pursued an agenda in which the role of the state is chiefly the protection of private property, the left's protectivism encompasses various forms of social protection: from welfare provisions to industrial policy, mild forms of trade protectionism and policies to accelerate the ecological transition and expand democratic participation.

Chapter 9 approaches the national question in relation to the rise and fall of globalisation. Confounding the prediction of many neoliberal theorists, national identity continues to play an important role for most citizens; indeed, this is now more evident, as the promise of a global cosmopolitanism has run its course. To counter the right's nationalism, the left should adopt what I describe as a democratic patriotism: a reassertion of belonging and commitment to the democratic political communities of which each one of us is a member, as a jumping-off point towards an authentically universalist politics. It is only through a re-localisation of political commitments and the construction of a 'provincial socialism' that appeals to people in non-urban and peripheral areas that the left can expand its appeal beyond urban middle classes and public employees.

The conclusion pulls together the various themes of the book, summarising its argument and advancing some recommendations for a post-pandemic socialist strategy. It argues that the coronavirus crisis has uncovered some key weaknesses of the populist right – its nefarious demeaning of science, irresponsible management of healthcare and prioritisation of business interests over citizens' welfare. This offers a strategic opportunity for a left breakthrough. To seize it, however, socialists will need to move past internecine struggles and the obsession with culture wars, to focus instead on developing the vision of a post-neoliberal society in which state protection and control are reinforced by democratic participation and guarantees of personal dignity. In other words, the left needs to pursue a 'socialism that protects', because society demands security from capitalist dislocation and control over its collective destiny.

# 1

# The Post-neoliberal Horizon

Understanding the new politics of the Great Recoil requires us to return to the question of ideology – ideology not in the form of Karl Marx's false consciousness, but as Antonio Gramsci conceived of it: a worldview that informs various political outlooks and is deeply interwoven with the commonsense prevalent at any given time.[1] The issue of ideology has remained below the political radar for decades: we were told that we lived in a post-ideological era, where politics was no longer guided by grand narratives, as had been the case in the nineteenth and twentieth centuries when liberalism, socialism and fascism emerged, but inspired instead by realism, pragmatism and consensus politics. But the impression of a post-ideological era was false. Ideological conflicts seemed to be resolved not because of the end of ideology, but because of the victory of a single ideology – neoliberalism – over all others; its triumph and subsequent colonisation of the public mind gave the false impression that ideology as such had disappeared.

Neoliberalism is a blanket term encompassing the political and economic doctrine that has held sway over the world since the end of the Cold War. Shaped by the ideas and teachings of conservative thinkers such as Friedrich Hayek, Ludwig von Mises and Milton Friedman, it came to command the political arena when Margaret Thatcher won

---

1   Antonio Gramsci, *Selections from the Prison Notebooks*, ed. and transl. Quintin Hoare and Geoffrey Nowell Smith (London: Lawrence & Wishart, 1971), pp. 326–30.

power in the UK in 1979, followed by Ronald Reagan in the United States the following year. As the prefix 'neo' suggests, neoliberalism involves a revival of nineteenth-century notions of laissez-faire economics that had been largely discredited after the 1929 crash and ensuing Great Depression. The novelty of neoliberalism lay in the fact that it broke with the Keynesian consensus of the post-war period, when both right and left agreed on the need for government intervention and the welfare state in order to guarantee basic standards of living to all, and to steer the economy towards socially desirable ends. Neoliberal policies of deregulation, privatisation, free trade and globalisation came to be widely adopted the world over under the aegis of the so-called 'Washington consensus', which reigned supreme between the fall of the Berlin Wall in 1989 and the financial crash of 2008. Neoliberalism acquired the status of a master ideology that inflected leaders and parties across the political divide. In the 1990s, Bill Clinton, Tony Blair, Romano Prodi and Gerhard Schröder all came to share Thatcher's commitment to free markets and property rights, in what became known as a Third Way between market conservatism and social democracy. The received wisdom of neoliberalism asserted that the market was more efficient than the state in delivering prosperity, and that policy-makers had to foster opportunity, entrepreneurialism, flexibility and openness.

The contemporary political horizon is defined by the collapse of this neoliberal consensus. The Great Recession of 2008–11 was followed by prolonged stagnation and now the corona-crash, and these together have profoundly upset the premises of the neoliberal project and its capacity to explain reality. Much as the emergence of stagflation – the coincidence of stagnation and inflation – in the 1970s presented an insoluble problem for Keynesian approaches, opening the way to monetarism and other capital-friendly policies, the current economic situation presents paradoxes that are impossible to solve within the neoliberal framework. With an economy marked by stagnation and deflationary pressures, which massive injections of liquidity and quantitative easing programmes have so far been unable to assuage, and while interest rates remain at an historic minimum, the neoliberal playbook of free competition seems unfit to address present dilemmas. While some authors have tried to capture this crepuscular phase as a partial readjustment of neoliberalism, as expressed by notions such as 'authoritarian neoliberalism' or 'punitive neoliberalism', my argument is that we have now entered a phase of 'post-neoliberalism', when the neoliberal horizon is crumbling around us, opening the way for a new set of ideological coordinates to replace it.[2]

Figure 1.1    Neoliberal thesis, populist anti-thesis, neo-statist synthesis

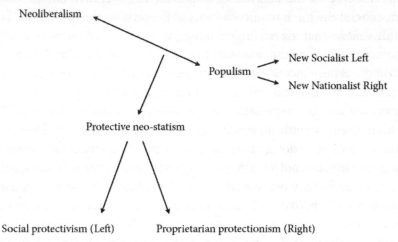

The contemporary ideological horizon is defined by the clash between neoliberalism and populism and the rise of an interventionist neo-statism which attempts to overcome this deadlock.

The crisis of the neoliberal consensus has manifested for many years in the rise of populist movements of the most disparate sort. From Occupy Wall Street to the Gilets Jaunes, from the new movements of the radical right to the resurgence of a socialist left, including Labour under Jeremy Corbyn and millennial socialism under the influence of Bernie Sanders and Alexandria Ocasio-Cortez, populism has been seen as the defining trend of contemporary politics. Despite their ideological differences, these various phenomena have shared a common enemy in neoliberalism and appealed to ordinary people against the elites. As I will argue in this chapter, the so-called populist moment has not been a phase of ideological convergence between right and left as argued by pro-market centrists seeking to smear socialists. On the contrary, it has been a phase of strong political polarisation between a new nationalist

---

2    Regarding these two perspectives, see respectively Ian Bruff, 'The Rise of Authoritarian Neoliberalism', *Rethinking Marxism* 26: 1 (2014), 113–29 and Will Davies, 'The New Neoliberalism', *New Left Review* 101 (2016).

right and a new socialist left, both moving away from the neoliberal centre in different directions.

Populism is crucial to understanding the genesis of the present political realignment. But capturing the spirit of post-neoliberal politics cannot stop at the analysis of populism as a negative counterpart of neoliberal elitism. It requires a focus on content, on the substantive political visions that are emerging out of the present crisis. Specifically, it involves exploring the neo-statism that has emerged out of the confrontation between neoliberalism and populism. It is in this neo-statism, namely a recuperation of the importance of state intervention, that we can find the key ingredients of an emerging post-neoliberal political order. The new battle for consensus, as will become clear, revolves around the notions of national sovereignty over the economy, social protection and democratic control. This protective statism is not a partisan ideology advocated by only one political camp, but more like a meta-ideological horizon, which, like neoliberalism at its zenith, infuses the entire political space.

Contemporary ideological commonsense is no longer just neoliberal, but increasingly neo-statist. The main political tendencies dominating the Western political landscape must all address the basic concerns at the heart of contemporary neo-statism: shelter from the vagaries of the global economy, protection from the international market, the economic development of depressed regions, democratic control over all levels of government, health and social security, and the provision of basic goods that cannot be left to the market. Hence, the new framework offered by neo-statism seems to offer a response to many urgent issues that neoliberalism appears unequipped to address. But while prefiguring a new post-neoliberal consensus, neo-statism is also a battlefield in which very different visions of the state and its mission are emerging; and a space in which new burning ethical and political dilemmas are coming to the fore.

## The Populist 2010s

The rise of populism in its multifarious and contradictory forms has been the most important political manifestation of the declining ideological hegemony of neoliberalism. According to theorists like Chantal

Mouffe and Cas Mudde, the 2010s were a 'populist moment' or 'populist zeitgeist' in which populism seems to have been stronger and more prominent than ever.[3] Scholars have battled over the exact meaning of the term, some seeing it as an ideology, albeit a thin one,[4] while others have interpreted it as a 'discursive logic',[5] or as a matter of style or rhetoric;[6] some attributing populism only to the nationalist right, while others have understood it as a generalised political tendency. This scholarship tends to share a formalistic approach,[7] identifying minimum common characteristics of populist movements, such as their reliance on the rhetorical opposition between people and the elite, rather than exploring the structural and class underpinnings of these phenomena.

When the media speak of populism, they are usually referring to the populist right represented by the likes of Donald Trump in the United States, Matteo Salvini in Italy, Jair Bolsonaro in Brazil, Viktor Orbán in Hungary, and their political allies in several other countries. Using chauvinistic arguments and xenophobic rhetoric targeting migrants, foreigners and all varieties of minorities, this new brand of right-wing politics achieved spectacular success in the second half of the 2010s. The victory of the Leave campaign in the 2016 Brexit referendum and Boris Johnson's subsequent rise to power; the election of Donald Trump as 45th US president in November 2016; the rise in popularity of Salvini in Italy in the aftermath of the general elections of March 2018; the election of Jair Bolsonaro in the Brazilian presidential elections in November 2018 – were all key populist moments of the last decade. They have informed the impression that we live in an 'age of anger', to use the words of Indian essayist Pankaj Mishra, in which popular discontent plays all too easily into the hands of right-wing demagogues who are ready to use all the basest tactics to shore up their power: circulating

---

3   Cas Mudde, 'The Populist Zeitgeist', *Government and Opposition* 39: 4 (2004), pp. 542–63; Chantal Mouffe, *For a Left Populism* (London: Verso, 2019).

4   Ben Stanley, 'The Thin Ideology of Populism', *Journal of Political Ideologies* 13: 1 (2008), 95–110.

5   Ernesto Laclau, *On Populist Reason* (London: Verso, 2005).

6   Michael Kazin, *The Populist Persuasion: An American History* (Ithaca, NY: Cornell University Press, 2017).

7   Yannis Stavrakakis, 'Antinomies of Formalism: Laclau's Theory of Populism and the Lessons from Religious Populism in Greece', *Journal of Political Ideologies* 9: 3 (2004), 253–67.

fake news, scapegoating minorities and pandering to all sorts of social anxieties.[8]

But populism is not a phenomenon associated only with the nationalist right. For example, while the 2018 elections in Italy briefly put the League and Salvini in government, it was the populist but centrist Five Star Movement that commanded the largest number of seats in the Italian parliament; indeed, it controlled many government posts, including the office of prime minister, held by self-described 'people's lawyer' Antonio Conte, who has run the country during the pandemic in a centre-left coalition with the Italian Democratic Party, until being replaced by a tech-nocratic government led by the former European Central Bank chief Mario Draghi. Furthermore, in recent years populism has been associated with many left-wing campaigns and political parties, often described as manifestations of a 'left populism'. If anything, the leftist version of populism can claim a longer history than its national-populist doppel-gänger. Populism has been entrenched in Argentina and other countries since the mid twentieth century. Today, to most people in Latin America, populism means the populist left of the 2000s and figures like Hugo Chavez and Luiz Iñácio Lula da Silva. Similarly, in the United States, populism has a progressive tradition, embodied by the proto-socialist People's Party of the late nineteenth century, which brought together farm workers and industrial workers against moneyed elites and robber-barons, and for a decade represented an alternative to the Democratic Party.

Building on this tradition of progressive populism, there has been much debate in recent years on the need for a 'left-populism' as a means of developing a coherent response to the Trumpist right. Chantal Mouffe has argued that 'instead of seeing the populist moment only as a threat to democracy, it is urgent to realize that it also offers the opportunity for its radicalization'.[9] Similarly, Grace Blakeley in the UK has written that the left 'must develop a populist narrative, which shows that working people are being made worse off by an exploitative and extractive capi-talist model that sees wealth and power concentrated in the hands of a tiny elite'.[10] In the US, figures such as left journalist and essayist Thomas

8    Pankaj Mishra, *Age of Anger: A History of the Present* (London: Macmillan, 2017).
9    Mouffe, *For a Left Populism*.
10   Grace Blakeley, *Stolen: How to Save the World from Financialisation* (London: Repeater, 2019).

Frank have argued that the Democratic Party has lost ground because it has betrayed working people by focusing on the constituency of urban professionals, and that it is necessary to embrace populism rather than reject it.[11] Similarly, Harvard economist Dani Rodrik has counterposed to the cultural populism he attributes to the right an economic populism he associates with the left.[12]

Movements such as Podemos, La France Insoumise, Syriza and Labour under Corbyn were all seen as progressive incarnations of this populist moment with the adoption of populist discourse providing a means to revive traditional redistributive motives of the left.[13] Since 2010, social movements from Occupy Wall Street to the French Gilets Jaunes have embraced egalitarian populism in a redoubled form. Wearing the safety vests of road workers, French protesters have emphatically demanded that power be taken away from Macron, 'le président des riches', and returned to the people. Thus, contemporary politics is marked not only by the conflict between neoliberalism and populism, but by the competition between two radically alternative strands of populism. Trump's former strategist, Steve Bannon, was not too far off the mark when he said that the defining political fight of our times was between the nationalist populism represented by Trump and his European allies and the socialist populism he identified with Jeremy Corbyn and Bernie Sanders.[14]

The question of whether the left should 'go populist' occupied much debate among progressives during the 2010s. Many on the left resisted such a move, insisting it would amount to pandering to the nationalism and xenophobia of the right. This suspicion was echoed in tirades by neoliberal centrists such as Tony Blair's protégé Yascha Mounk, who argued that left-wing populists were just the same as right-wing populists – echoing a customary neoliberal trope in which political extremes

---

11   Thomas Frank, *Listen, Liberal: Or, What Ever Happened to the Party of the People?* (London: Macmillan, 2016).

12   Dani Rodrik, 'Populism and the Economics of Globalization', *Journal of International Business Policy* 1: 1–2 (2018).

13   Yannis Stavrakakis and Giorgos Katsambekis, 'Left-Wing Populism in the European Periphery: The Case of SYRIZA', *Journal of Political Ideologies* 19: 2 (2014).

14   Bannon made this declaration during the Munk debate held in Toronto in November 2018 with *Atlantic* staff writer David Frum. Munk Debate: The Rise of Populism, available at youtube.com.

join hands, all to reaffirm the importance of the political centre. But these discussions betrayed a fundamental misunderstanding.

References to a populist left and right did not mean that they were converging ideologically in a sort of cross-over populism. If anything, the populist moment has been marked by strong political polarisation with a new 'real left' and 'real right' moving further apart from the neoliberal centre. The explanatory power of the idea of a populist moment lay in the fact it captured first and foremost a commonality of structural conditions which carried the need for similar strategies and rhetoric developing at opposite ends of the political spectrum. It reflected the gaping divide between an economic oligarchy that had amassed the spoils of neoliberal globalisation and the vast mass of people, who had seen their conditions stagnate or decline. It was from this impoverished working class and the squeezed middle class that both the new right and new left emerging in the populist moment strove to draw new bases of support. Populist discourse mobilised by new political actors thus contained an implicit class, or 'plebeian', appeal. It suggested that the centre of gravity in the battle for electoral consensus had moved from the aspirational middle class that was the decisive swing electorate at the height of the neoliberal era to voters affected by socioeconomic decline.

Some recent events seem to point to the fact that this populist moment may be fading, giving way to a post-populist phase. The coronavirus pandemic has negatively affected many leaders and groups that are part of the populist right because of the perception of their mismanagement of the pandemic, and of the irresponsibility of an anti-science libertarianism that the right has often stoked. Furthermore, Trump's humiliating exit from the White House in the aftermath of the Capitol Hill riots may hamper the appeal of right-wing populists in the short term. At the same time, many centrist and left-populist political efforts have been defeated, or have entered into centre-left alliances – for example, the Five Star Movement alliance with the Italian Democratic Party, and the alliance between Podemos and the Spanish Socialist Party. Populism seems to have been either defeated or normalised.

These tendencies do not mark the 'end of populism' in any absolute sense. Populism is a perennial feature of mass democracies, in which the notion of the people constitutes the universal subject.[15] In turn, the

---

15   Ernesto Laclau, *On Populist Reason* (London: Verso, 2015).

character of populism varies according to historical circumstances. In the twentieth century, it was an anomalous political tendency in Latin American countries facing economic underdevelopment and with high shares of the population living off the informal economy. In the twenty-first century, it appears in the core countries of the capitalist West, afflicted by 'hyperdevelopment' in a landscape of stagnation, falling living standards and apparently intractable environmental problems. Finally, populist orientations can have radically different manifestations depending on the ideologies they are associated with – hence the risk in reducing to the same 'populism' phenomena that otherwise have little in common. Yet, it is apparent that at a moment when populism seems to have reached saturation point, inflecting virtually all political actors and voicing widespread discontent at neoliberalism, this notion alone is not sufficient anymore to capture the underlying logic of contemporary politics.

The theoretical effort needed to make sense of the new political horizon in the aftermath of the pandemic requires us to overcome this misunderstanding of populism as a purely negative moment, or as a cauldron in which left/right political differences are eliminated. Furthermore, it is necessary to go beyond the formalism that has dominated debate on populism and capture the concrete political positions, and the new class alignments, that have emerged out of the populist moment. To this end, in the continuation of this chapter we shall examine more closely the three major actors on the contemporary political stage: the nationalist right, the socialist left and the neoliberal centre.

## The Nationalist Right

There is little doubt that the most significant political trend in recent years has been the rise of the nationalist right. It has been such a striking trend that many commentators in the press and academia have come to view it as synonymous with 'populism' per se. The victory of Boris Johnson after the Brexit ordeal, on the back of a strong anti-immigration campaign; the rise to power of Donald Trump in the United States and of Jair Bolsonaro in Brazil; the dominance of national-populists in Eastern Europe; the strong popularity of Marine Le Pen in France, Matteo Salvini in Italy and the neo-Francoist Vox party in Spain – have all created the impression that, at least until the Covid crisis began to build in 2020, national populism was an unstoppable political force bound to engulf countries all around the world.

What is novel about this new nationalist right is the way in which it has departed from the dominant approach of conservatism in the 1990s and 2000s, which was to accept the neoliberal framework. This shift has been seen at different levels: in economic policy as much as in social and cultural policy. Some leaders of the populist right have abandoned adherence to strict monetarism, which was prevalent at the height of the neoliberal era. They have accepted the need for some fiscal deficit, especially in the aftermath of the pandemic, leading some people to speak of a right-wing Keynesianism. Furthermore, they have broken with the free trade creed of neoconservatives, as seen in Trump's protectionism and Johnson's embrace of the idea of an activist state. While the populist right is still in line with other neoliberal tenets, such as low taxation, this shift in economic policy is a remarkable break with the legacy of Reagan and Thatcher.

However, more symbolic has been the populist right's departure from neoliberal consensus on social and cultural issues. National populists have adopted a communitarian discourse infused with xenophobia, misogyny and chauvinism, as a means to intercept the growing anger and resentment of disgruntled workers and the declining middle class. The toxic nature of this discourse has led to the perception that national-populism is ultimately just a contemporary recrudescence of twentieth-century fascism – a kind of Nazi-populism, if you will. References to the 1930s and to an impending fascist menace have routinely peppered commentaries about Trump and his international sympathisers. Former US secretary of state Madeleine Albright attacked Trump vehemently in a book emphatically titled *Fascism: A Warning*.[16] American philosopher Jason Stanley, in his book *How Fascism Works*, identifies the rhetoric of Trump and others as typically fascist.[17]

Many politicians who feature on the frontline of the 'nationalist international' have indeed often flirted with openly fascist movements and ideas. In the United States, Trump has sometimes deployed overtly fascist rhetoric, indulged neo-Nazi groups such as Richard Spencer's

---

16 Madeleine Albright, *Fascism: A Warning* (London: HarperCollins, 2019).
17 Jason Stanley, *How Fascism Works: The Politics of Us and Them* (New York: Random House, 2020).

National Policy Institute and Gavin McInnes's Proud Boys, and given credence to far-right conspiracy theories such as those associated with QAnon.[18] Fascist movements have clearly felt emboldened by Trump's election. The 6 January 2021 Capitol Hill riots, incited by Donald Trump with the participation of far-right militias, seemed to confirm the worst fears about a new fascism. In Italy there have been frequent meetings between Matteo Salvini and members of the neo-fascist groups CasaPound and Forza Nuova; and in Hungary, Orbán has known ties to the neo-Nazi Jobbik party.

It is true that some contemporary right-wing populists may eventually go down the road of outright fascism. As things stand, however, right-wing populism generally has a greater resemblance to nineteenth-century rabid conservative nationalism than to twentieth-century fascism. Although it has adopted many of the toxic themes of fascism, contemporary right-wing populism lacks the reactionary element of a 'revolution against revolutions'. More generally, it is doubtful whether the Trumpists fully embody the defining characteristics of fascism identified by Poulantzas: its overt biological and/or cultural racism; its militarism and will-to-conquer; its totalitarian and anti-democratic spirit.[19]

While often engaging in dog-whistle racism, the new nationalists have mostly stopped short of explicitly affirming white supremacism. In their approach to foreign policy, they appear more doggedly isolationist than bent on war and invasion. It is telling that, while often issuing threats to foreign enemies, such as Iran, Trump did not embark on any new armed conflicts – a signal achievement for a US president, given the record of recent decades. More complex is the attitude of the populist right regarding democracy. So far, most right-wing populist movements seem bent more on plebiscitary democracy than outright dictatorship. Trump's attempt to subvert the 2020 election results, however, suggests that their celebration of democracy is purely opportunistic.

Rather than outright fascists, right-wing populists are better understood as 'illiberals'. The term 'illiberal democracy' was approvingly

---

18   QAnon is a conspiracy theory which claims that US politics is dominated by a corrupt deep state allied with the Democrats and engaging in paedophilia and Satanism.

19   Nicos Poulantzas, *Fascism and Dictatorship: The Third International and the Problem of Fascism* (London: Verso, 2019), pp. 254–6.

coined by Hungarian prime minister Viktor Orbán in a 2014 speech, expressing his refusal of liberal values, and has since been used by liberal theorists to express the nature of Orbán-style populism.[20] Besides Orbán, this illiberalism has also been attributed to Russian president Vladimir Putin, who has been accused of overtly and covertly giving succour to his international allies in Europe and America while explicitly claiming that the hegemony of liberalism was over.[21] Yale historian Timothy Snyder has sounded the alarm on the rise of illiberal regimes in Europe and America, singling out Putin's despotism as one of the main international drivers of this phenomenon.[22] For Takis Pappas, the right-wing populists' pursuit of an 'illiberal democracy' is what distinguishes them from full-blown fascists.[23] While fascism is non-democratic illiberalism, because it is both against civil liberties and democracy, populism is democratic illiberalism: it continues to nominally embrace democratic methods while attacking civil liberties and political institutions.[24]

The Covid pandemic led the nationalist right to radicalise its discourse, and in particular its criticism of science and experts. Nationalist leaders the world over have embraced conspiracy theories and winked at the anti-vaccination and anti-mask movements. They have pandered to fears of a fictitious communist enemy and stoked the flames of anti-China sentiment. Following their anti-elite instinct has, however, sometimes led national-populists to embrace untenable positions, leading to internecine culture wars within the right and an increasing divergence between hardcore right-wing populists like Trump and more moderate ones like Johnson. The radicalisation of the nationalist right is a reflection of despair more than a demonstration of strength; it reveals the weakness of what, until 2019, looked like the unstoppable rise of nationalism. This moment of the right's retreat may open new opportunities for the left, whose embrace of populism has been aimed at

---

20   Viktor Orbán speech on illiberalism, in Timothy Snyder, *The Road to Unfreedom: Russia, Europe, America* (London: Tim Duggan, 2018).

21   Lionel Barber and Henry Foy, 'Vladimir Putin: Liberalism Has "Outlived Its Purpose"', *Financial Times*, 27 June 2020.

22   Snyder, *Road to Unfreedom*.

23   Takis S. Pappas, 'Populist Democracies: Post-Authoritarian Greece and Post-Communist Hungary', *Government and Opposition* 49: 1 (2014).

24   Jan-Werner Müller, *What Is Populism?* (London: Penguin, 2017), p. 58.

the construction of a people built around a logic of equality and inclusion rather than discrimination.

## The Socialist Left

The rise of a nationalist right has been paralleled on the opposite
political front by the rise of a new socialist left. The foundation of
Podemos, an avowedly left populist party in Spain in 2014; the
victory of Syriza in the January 2015 Greek parliamentary elections;
the election of Jeremy Corbyn as Labour leader in the UK in May
2015 and the strong performance for Labour in the 2017 national
elections; Bernie Sanders' inspiring primary campaign in 2016; and
the creation of La France Insoumise, with its leader Jean-Luc
Mélenchon coming close to entering the second round of the French
2017 presidential elections – this rapid succession of events, created
the impression that there was a strong revival of the socialist left in
the populist moment. While most of the politicians and parties
involved were previously confined to the radical left, in the aftermath of the 2008 financial crash they managed to conquer a larger
base of support profiting from widespread socioeconomic distress
and discontent at mainstream centre-left parties.

The feature that defines this new socialist left against the mainstream
centre-left is its hostility towards the Third Way adopted by several
social-democratic formations in the 1990s, including those of Clinton,
Blair and Schröder. The socialist left has vehemently denounced the
neoliberal conversion of the centre-left, and in particular its complicity
in the demolition of the Keynesian welfare state, with disastrous effects
for many working people. To correct what they perceive as a betrayal of
the true mission of the left, the leaders of this 'newest left' – sometimes
described as a 'purple wave', after the colour used by Podemos in reference to the 'pink wave' of Latin American left-populism of the 2000s –
have advocated policies with a strong democratic socialist flavour. They
have called for investment in public health and public education, an
extension of social benefits and a return of the state as a driver of
economic activity. Furthermore, they have taken aim at the rich and at
the financial system as a whole, demanding higher taxation of the
wealthy and a reining in of global corporations.

This reprise of redistributive themes has led to a debate about the return of socialism, as seen in the many discussions of democratic socialism, twenty-first-century socialism, or 'millennial socialism' (in the sense of a socialism for the millennial generation). What is at stake in the current left revival is not merely a resuscitation of the socialism of old, but the adaptation of traditional socialist priorities to a society marked not only by extreme inequality, but also by social atomisation and low levels of political participation. It is a socialism whose populism consists mainly in a unifying appeal to the people as a means to make up for the weakness of class organisation, at a time when trade union membership has fallen to a historical low. This left resurgence has been met with disapproval from liberal commentators almost equalling that of the nationalist right – not least because it has shown that, despite decades of neoliberalism, criticism of capitalism has a renewed appeal.

Compared with the strong success of the new nationalist right, the electoral record of this new left has been rather disappointing. In the Anglo-Saxon world, both Corbyn and Sanders were defeated in 2019–20 – though after marking the best performances for overtly socialist candidates in both of their countries for several decades. Although some would like to paint Corbyn as a new Michael Foot – in other words, as marking a lurch to the left that ended in failure for Labour – this ignores some significant facts. While the 2019 elections were a disaster for Labour, in the 2017 polls Corbyn came close to beating the Tories, despite strong internal opposition from sections of the party apparatus that openly boycotted him. Similarly, in 2016, Bernie Sanders surprised commentators by coming close to snatching away the Democratic nomination from Hillary Clinton, whose victory was largely owed to the support she received from party grandees in the Democratic National Congress.

The fact that politicians like Sanders and Corbyn who, until their populist transmogrification, were seen as marginal figures of the radical left, were able to contend for power at a national level was remarkable, despite their ultimate failure. Moreover, left-populist formations in other countries did manage to reach government. In Greece, post-communist Syriza won two elections, in January and September 2015, its leader, Alexis Tsipras, governing the country as prime minister until 2019 in a progressive government that was nevertheless criticised by the hard left for capitulating to the pressures of the Troika.[25] Meanwhile, following its foundation in 2014 in the wake of the Indignados movement, Podemos moved firmly into position as the third-largest party in Spain – ultimately, in January 2020, forming a government with the socialist PSOE.

There are some parallelisms between this socialist–populist wave and other parties such as Italy's Five Star Movement. The formation founded by comedian Beppe Grillo is not a movement that can be easily catalogued as on the left, much less as socialist, eschewing all talk of ideology. It is one of the phenomena to have emerged out of the populist decade that strongly corresponds to a sort of ideal-typical 'pure populism'. It has attracted supporters with political leanings all over the political map – nationalist, conservative, socialist and social-democratic – if, indeed, they had any previous political affiliation at all. Its central political pitch has been an anti-elitist opposition to the political class. Its eclecticism and post-ideological character are underlined by the fact that, before entering a coalition government with the Democratic Party (PD), it was in coalition with radical right-wing Lega, posing little resistance to the hard line of Salvini on closing harbours to migrants. Nonetheless, the Five Star Movement has been responsible for pushing a number of policies that have redirected Italian political mobilisation towards social-democratic ends. It has created a citizen wage that supports over a million poor households in Italy and Prime Minister Conte's second government has supported decisions that mark a rupture with the neoliberal consensus, including the partial renationalisation of Italy's motorways. Thus, while many candidates of the new socialist left have ultimately been defeated, and more centrist formations such as the Five Star Movement are experiencing declining support at the polls, it would be wrong to hastily conclude that populism cannot work for the left. In fact, only the left parties that have embraced populist discourse have managed to overcome their electoral marginalisation.

---

25   The European Troika is a colloquial term used to describe the decision group formed by the European Central Bank (ECB) and the International Monetary Fund (IMF) and the European Commission (EC), which was involved in the bailout negotiations in Greece, Cyprus, Ireland and Portugal, imposing punitive austerity measures.

Table 1.1    Political Actors in the Great Recoil

|  | Socialist left | Neoliberal centre | Nationalist right |
|---|---|---|---|
| **Sovereignty** | Popular sovereignty; democratic autonomy; egalitarian state; state capacity | Supra-national governance; defence of global integration and European Union (EU); support of multilateral institutions (ECB, IMF, WB, WTO, UN) | National sovereignty; territorial sovereignty; White supremacy; ethnic democracy |
| **Protection** | Social protectivism; labour and environmental protectionism; anti-globalisation; nationalisation of strategic industries; jobs guarantee; social welfare and health; politics of care | Free trade; no state subsidies; suspicion towards protectionism | Proprietarian protectionism; trade tariffs; bilateralism; regressive taxation; Sinophobia; law and order policies; defence of local capitalist class; socialism for the rich |
| **Control** | Environmental regulation; wealth taxation; unions on corporate boards; social movements; citizens' participation | Technocracy; virtual town hall meetings; civil society participation | Border controls; anti-migrant policies; strengthening of executive power; plebiscitary democracy |

Despite its failings, the emergence of a new socialist left with populist characteristics proves that the lurch to the extreme right is not a foregone conclusion in the era of the Great Recoil. Socialist policies have been demonstrated to have broad appeal among voters, who now covet state protection from health and economic insecurity. This is all the more significant given the way in which, since 1989, neoliberals have demonised socialism through 'red scare' tactics. Testifying to this rebalancing is the fact that even centre-left parties such as the Democratic Party in the United States and the new president, Joe Biden, and the PSOE in Spain have been forced to redirect their agendas in a left direction, promising to champion the priorities of workers, neglected for so long in favour of corporate interests. A centrist, on the model of Clinton and Obama, since becoming president Joe Biden has unveiled ambitious spending plans and a far-reaching green deal, often jointly described as 'Bidenomics', which point to a departure from the neoliberal consensus.

Biden's economic programmes include a $2 trillion infrastructure investment plan, higher taxes on corporations, and action against tax havens. These policies show that the centre-left is realigning itself, to a great extent in response to the growing influence of the socialist wing of the Democratic Party. Thus, while the political situation may look dire for the left, the electoral viability of progressive economic policies in the longer term should not be underestimated.

## The Neoliberal Centre

The feature shared by the nationalist right and the socialist left, which lies at the core of their populist orientation, is their hostility towards the neoliberal centre. The neoliberal centre – a category that includes many formations and politicians that adopt a free market stance and preach political moderation – was the dominant actor during the 1990s and early 2000s, when the alternative between centre-left and centre-right governments seemed a matter of taste rather than substance (like the difference between Coca-Cola and Pepsi, according to Slavoj Žižek's quip), neoliberal policies always being part of the package. Since the 2008 economic downturn, however, pro-market centrists have been on the back foot, as public opinion has grown increasingly critical of neoliberal globalisation and the devastating effects of the policies it entails, including privatisation and deregulation.

If anything, this defensive repositioning has become more pronounced amid the Covid-19 pandemic, since free markets have failed spectacularly to provide essential health goods and services. It is true that the emergency situation, by revealing the incompetence and recklessness of the nationalist right, seems to have given a new lease of life to the politics of competence and expertise – something on which centrist politicians have long prided themselves. The consolidation of Angela Merkel's reputation for clear-headed and compassionate moderation and the growing popularity of centrist figures like Jacinda Ardern in New Zealand and Justin Trudeau in Canada are indications of this trend. Yet the profound socioeconomic pain inflicted by the corona-crash and the new Keynesian interventionism and welfare support that are now being demanded, evidently go against the laissez-faire creed espoused by free market centrists.

A sense of disorientation is engulfing contemporary liberalism. In works such as Edward Luce's *The Retreat of Western Liberalism*, William A. Galston's *Anti-Pluralism* and Patrick Deneen's *Why Liberalism Failed*, liberal scholars have argued that liberalism faces an existential crisis, and that populists' success derives from liberalism's decline.[26] But the root causes underpinning this correlation between a fading liberalism and a growing populism remain unexplored. While liberals are quick to denounce the political illiberalism of the populist right, they often fail to notice how discontent at the liberal order stems from the disastrous effects of neoliberal economic doctrines themselves – 'actually existing liberalism', as it might be called: the concrete form that liberal doctrine has acquired in the early twenty-first century. The depiction of populism as a pathology often found in the liberal news media and academia seems to be part of a strategy to deflect blame; it overlooks the unforgiving structural circumstances from which the populist moment emerged as a reaction against the free market extremism of neoliberal governments.

The suspicion of liberal centrists towards populism in all its forms is strongly reciprocated. As we have seen, what sets both the socialist left and the nationalist right apart from their predecessors is a strong opposition to neoliberalism. The dominant trends of their political discourse are post-neoliberal, because they involve a negation of the key neoliberal reservations against government intervention and in favour of prudent fiscal policy and limited social spending. Whereas neoliberalism celebrates freedom of movement of all economic factors (capital, labour and commodities) in the global arena, populist challengers have often questioned whether free markets work for the collective or national good. Whereas neoliberalism waxes lyrical about the advantages of openness, populists on the left and the right have signalled the value of protecting society by advocating economic protectionism; whereas neoliberalism is informed by a preference for cosmopolitan globalisation, right-wing populists have reclaimed the importance of locality, nationality and place-based identity; whereas neoliberals see the state as a mere referee, praising the self-organisation of private firms and civil

---

26   Edward Luce, *The Retreat of Western Liberalism* (London: Abacus, 2018); William A. Galston, *Anti-Pluralism: The Populist Threat to Liberal Democracy* (New Haven, CT: Yale University Press, 2018); Patrick J. Deneen, *Why Liberalism Failed* (New Haven, CT: Yale University Press, 2019).

society, left-wing populists have called for an interventionist state; and, finally, where neoliberals have long preached and practised antisocial monetarism, populists advocate Keynesian monetary expansion, deficit spending and debt monetisation advocated by Modern Monetary Theory.[27] In short, twenty-first-century populist discourse is fundamentally the antithesis and inversion of neoliberalism: populism = anti-neoliberalism. Yet, this has also been populism's apparent limit, the fact that it tends to stop at the level of countercultural contestation, instead of rising to the challenge of constructing a truly counter-hegemonic project.[28] It from this necessary negative moment that a post-neoliberal statism is now developing its positive form.

## A New Ideological Era

The negation of neoliberalism that lies at the core of the populist moment is represented differently within the nationalist right and the socialist left. The right mostly takes aim at cultural neoliberalism – the openness and tolerance with respect to cultures and genders that was one of the components of so-called progressive neoliberalism discussed by Nancy Fraser.[29] While it has denounced and abandoned the neoliberal commitment to global free trade it has clearly conserved the neoliberal emphasis on low taxation and lax labour regulation. Conversely, the left has not only attacked free trade in the name of environmental and social protectionism, but has also denounced the system of flexible labour regulation and casualisation that has dominated markets for employment since the 1980s. On the other hand, it generally retains the same favourable view of multiculturalism and immigration espoused by the neoliberal centre-left. From the collision between neoliberal thesis and populist antithesis a novel synthesis is now emerging, in the form of a protective neo-statism that aspires to displace neoliberalism in its role of defining our shared ideological horizon.

---

27   Modern monetary theory is a heterodox post-Keynesian theory that turns upside down much of the received wisdom on the quantitative theory of money, advocating large deficits financed by monetary expansion.

28   Michael Lind, *The New Class War: Saving Democracy from the Managerial Elite* (London: Penguin, 2020)

29   Nancy Fraser, 'Progressive Neoliberalism versus Reactionary Populism: A Choice that Feminists Should Refuse.' *NORA-Nordic Journal of Feminist and Gender Research* 24: 4 (2016), 281–4.

Figure 1.2    Title: Ideological long waves in the twentieth and early twenty-first century

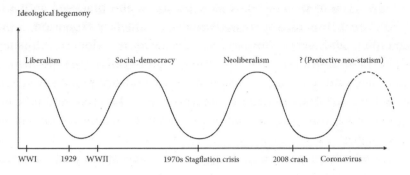

Like the economy, ideology is defined by long waves lasting for around forty to fifty years, with periods of rising hegemony succeeded by phases of decline. After the early twentieth-century crisis of liberalism and the crisis of social democracy in the 1970s and 1980s, we seem to be witnessing a new moment of ideological transition.

We can best approach this trend of historical transformation of ideologies through the notion of ideological cycles, similar to the long waves discussed by Soviet economist Nikolai Kondratieff, each lasting for around fifty years.[30] Successive historical eras have been defined by different ideological hegemonies that have often emerged in opposition to pre-existing dominant ideologies. We can begin from the liberal era of the nineteenth and early twentieth centuries, which was dominated in various European countries by liberal formations informed by the idea of laissez-faire market individualism, putting the conservative right mostly on the defensive.[31] Its master-signifier was freedom. The liberal era ended in the disasters of world wars and global depression and its place was taken by its old socialist adversary – democratic in the West, authoritarian in the East – whose master-signifier was justice. In the face of capitalist crisis, Red Russia became the purveyor of a state-centred and highly repressive socialism in one country. At the same moment, Roosevelt was fashioning his progressive New Deal, which prioritised pro-labour policies and social-democratic public spending (as, for a briefer period, did Léon Blum's Popular Front government in France). With liberalism in crisis, fascist nationalism emerged as a

---

30    Nikolai Kondratieff, 'The Long Waves in Economic Life', *Review of Economics and Statistics* 17: 6 (1925), 105–15.

31    Immanuel Wallerstein, *The Modern World-System IV: Centrist Liberalism Triumphant, 1789–1914* (Berkeley, CA: University of California Press, 2011).

right-wing reaction against the rise of socialism, appropriating part of the discourse of working-class movements. In the aftermath of World War II, socialism developed on both sides of the Iron Curtain. In most countries of Western Europe, class compromise took the form of a social-democratic pact between capital and labour and led to the so-called *trente glorieuses* – the golden age of economic growth experienced by capitalism between 1945 and 1975; in the USSR and its satellites, it was expressed in a communist command economy and policies of social welfare.

The oil shocks and crises of the 1970s signalled the collapse of the social-democratic era, once again opening the terrain for the birth of a new ideological order. The battle for hegemony was won by neoliberalism, informed by thinkers such as Friedrich Hayek, Karl Popper and Milton Friedman. These thinkers took aim at what they saw as a wasteful and authoritarian socialist world. Neoliberal ideology was swiftly implemented by a new brand of conservative politicians – most importantly Margaret Thatcher in the UK and Ronald Reagan in the United States, who ensured that neoliberalism became the dominant economic and political doctrine among policymakers. Once again, the master-signifier of this era was 'freedom' – or, more precisely, 'market freedom'. This was accompanied by a number of connected terms – 'openness', 'opportunity', 'entrepreneurialism' – that conspired to project the narrative of a triumphant era of open markets. The rise of anti-neoliberal populism in the 2010s, fuelled by widespread discontent at ballooning inequality, marks the low point of this ideological era. Populism is neoliberal society recoiling upon itself.

We now stand at a similar moment of ideological, or better meta-ideological, transition, in the sense of a systemic change in ideological space that embraces both political poles. It is a moment in which neoliberalism seems on the point of giving way to a neo-statism, which is destined to reshape political discourse and radically transform society's expectations and political priorities. While, amid the frenzy of the present ideological interregnum, we cannot yet affirm with any certainty whether this shift in political common sense will have a progressive or reactionary momentum, the new keywords of the discourse of protection and control provide an inkling of the new world that is emerging out of the Covid crisis.

## Statist Signifiers

To study post-neoliberal ideology, I follow the framework of discourse analysis, examining the speeches, public declarations, policy documents and campaign messages of Western political leaders, and approaching them as texts that are part of a larger ideological discourse. The study of political discourse offers a vantage point from which to investigate political ideology – and explore the changes in values and worldviews that are emerging in the present moment. One of the problems with the debate on populism that has developed in recent decades is that it seems to only scratch at the surface of the actual content of contemporary ideology. As we have previously signalled, this scholarship is dominated by a formalistic approach, which reduces the contents of populism to an anti-elite, anti-establishment posture, combined with the pursuit of a discourse of the people. It thereby makes little headway in capturing the concrete demands, visions, values, but also class coalitions and antagonisms, that lie at the centre of post-neoliberal politics and spell out their positive content.

This formalism is visible in the work of the most influential theorist of populism, Ernesto Laclau, an Argentinian theorist who fled to exile in England to escape military dictatorship. The work of Laclau offers the most sophisticated and explicit theorisation of populism as a discursive phenomenon. In *On Populist Reason*, his best systematisation of this argument, Laclau asserts: 'by "populism" we do not understand a *type* of movement – identifiable with either a special social base or a particular ideological orientation'.[32] Laclau proposed instead an approach to populism as a certain 'political logic'.[33] This means that populism is not an ideology as such, but rather a discursive dynamic that, in different circumstances, will articulate different ideological contents. This goes a long way to explaining why populism seemingly never offers itself in a pure form, as it were, but in alloys uniting disparate and sometimes seemingly irreconcilable ideological elements: from working-class communism and socialism to middle-class radicalism and reactionary bourgeois conservatism. Hence the quintessentially hybrid and eccentric character of populist politics.

What is central to populism, according to Laclau, is its appeal to the people, defined as the totality of the political community, and the connected

---

32   Laclau, *On Populist Reason*, p. 177.
33   Ibid.

construction of a 'popular identity'. This 'popular identity' – as distinct from other social identities that are mobilised in the political arena, such as class identity, religious identity and gender identity – is marked by its all-inclusive character, which allies various constituencies and their disparate demands. This unity develops through a 'chain of equivalence' – a process of concatenation that binds together disparate grievances in opposition to a single power system. Taking his cue from Jacques Lacan's psychoanalysis and the linguistics of Saussure, with their insistence on the arbitrary nature of the coupling between signifier and signified, Laclau famously argues that this unifying effort coalesces around an 'empty signifier'.[34] This is a symbol that, precisely by virtue of its indeterminacy and apparent mean-inglessness, becomes the catalyst of a process of symbolic and political aggregation.[35] This theory has provided useful insights into the logic of mobilisation for national–populist leaders like Donald Trump and left-populist parties such as Podemos, and the way such mobilisation revolves around a unifying appeal to the people against the establishment, which studiously avoids traditional political signifiers. But to understand the shape of post-neoliberal politics it is necessary to move beyond this formal-istic theory of populism and the connected view of contemporary politics as a collection of empty signifiers. It is instead time to approach the substan-tive contents that are emerging on the post-neoliberal horizon and how they project a new political imaginary.

The discursive horizon of the Great Recoil is defined by the neo-statist triad of *sovereignty*, *control* and *protection*, the master-signifiers of our era. Issues of sovereignty are mobilised to reassert the primacy of the state and of political power over private power, as well as the primacy of national space. These notions have been voiced not only by 'exiters' and anti-globalists, but also in the context of social and environmental campaigns and calls for energy sovereignty, technological sovereignty, food sover-eignty, democracy and local government. The demand for a restoration of popular sovereignty reflects a perception of the weakness of the nation-state and its inability to function as an effective agency guaranteeing people's security, amid the present phase of organic crisis of capitalist democracies. It involves a reaffirmation of the principle of authority, in

---

34   Ferdinand de Saussure, *Course in General Linguistics* (New York: Columbia University Press, 2011); Jacques Lacan, *Écrits: A Selection* (London: Routledge, 2001).

35   Laclau, *On Populist Reason*, p. 28.

contrast with the libertarian anti-authoritarianism dominant in the neoliberal era, in a negation of the framing of the state as wasteful and impotent.

Terms such as 'protection' and 'control' are strongly connected to this rehabilitation of the principle of political authority and order. 'Protection' is associated with a demand for security in a world full of danger and fear, whose central driver, unlike the desire for risk-taking in the pursuit of wealth that defined the neoliberal era, is economic precarity and status anxiety: a profound fear of decline, substitution, or even annihilation, as expressed by environmental movements campaigning for climate justice. This demand features broadly in contemporary political discourse around all forms of protection, from protection against the coronavirus to environmental protection, on the left, to the protection of cultural identity against migrants, on the right. Finally, the issue of 'control' echoes from the Brexit campaign on retaking national control of borders and laws, to demands for workers' control and social movements' struggles for a real democracy. This demand reflects an anxiety about a world that feels increasingly chaotic, in which the desire to regain some steering capacity at a collective level has become singularly urgent.

Figure 1.3   The neo-statist discursive triad

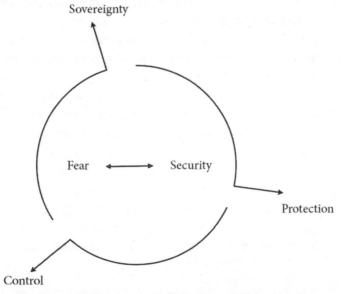

Neo-statist discourse centres on three recurring terms: sovereignty, protection and control. All of them are connected to the growing demand for security (in its manifold variations: social, environmental and geopolitical).

The terms featuring in the neo-statist triad are not mere 'empty signifiers' – in other words, terms whose content is arbitrary, and ultimately irrelevant. Rather, their distinctive aspect is that they do indeed carry 'signifieds': specific meanings that are secreted through their deployment in political philosophy and political history. For example, the notion of control revolves around issues of mastery, domination and ownership, including the operation of various state apparatuses. Talk of control, in this sense, is distinct from talk of 'freedom'. It implies a different vision of society, and projects different priorities and preoccupations. On the other hand, these terms can be assigned different specific connotations, by qualifying them and emphasising certain aspects of their content over others. When speaking of security, for example, the nationalist right is referring chiefly to law and order – security from crime. The socialist left, on the other hand, will emphasise issues of social and environmental security. If they share a common jargon, it is because the socialist left and nationalist right *live in the same world* and face the same fundamental social dilemmas at a time marked by the triple threat of economic, climate and health crises. What matters for the purposes of political programmes and strategies is how various political forces 'fill' these signifiers with specific meanings, and in turn how these meanings offer a response to dominant social anxieties. To begin addressing these questions in the next chapter we will explore the crisis of neoliberal globalisation, which constitutes the historical background against which these ideological shifts can be best understood.

# 2

## Global Blowback

The coronavirus crisis marks a tipping point in the decline of neoliberal globalisation that has important consequences for contemporary politics and ideology. In just a few weeks in February and March 2020, what initially looked like a local epidemic affecting a limited region of Asia – a passing threat like the one posed in previous years by SARS, MERS and H1N1 – became a severe global pandemic. The spread of the virus grew rapidly out of control and billions of people had to go into lockdown in order to 'flatten the curve' of contagion, and protect the intensive care units of healthcare systems around the world from a sudden, overwhelming influx of gasping patients. With empty streets and shopping malls, the routine wearing of surgical masks and large trucks sanitising walkways, the landscape of major cities was transformed. Several countries closed their borders, while planes remained earthbound. The health crisis was soon compounded by a major economic depression. Many countries underwent their largest drop in employment in history. Entire industries, and in particular the tourism sector, heavily dependent on international travel, ground to a halt, while governments and central banks tried desperately to stem economic collapse by pumping enormous sums of money into the economy.

The event has been described as an 'exogenous' shock – one originating outside the system it affects, an unprecedented and unrepeatable 'black swan' event, violently upsetting well-established equilibria. However, the explosion of the pandemic and its consequences are anything but exogenous to society; they are merely accelerating developments that were already years in the making. The Covid-19 pandemic has shone a light on the follies of the neoliberal system and the risks of global interconnectedness. From business travellers becoming superspreaders to the shortage of beds and ventilators – due to austerity cuts to public services – and the social inequality between those able to 'smart-work' and those forced to risk infection in factories and warehouses or be laid off, this emergency has been a damning test of the fraught promises of a neoliberal and globalised world. Moreover, this crisis should not be taken as a one-off. Rather, as many people have come to realise, it offers a cautionary tale about coming global emergencies, as represented in a viral internet meme in which the wave of Covid-19 is followed by even higher and more destructive waves: the recession, climate change, biodiversity collapse. The health emergency has served to connect the dots of a failing global order.

Economic globalisation – the growing interconnectedness of the economy at a planetary level – has been the most vaunted product of the neoliberal order. During the 1990s and early 2000s, it looked like an unstoppable phenomenon, bound to integrate even the most remote recesses of the planet into a global market, while condemning the countries, companies and individuals who did not follow its imperatives to irrelevance. Nonetheless, in a world traversed by multiple shocks, it is precisely this monument to neoliberalism's ingenuity and ambition that stands in peril. Already in the aftermath of the 2008 financial crisis, and during the austere 2010s, economists had noticed a tendency towards 'slowbalisation' – the slowing of globalisation. Global growth slackened, foreign direct investments dipped and even global trade – a key indicator of global interconnectedness – itself receded. The coronavirus crisis has only intensified this tendency, producing a dip in global trade, the upsetting of global supply chains, growing economic protectionism, and signs of increasing 'uncoupling' between the Chinese and Western economies.[1]

This state of affairs is central to any understanding of ideological transformation attending the Great Recoil. As this chapter will show, the multiple inequalities engendered by globalisation have been key drivers

---

1   Katherine Hill, 'The Great Uncoupling: One Supply Chain for China, One for Everywhere Else', *Financial Times*, 6 October 2020.

of the social discontent that has fuelled the rise of populist movements in the 2010s. Globalisation's drive towards externalisation and flexibility has redrawn the economic map of the world according to the principle of cost-minimisation of production inputs, especially labour. In order to sell on world markets and insulate their profits from taxation, companies have relocated, outsourced their labour, offshored their factories and taken advantage of the special export zones and tax havens that were created all over the world during the neoliberal era. The net result has been a spectacular rise in inequality. A very few have been able to amass huge wealth, while workers' wages have been pushed to the bottom; economic risks have sharpened; and the gulf has grown massively between rich, globalised cities and a diffuse global periphery ravaged by impoverishment and decline. These huge social dislocations, combined with a perception of exposure to uncontrollable and anti-democratic forces, lie at the heart of the global agoraphobia that informs contemporary politics.

## United under One World Market

Popularised by Harvard business professor Theodore Levitt in the mid 1980s, the term globalisation served to capture the progressive engulfing of ever more nations into a global market under the aegis of the United States as the uncontested global superpower after the collapse of the Soviet bloc. In fact, this is not the first globalisation in history, nor probably the last.[2] As Fernand Braudel and other theorists of the 'world-system' such as Immanuel Wallerstein and Giovani Arrighi have documented, from the Genoese to the Dutch Empire and the Victorian age, societies have undergone successive waves of international integration and trade liberalisation.[3] But the wave of globalisation occurring after

---

2   Theodore Levitt, 'The Globalization of Markets', in Robert Z. Aliber and Reid W. Click, eds, *Readings in International Business: A Decision Approach* (Cambridge, MA: MIT Press, 1993).

3   Fernand Braudel, *Civilization and Capitalism, 15th–18th Century, vol. III: The Perspective of the World* (Berkeley, CA: University of California Press, 1992); Immanuel Wallerstein, 'Globalization or the Age of Transition? A Long-Term View of the Trajectory of the World-System', *International Sociology* 15: 2 (2000); Giovanni Arrighi, *Chaos and Governance in the Modern World System* (Minneapolis, MN: University of Minnesota Press, 1999).

the fall of the Berlin Wall has been unequalled in magnitude. For the first time in human history, almost the entire planetary economy has been subsumed into a unitary world market.

Neoliberal globalisation emerged from the ruins of the system created by the Bretton Woods Agreement – signed in 1944 as World War II was still raging in Europe, China and the Pacific – which until the 1970s had enforced strict control over currency and capital movements. Starting in the 1960s, the rise of multinational corporations and the increase in transnational capital mobility began to reshape the international economy. From just a few hundred at the end of World War II, multinational corporations grew in number to 30,000 by 1990 and then 100,000 by 2011.[4] The most disparate industries – from car manufacturing to food and beverages, retailing and social media – were progressively colonised by multinationals such as Nike, Coca-Cola and Nestlé, and more recently digital companies such as Apple, Facebook and Amazon; these became the public faces of globalisation, whose goods, services and brands were available virtually anywhere on the planet. Some of these companies are larger in financial value than many countries, affording them such enormous power that some commentators speak of 'corporate sovereignty' having surpassed that of nation-states.[5] According to the United Nations Conference on Trade and Development (UNCTAD), 80 per cent of global trade happens in 'value chains' linked to transnational corporations, and a third of it takes place *within* multinational companies, between their various national affiliates.[6]

The growth of corporations has been facilitated by free-trade agreements that have done away with many barriers to international commerce. While the original General Agreement on Tariffs and Trade, signed in 1947, already aimed at the liberalisation of trade through the reduction of tariffs, quotas and subsidies, important areas – such as agriculture, textiles and, most importantly, services – were not covered

---

4    Alfred D. Chandler and Bruce Mazlish, eds, *Leviathans: Multinational Corporations and the New Global History* (Cambridge: Cambridge University Press, 2005).

5    Joshua Barkan, *Corporate Sovereignty: Law and Government under Capitalism* (Minneapolis, MN: University of Minnesota Press, 2013).

6    United Nations Conference on Trade and Development, '80% of Trade Takes Place in "Value Chains" Linked to Transnational Corporations', 27 February 2013, at unctad.org.

by it. The World Trade Organization (WTO), created in 1995, went on
to supervise 95 per cent of the world's global trade. Its effect – combined
with that of the creation of regional free trade agreements such as the
Mercosur in South America (1991), the ASEAN Free Trade Agreement
(AFTA, incorporating Southeast Asian nations – 1992) and the North
American Free Trade Agreement (NAFTA – 1994), as well as ever
deeper integration in the European market – was the progressive elimination of ever more trade barriers.

As a consequence, global trade has grown spectacularly. Between
1985 and 2011, it more than doubled, growing by an average of 5.6 per
cent in excess of global GDP growth.[7] There are now countries, such as
Hungary and the Netherlands, whose volume of global trade (combining imports and exports) is greater than their GDP, indicating a state of
extreme dependency on the vagaries of the global market. Developing
countries in Latin America and Africa have become global suppliers of
primary goods, oil, minerals and cash crops, while China has risen to
the status of 'factory of the world'. Export-processing zones or 'special
zones' – tax-free areas dedicated to the production of export goods –
have grown from 500 in 1995 to 5,400 in 2018, according to UNCTAD.[8]
Despite its present difficulties, global trade continues to be a formidable
force: the value of world merchandise stood at a towering US$19 trillion
in 2019 – equivalent to the GDP of the entire European Union.

Free trade and the rise of multinational corporations have been key
factors fuelling the pervasive financialisation of the economy. Informed
by the recommendations of English theorist and 'economic diplomat'
John Maynard Keynes, the Bretton Woods Agreement was designed to
limit international capital flows, which Keynes considered a cause of
macroeconomic destabilisation. Furthermore, taking a lesson from the
Great Depression, many countries had imposed strict regulations on the
banking sector; the landmark Glass–Steagall legislation, passed in the
United States in 1933, separated commercial from investment banking.
During the decades after World War II, governments implemented
controls on capital flows and currency holdings. For instance, when

---

7    Dani Rodrik, *Straight Talk on Trade: Ideas for a Sane World Economy* (Princeton,
NJ: Princeton University Press, 2017).

8    United Nations Conference on Trade and Development, *World Investment Report
2019 – Chapter IV: Special Economic Zones*, 2019, at unctad.org.

travelling abroad, citizens could only exchange limited amounts of cash. Neoliberalism demolished all such Keynesian rigidities that stood in the way of international market arbitrage and speculation.

In the aftermath of the oil shocks of the 1970s and the end of the Bretton Woods gold standard, OECD countries underwent a sustained liberalisation of their financial systems. The growth of the Eurodollar market in the 1960s and 1970s and the ensuing deregulation of financial services in London in 1983, led to the famous 'Big Bang' in the London Stock Exchange. In the United States, under Ronald Reagan, requirements for savings and loans were relaxed and the Depository Institutions Act of 1982 deregulated mortgage lending. In the 1990s, Bill Clinton would further shake up the industry, repealing the Glass-Steagall Act. These measures were accompanied by a relaxation of controls over international capital mobility. Global capital flows more than quadrupled between 2000 and 2007 and continued growing even after the 2008 crisis. Global market capitalisation was estimated to be $90 trillion in 2019, while gross cross-border capital flows accounted for over 20 per cent of global GDP: a colossal river of money that can wreak havoc in countries experiencing sudden inflows and outflows.

These global economic trends were accompanied at the national level by a progressive weakening of social protections established during the social-democratic era. In the post-war years, the capitalist West experienced a golden age of growth and rising productivity; demand was maintained by Keynesian government spending while wages were driven up by strong unions. This social-democratic compact reduced inequality and curbed the managerial autonomy of industrialists and the property rights of the wealthy. But this was not to last. Starting in the 1970s, neoliberals introduced an ever-greater degree of monetarism into the system while attacking the power of unions. Even in continental Europe, where social democracy remained dominant throughout the 1980s and 1990s, social-welfare provisions were reduced and made ever more conditional on job-seeking. German social democracy caved in to neoliberal flexibility by passing the 'workfare' package of the Hartz IV labour reforms in the early 2000s. Labour deregulation came to allow for all sorts of part-time, casualised or 'zero-hour' contracts, offloading risks onto workers. The so-called 'pact between labour and capital' of the post-war period, forged amid fear of the Soviet Union, which guaranteed rising living standards for workers was thus progressively dismantled. The institutions that had guaranteed social stability and presided over sustained growth during the so-called *trente glorieuses* – the years of the economic miracle grown on the rubble of World War II – were seen as out of kilter with the logic of international competitiveness and the connected imperative of suppressing salaries and social guarantees.

The buzzword 'globalisation' served to give these different economic 'reforms' the allure of a civilisational project. Globalisation was predicated on the promise of universal prosperity: it would not just lift people in Third World countries out of poverty, but also provide better jobs for workers living in the old trinity of the capitalist system – the United States, Europe and Japan. While many added-value manufacturing jobs would inevitably be relocated offshore, highly skilled and better-paid jobs in the service industry would become available. Opening countries to the global market would not only render companies more efficient, and hence make consumers happier; it would also force governments to abandon unsustainable deficit-spending and tax-payer support for failing industries, providing an effective 'external constraint' to deter irrational and wasteful economic practices. Resisting globalisation would be framed as reactionary or nostalgic, given the momentum behind it. All politicians could do was to manage it, making national economies more export-friendly and globally competitive.

As argued by the former vice president of Bolivia, Álvaro García Linera, for many people globalisation ultimately became 'a political and ideological horizon to channel collective hopes into a unique destiny where all possible expectations of improvement can become reality'.[9] Neoliberal evangelists not only saw 'the global triumph of the free market as the "natural" and irreversible destiny of the world'; they also painted globalisation as a moment of 'redemption of humanity'.[10] In the teleological vision of a Hegelian end of history proposed by American political scientist Francis Fukuyama, globalisation was to be the last step in the development of the World Spirit, affirming the civilisational supremacy of liberal societies.[11] United under the umbrella of global

---

9   Álvaro García Linera, 'La globalización ha muerto', *Educere* 21: 68 (2017).
10   Ibid.
11   Francis Fukuyama, *The End of History and the Last Man* (London: Simon & Schuster, 2006).

capitalism, humanity would overcome its atavistic particularisms and recognise its shared interests. Global economic integration would be the pathway to a more peaceful and rational world. Commercial bonds of economic interdependence between countries, shouldered by the international interests of global finance, would be the best insurance policy against war.

Globalisation was also a utopia in the literal sense of the word – that is, as a non-place. It promised to obliterate geographical distance and erode parochial, place-based identities. Its practical driving force was what Marxist geographer David Harvey named 'time–space compression' – in other words, the shortening of travel times and instantaneous communication.[12] Indeed, thanks to the accelerating pace of transportation and information transmission, the space of global flows, epitomised by the internet, seemed bound to prevail over the space of places.[13] This elision of time would result in a shrinking of space, a victory of speed over terrain.[14] The overcoming of barriers and distances would eventually be complete, leading to what one *New York Times* columnist and globalisation apologist, Thomas L. Friedman, called a borderless 'flat earth' of endless opportunities.[15] Regardless of whether one lived in Baltimore, Jakarta, Mumbai, or Cape Town – so the argument ran – the world would eventually resemble the global village envisioned by Marshall McLuhan, under festoons filled with the faces of celebrities and the logos of global brands.[16] As history came to an end, geography and geopolitics would themselves breathe their last.

## Globalisation in Shreds

Amid the dark atmosphere of the present, with societies caught in multiple systemic crises and globalisation on the retreat, the wisdom of

---

12  David Harvey, *The Condition of Postmodernity* (Oxford: Blackwell, 1989).

13  Manuel Castells, 'The Space of Flows', in his *The Rise of the Network Society: The Information Age: Economy, Society and Culture, Vol. 1* (Cambridge, MA: Blackwell, 1996).

14  Ibid.

15  Thomas L. Friedman, *The World Is Flat: A Brief History of the Twenty-First Century* (London: Macmillan, 2006).

16  Marshall McLuhan and Bruce R. Powers, *The Global Village: Transformations in World Life and Media in the 21st Century* (Oxford: Oxford University Press, 1989).

hindsight allows us to assess these shining promises with a cooler eye. It is true that globalisation has had positive results in emerging economies. The inclusion of China and other developing countries in the world market has taken hundreds of millions out of rural poverty and created a sizeable middle class. However, the growth record under neoliberalism (1979–2008) was considerably lower than that achieved under the Keynesianism that defined the Bretton Woods era (1946–71), with its fixed exchange rates and limited capital mobility. Furthermore, globalisation has contributed to a spectacular increase in social inequality, magnified by the enormous scale on which the economy now operates.[17] In 2020, it was documented that 2,153 billionaires had more wealth than the 4.6 billion people making up 60 per cent of the world's population. Between them, they controlled US$10 trillion, and Jeff Bezos, one of the world's richest people, was projected to become the world's first trillionaire in the 2030s. In fact, in America and Europe wages have long stagnated; the labour share in national income has been steadily decreasing since 1990, while the capital share has been growing and growing. In this context, globalisation seems to have lost much of its former ideological allure. It is no longer perceived as a force for prosperity, but as the prime source of many threats that have put society's well-being in peril.

These strains of globalisation have been vividly revealed in the wave of crises of the 2010s and 2020s. The 2008 financial deflagration caused a great recession that disproportionately affected America, and especially Europe, and led to growing unemployment, stagnating wages and millions of people unable to pay their rent or mortgage. Public services were cut to the bone under the aegis of austerity, leading to infant poverty, and now to thousands of unnecessary deaths due to unpreparedness in the face of the pandemic, in a landscape of devastated education and welfare services. From a macroeconomic perspective, the 2020 coronavirus crisis is far worse than the 2008 slump and more similar to the Great Depression of the 1930s. The simultaneous fall in production and consumption during the repeated wave of lockdowns between 2020 and 2021 resulted in a deep economic contraction. The fall in GDP in 2020 was just below 10 per cent in OECD

---

17    Thomas Piketty, *Capital in the Twenty-First Century* (Cambridge, MA: Harvard University Press, 2018).

countries – something unseen since World War II. Things could get far worse, with unemployment ballooning and the possibility of a new financial crisis.

Despite the enormous stimulus packages totalling US$5 trillion, in the United States and around half that amount in the European Union, and massive government interventions to support household incomes and corporate liquidity, prospects remain bleak. As economists like Nouriel Roubini have argued, we may be heading for a 'Greater Depression' marked by mass unemployment, deflation and widespread bankruptcies.[18] Neoliberal voices insist this is just a bump in the road, but it is clear that this crisis poses an existential challenge to globalisation as we know it.[19] After the slowdown of global economic integration experienced in the 2010s, we are likely to see a phase of outright 'deglobalisation' – a global convulsion resulting in a lasting reduction in global economic interconnectedness: logistics chains are shortening, companies are reshoring and national economic interventions are multiplying. In the long run this trend could potentially lead to markets more closely focused on specific countries and their immediate geographical region, in order to ensure greater economic and environmental 'resilience'.[20]

The problems faced by globalisation are paradoxically a product of its own success – a result of the fact that it has saturated the entire planet after drawing one country after another into its grasp. There are now no new markets left to open up. The garment factories of the Buriganga River in Bangladesh and the furniture factories around Ho Chi Minh City in Vietnam – some of the most recent sites of global integration – are a sort of Hercules column Western neoliberal capitalism cannot overcome. Ironically, and tragically, both are under threat from rising sea levels due to climate change. Meanwhile, natural resources – mines, forests and fisheries – are overexploited, large areas of the planet subject

---

18   Nouriel Roubini, 'Ten Reasons Why a "Greater Depression" for the 2020s Is Inevitable', *Guardian*, 29 April 2020.

19   Henry Farrell and Abraham Newman, 'Will the Coronavirus End Globalization as We Know It?' *Foreign Affairs* 16 (2020); John Allen, Nicholas Burns, Laurie Garrett et al., 'How the World Will Look After the Coronavirus Pandemic', *Foreign Policy*, 20 March 2020.

20   'Impact of the Pandemic on Trade and Development', UNCTAD, 19 November 2020, at unctad.org.

to excessive construction, and climate catastrophe lies on the horizon. There is no more profitable 'low-hanging fruit' to be picked. Some investors hope that digital technologies will give a new lease of life to capitalism, opening an unexploited space in which it might thrive, an intensification of productivity and exploitation making up for the impossibility of further spatial extension. Others look to the 'lawless sea', in which libertarians like Peter Thiel want to erect autonomous floating cities. Others still set their gaze towards the sky – focusing on the moon, Mars and other planets and asteroids that Tesla's founder Elon Musk, among others, hopes to mine, and one day even colonise. In the meantime, though, global capital is in danger of asphyxiation in a world whose every recess it has colonised.

The crisis of globalisation has important geopolitical implications. What came to be known neutrally as 'globalisation' was in fact US-led globalisation, whose stability depended on the unrivalled status of the United States as world hegemon after the collapse of the Soviet Bloc. China's tremendous growth in recent decades and its consequently rising international status, combined with the progressive decline of the United States, are upsetting the balance of international relations. The financial difficulties of the United States – the prospect of a devaluation of the dollar, the collapse in US domestic saving and a gaping current account – may even lead to the loss of the dollar's status as international reserve currency.[21] The so-called 'Opening of China', propitiated by a meeting between Mao and Nixon in 1972 and set in motion by reforms initiated in 1978 by Deng Xiaoping, was instrumental in setting the conditions for a truly world market hinged on the Sino-American axis. In recent years, the country has moved beyond the low-cost manufacturing that caused the term 'Made in China' to be associated with cheap, poor-quality products. It has shifted towards the domestic market and towards high technology; in artificial intelligence, for example, China now has a considerable edge over the United States.

As in previous crises of the world system, we are witnessing an intensification of inter-power rivalries.[22] The growing self-confidence of

---

21   Stephen Roach, 'The End of the Dollar's Exorbitant Privilege', *Financial Times*, 5 October 2020.
22   Iftikhar Ahmad, Giovanni Arrighi and Beverly J. Silver, *Chaos and Governance*

China, demonstrated by huge investments in Africa, the gigantic Belt and Road Initiative logistics project and its assertiveness in the South China Sea, is a major worry for the United States, which fears an anticipated end of the 'American Century'. The Trump administration's trade war with China was a sign of a change in attitudes that may not be entirely reversed by Biden's administration. This escalating confrontation may turn out to be the first stirrings of a new Cold War, which may eventually escalate into a 'Thucydides Trap' – the tendency of the declining hegemon to spark an all-out conflict against a rising rival.[23] In the coming years, it can be expected that the United States and China will try ever more urgently to assert their respective spheres of influence, forcing other countries, including those in the European Union, to make a binary choice about which power they should submit to. Some hope that the end of unipolar globalisation under US hegemony will lead to a more pluralistic multipolar world. Nonetheless, considering the resentment nursed by the United States as a declining hegemon and the ever more aggressive ambitions of the Chinese state, the reality of a Balkanised globalisation may prove far less hospitable than such expectations suggest.

## Externalisation and Offshoring

To understand the strains produced by neoliberal globalisation, coming fully into view precisely at the moment of its decline, it is essential to appreciate in detail how the world market has refashioned economies and societies. Only by looking at the direction of travel at its moment of expansion can we estimate the orientation of globalisation's retreat in the moment of the Great Recoil. Neoliberal *exopolitics* was pervaded by an outward push, scattering around the world everything that was previously contained within the cages of various social units. Free market economists advised a reorientation towards exports, praising financial markets and supra-national institutions for imposing *external*

---

*in the Modern World System* (Minneapolis, MN: University of Minnesota Press, 2008).

23    Patrick Wintour, 'US v. China: Is This the Start of a New Cold War?', *Guardian*, 22 June 2020. The notion of Thucydides's trap was coined by Graham Allison in his book *Destined for War: Can America and China Escape Thucydides's Trap?* (Boston: Houghton Mifflin Harcourt, 2017).

constraints on national budgets. The imperative for managers, companies and governments was *externalisation* – a catch-word peppered throughout the pages of financial newspapers and MBA syllabi.

Externalisation underpins many of the managerial innovations introduced during the neoliberal era: outsourcing, contracting out, offshoring of businesses and manufacturing facilities. Such terms semantically reflect this outward thrust and the intention of escaping the bonds imposed by pre-existing social units. The new spirit of capitalism described by Luc Boltanski and Eve Chiapello centred on 'outsourcing, the creation of subsidiaries, relocations'. It had a predilection for 'lean firms working as *networks* with a multitude of participants' with 'a slim core surrounded by a conglomeration of suppliers, subcontractors, service providers, temporary personnel making it possible to vary the workforce according to the level of business and allied firms'.[24] In line with this model, many companies were radically restructured, outsourcing entire departments, functions or activities that had previously been handled in-house to third parties, to achieve greater 'flexibility' and concentrate on the activities deemed most profitable.[25] Thus, for example, a tech company might externalise its manufacturing process to other firms, which in turn outsource provision of basic materials to other companies, leading to a complex 'value chain' of suppliers and sub-suppliers, often comprising hundreds of firms located in several dozen countries. Take, for instance, the iconic case of an Apple iPhone – designed in Cupertino, California and assembled near Shenzhen, in China with rare earth materials from Inner Mongolia and hand-mined cobalt and coltan from war-ravaged Congo; and then sold all over the world in elegant shops.

The efficiency gains, and connected profit margins, achieved through global outsourcing were by and large premised on the disempowerment of organised labour, by its nature reliant on 'union density' and the physical concentration of workers in crowded workplaces. The neoliberal restructuring of firms led to the 'closure of numerous "great bastions" of trade unionism (coal mines, iron and steel, shipyards, automobiles,

24    Luc Boltanski and Eve Chiapello, *The New Spirit of Capitalism* (London: Verso, 2018), pp. 73, 74. Emphasis in original.

25    William S. Milberg and Deborah Winkler, *Outsourcing Economics: Global Value Chains in Capitalist Development* (Cambridge: Cambridge University Press, 2013).

etc.), or their subjection to severe job cutbacks'.[26] The net result of these moves was the scattering of workers across smaller firms that tended to be less unionised and did not have a tradition of resistance.[27] In fact, for many firms, externalisation has meant relocation and offshoring – the moving of plants and activities to countries with lower wages. New industrial centres have mushroomed in developing countries with poor working conditions and low pay: from the *maquiladoras* producing components for the US car industry in Mexico, to the ghastly and some-times deadly textile factories in Southeast Asia producing clothes sold by Western brands. This trend has severely undercut employment opportunities for the working class in the global North, turning many industrial communities into rust belts blighted by despair and drug addiction.

The outsourcing revolution is strongly tied to the drive towards exports. Neoliberal politicians have waxed lyrical about the benefits of an export-oriented economy, insisting that a strong export sector would allow countries to specialise in the activities in which they were most productive, benefiting both consumers, who would be able to purchase goods at lower prices, and workers, who would be able to find well-paid jobs in high-added-value production. Export – namely the production of goods and services to be consumed externally – is driven by the constant quest of capital to pursue the 'optimal allocation' of resources, resulting in extreme specialisation in a global system of production.[28] Entrepreneurs strive to exploit the so-called 'factor endowment' of each country and region, whether it is land, minerals or skilled labour. This often leads to a situation akin to monoculture, in which, by overempha-sising certain areas of production, countries abandon others that, while essential for local consumption – from food to clothing and machinery – are suboptimal in terms of international competition. This has plunged not only peripheral but also many semi-peripheral countries into a 'development trap', in which they are incapable of lifting themselves from the type of low-value production on which they have become over-dependent.

26  Ibid., p. 292.
27  Ibid.
28  Optimal allocation is a notion used to express the way in which capital has to be invested in the most profitable activities.

Even more dismal have been the consequences for wages. The focus on exports and the imperative to be internationally competitive has meant that companies have had to fight tooth and nail against their international competitors, which mostly take the form of gigantic multinationals that are able to leverage huge economies of scale. The easiest option is to minimise costs, and in particular the cost of labour, engendering a global 'race to the bottom' in which workers are inevitably the victims. Furthermore, an export-oriented economy translates into a disregard for the domestic market. By definition, producing goods for export entails renouncing their local consumption. In an export-oriented economy, multinationals do not have to concern themselves too much with domestic demand in their country of incorporation. If anything, domestic demand needs to be kept under control, as it would probably imply a rise in wages, which would in turn undercut international competitiveness. Whereas, under Fordism, companies had a vested interest in their home country being economically prosperous and their workers well paid, enabling them to purchase their cars and washing machines, this reciprocity of interests has now been severed.

Externalisation is ultimately also the core logic of financialisation. As we have seen, while the Bretton Woods Agreement aimed at enclosing finance within national boundaries, as advised by Keynes, neoliberal globalisation has unleashed the genie of financial markets. The most evident consequence has been the emergence of offshore tax havens such as the Bahamas and the Cayman Islands, where companies are 'domiciled' in order to escape the control of national treasuries and skirt their financial regulations. These 'secrecy jurisdictions' resemble pirate strongholds that suck money away from local economies to store it in virtual vaults controlled by the super-rich.[29] It is here that digital companies such as Amazon, Facebook, Google and Apple, as well as wealthy individuals who have become fiscal exiles, hide their enormous treasure troves. According to Oxfam, internationally, only 5 per cent of state revenues come from corporate tax, while wealthy individuals avoid one-third of their tax liabilities on average. Tax havens short-circuit national sovereignty, preposterously claiming it for territories that are

---

29   Nicholas Shaxson, *Treasure Islands: Uncovering the Damage of Offshore Banking and Tax Havens* (New York: St Martin's, 2011).

autonomous only in name, as a ruse to keep the tax collector at bay.[30] Many financial operations attributed to fiscal havens are in fact performed in the City of London or Manhattan, for which tax havens act as mere flags of convenience.

The drive for externalisation in the management of firms, commerce and finance has allowed global capitalism to create new profit opportunities predicated on skirting the obligations to workers and local communities. Needless to say, this restructuring has sown the seeds of profound instability, resulting in a net loss of social protection and democratic control that is now generating a backlash against global capital. The imperative of externalisation and global outsourcing has created an army of outsiders – workers who are deprived of the steady wages and guaranteed coverage of collective bargaining that were taken for granted during the social-democratic era, making them particularly vulnerable to economic downturns. These growing ranks of excluded and impoverished precarious workers have, unsurprisingly, become neoliberal globalisation's most discontented cohort.

From the managers' perspective, the key reason behind the drive towards externalisation was the intention to offload the risks previously borne by companies onto workers and society as a whole. But offshoring has also created altogether new risks connected with the exposure to global disruption – especially in the case of economic crises, conflict and environmental disaster. This can be seen most clearly in the case of manufacturing and logistics. The drive to reduce excess capacity and aim for the goal of 'just-in-time' supply chains, which lies at the heart of outsourcing practices, has caused companies to reduce their stocks and warehouse space to the bare minimum. While allowing fixed costs to be lowered this tactic can prove dangerous in emergency situations where supply chains are disrupted. The Suez canal obstruction of March 2021 was yet another reminder that unforeseen events can clog the arteries of global trade. The coronavirus crisis and Brexit disruption showed that these vulnerabilities could potentially even undermine food security, especially in countries like the UK which imports more than half of their agricultural products.[31] The same is true of the unpredictability

---

30    John Urry, *Offshoring* (Hoboken, NJ: John Wiley, 2014).
31    Fiona Harvey, 'Food Security Plan After Brexit: Biggest Shake-Up to Farming in 40 Years', *Guardian*, 16 January 2020.

produced by financialisation. The era of neoliberal globalisation has seen a litany of banking crises: the 1997 Asian financial crisis; the ensuing financial crises in Ecuador, Argentina and Russia; the dotcom bust of 2000; the financial crisis of the late 2000s. Due to the absence of robust capital controls acting as a firewall between different financial systems, capital flight and the 'financial contagion' that results from it can cripple banking systems, devastating businesses and families.

The extreme fragility that represents the flipside of the agility of the new spirit of capitalism is not unknown to the capitalist class. It has been addressed by neoliberal management scholars in discussions of 'resilience' – in other words, the ability to manage disruption and ride out difficult circumstances.[32] Using this term, business experts have argued that entrepreneurs should not merely look at quarter-on-quarter earnings, but at the ability to manage threats and recover from crisis – overemphasising efficiency can put companies in peril.[33] Likewise, growing concern about global capitalism's viability is signalled in current discussions of on-shoring and re-shoring: relocating businesses to their main countries of operation. In the aftermath of coronavirus, numerous countries made assessments of their vulnerabilities in key areas, such as pharmaceuticals, while some, including Japan, offered subsidies to their companies to reshore industrial production.

The most salient victim of externalisation is ultimately democracy, which by its nature is tied to location, to a specific territory over which a people asserts collective control. In this context, as British sociologist of mobility John Urry highlights, 'the flows of money, finance and manufacturing, services, security, waste and emissions, which are in various ways offshored are catastrophic for transparent governance'.[34] Besides being enemies of national sovereignty, offshoring and other practices of externalisation are also enemies of democratic authority, because they disentangle economic and financial activities from the scale at which state power operates. By globalising production, commerce and financing, offshored capitalism precipitates a game of smoke and mirrors whose ultimate aim is to hinder political accountability and fiscal transparency.

---

32   Kevin Grove, *Resilience*, (London: Routledge, 2018).
33   Roger L. Martin, 'The High Price of Efficiency' *Harvard Business Review*, January-February 2019. https://hbr.org/2019/01/the-high-price-of-efficiency
34   Urry, *Offshoring*, p. 89.

## Rebellion in the Peripheries

Within each country, global economic integration has opened up deep geo-economic fractures, widening the gap between large cities and small towns, or what economic historian Michael Lind describes as 'hubs' and 'hinterland'.[35] Regions that were attractive to global capital because of their prominence in a given economic activity – from finance to high-tech manufacturing and tourism – have flourished. 'Global cities' – such as Barcelona, Milan, Amsterdam and London in Europe; New York and San Francisco in the United States; Singapore, Beijing and Tokyo in Asia – have profited immensely from their role as international hubs.[36] But this rise has had its counterpart in the impoverishment of the hinterland: of more geographically and economically peripheral areas that are badly connected to global circuits, or otherwise unable to offer 'unique value' to global consumers and investors.

Pressing outwards, in accordance with the logic of externalisation, neoliberal globalisation has widened the gap between the centre and the margins, between the networked global metropolis and the impoverished periphery, while that periphery has unsurprisingly come to be at the heart of many populist insurgencies. It was the peripheral areas of the UK, from Sunderland to Lincolnshire, that provided the strongest electoral ground for Brexit, while the peripheral states of the Midwest rust belt contributed to Donald Trump's victory in 2016. The time-honoured urban–rural cleavage is coming back at the very centre of contemporary politics, at a time marked by a 'revenge of geography', in which the space of places is reasserting its primacy over the space of flows.[37] As books like *What's the Matter with Kansas?* and *Hillbilly Elegy* make vividly clear, ex-urban areas have been afflicted by a wave of social decline and despair that has pushed many in working-class communities into the hands of the

---

35   Michael Lind, *The New Class War: Saving Democracy from the Managerial Elite* (London: Penguin, 2020).

36   Saskia Sassen, *Global City* (New York: Princeton University Press, 1994).

37   The phrase 'the revenge of geography' was coined by Robert Kaplan to discuss the role that physical geography and geopolitics play in international relations. Robert D. Kaplan, 'The Revenge of Geography', *Foreign Policy* 172 (2009), 96–105. Here the term is used more broadly to speak of the returning concern for geographic factors in contemporary society.

hard right.[38] The sprawling neoliberal province, the 'flyover country' that has become the object of ridicule in *Borat* and countless other movies and TV series is now taking its revenge on the globalised towns it blames for its marginalisation.

The neoliberal periphery is not defined only in terms of geographic remoteness, but also in relation to economic marginalisation. It comprises such disparate areas as the Appalachians in the United States and the northern *banlieues* of Paris, the north-east of England and Italy's Mezzogiorno. In the European Union, many of the poorest regions are those on the southern Mediterranean seaboard, such as Andalusia, Calabria, Sicily and the Peloponnese – far from the so-called 'Blue Banana' that stretches from Liverpool to Milan, where most of the urban population and high-value-added employment opportunities are concentrated. Often, however, rather than geographic remoteness, it is reliance on manufacturing that condemns an area to peripheral status. This is true of the so-called rust belt states of the United States – Michigan, Ohio, Indiana and Illinois – and their equivalents in the north of France and the north of England: places that have lost steady and well-paid manufacturing jobs due to offshoring and automation.

These ex-urban and peri-urban places are part of 'the hinterland', which American writer Phil A. Neel describes as 'a heavily industrial space – a space for factory farms, for massive logistics complexes, for power generation, and for the extraction of resources from forests, deserts, and seas'.[39] It is a space where 'large-scale industrial extraction, production, and initial processing of primary products' takes place these days.[40] While large cities, integrated into global networks, have become sites for high-value economic activities in the fields of finance, technology and knowledge professions, the hinterland is tied to forms of production that have been devalued and marginalised in the present digital economy, such as manufacturing and agriculture. The hinterland has been disproportionately affected by recent economic crises. As Brookings Institution senior fellow William A. Galston notes, 'In the

---

38  Thomas Frank, *What's the Matter with Kansas? How Conservatives Won the Heart of America* (New York: Picador, 2007); J. D. Vance, *Hillbilly Elegy* (New York: HarperCollins, 2016).

39  Phil A. Neel, *Hinterland: America's New Landscape of Class and Conflict* (London: Reaktion, 2018), 17.

40  Ibid., 18.

first five years after the Great Recession, only 35 percent of job gains were in [rural] counties, versus 64 percent in counties with populations of five hundred thousand or more.'[41] Furthermore, non-metro areas are far more dependent than metropolitan areas on manufacturing activities that have been devalued under neoliberalism and are highly exposed to international competition.[42]

Many recent protest movements have thematised this suffering of the periphery. The 2018–19 Gilets Jaunes protest movement in France enjoyed strong support in suburban areas and small centres, famously turning provincial roundabouts into protest barricades. According to French geographer Christophe Guilly, protestors clad in yellow vests have exposed a deep rift between the city and the countryside.[43] While 40 per cent of the population in urban areas control two-thirds of GDP, the remaining 60 per cent are left with a meagre third. As they become integrated into the global value chains of finance, information technology, services and tourism, urban centres sever themselves from the countryside, which becomes increasingly useless from the viewpoint of global capital.

In times of globalisation, living in this expanded periphery is a recipe for both destitution and disenfranchisement. The systematic externalisation of the economy has made manufacturing workers feel superfluous and disposable, their jobs always on the verge of being offshored. This trend is compounded by a perception of the loss of democratic voice and control – which, as we have seen, is a by-product of externalisation. In a world in which decision-making is in the ever more remote hands of businessmen, technocrats and aloof politicians living in global cities or 'offshore', where an increasing number of economic forces appear to have escaped the scope of democratic decision-making and public oversight, those who live on the periphery are bound to feel like mere objects of economic and political life, with little say over their destiny.

It is only in light of this experience of neglect and loss, experienced most sharply in the global periphery, that we can interpret the culture war between conservatives and progressives, and the way it maps onto the

---

41   William A. Galston, *Anti-Pluralism: The Populist Threat to Liberal Democracy* (New Haven, CT: Yale University Press, 2017), p. 68.

42   Jonathan A. Rodden, *Why Cities Lose: The Deep Roots of the Urban-Rural Political Divide* (London: Hachette UK, 2019).

43   Christophe Guilluy, *La France périphérique. Comment on a sacrifié les classes populaires* (Paris: Flammarion, 2016).

rural–urban divide. According to scholars including Pippa Norris and Ronald Inglehart, cultural conservatism is the key driver behind populist rebellions which see neoliberal modernisation and progressive values as a threat to identity and tradition.[44] While no doubt cultural conservatism has been a major factor in fuelling right-wing populism, it is simplistic to think that the populist rebellion is predominantly a cultural issue, when it stems first and foremost from widening social inequality.[45]

An example of this misconception can be seen in the argument advanced by centrist commentator David Goodhart that the Brexit referendum uncovered a newly salient divide between 'Somewheres' and 'Anywheres'.[46] Anywheres – a code word for the 'metropolitan elite' – are between 20 and 25 per cent of the population, while Somewheres make up around 50 per cent, giving them significant electoral power. Anywheres tend to live in London or other big cities, are highly educated and well-travelled, and do not have a strong attachment to place. Somewheres, people of lesser income and education, live in more peripheral areas, from rural Scotland to Cornwall. They have a strong attachment to place and tradition, and feel uneasy about the transformations imposed by globalisation, for which they blame Anywheres.[47] In this narrative, the opposition between country and city is reduced to a matter of values and attitudes dividing urban progressives and rural conservatives, a perspective negating that of Thomas Frank in *What's the Matter with Kansas*, which holds that it is economic disarray and social despair that leads peripheral constituencies to embrace conservative views.[48]

The dissatisfaction with neoliberalism, felt most acutely at the periphery, has clear socioeconomic causes. It stems from the rollback of the state and the gutting of industry, resulting from the neoliberal logic of externalisation and the way it has disproportionately affected peripheral areas. Ignoring such socioeconomic realities in favour of an exclusive focus on cultural conflicts is akin to looking at the finger rather than the

---

44   Pippa Norris and Ronald Inglehart, *Cultural Backlash: Trump, Brexit, and Authoritarian Populism* (Cambridge: Cambridge University Press, 2019).

45   Thomas Frank, *Listen, Liberal: Or, What Ever Happened to the Party of the People?* (London: Macmillan, 2016).

46   David Goodhart, *The Road to Somewhere: The Populist Revolt and the Future of Politics* (Oxford: Oxford University Press, 2017).

47   Ibid. pp. 5–7.

48   Thomas Frank, *What's the Matter with Kansas?: How Conservatives Won the Heart of America* (New York: Henry Holt, 2005).

moon. Moreover, it is overlooked that the growth in global migration – what Goodhart sees as the burning issue for Somewheres – has been the direct result of the imbalances of globalisation. The asymmetries engendered by global economic integration constantly force people to relocate to other countries in search of jobs. The high degree of international specialisation means that workers have to move around to fill in for the 'input gaps' opening in different countries, depending on their position in the international division of labour. To make up for the lack of opportunities at home, Spanish, Greek and Italian engineers have had to move to northern European countries, Nepalese construction workers to the Middle East and African field and factory workers to Europe's shores.

Like other factors of production, labour is constantly propelled to the places where the highest returns can be made, in order to realise its value on the global market. But unlike that of commodities and capital, the flow of labour is far from unimpeded. Even at the height of neoliberal globalisation, governments mostly enforced strict rules on immigration, denying migrants residency and citizenship, thus forcing many of them to live off the informal economy or accept miserly wages. In other words, movement of labour has a far higher 'cost' than that of capital and commodities, in terms of the physical and psychological dangers, cultural ostracism and economic precariousness it entails. Yet, its possible benefits mean that emigration often remains an attractive option. The immigrant is thus the figure in which globalisation's pressures and contradictions are personified. This goes a long way to explaining why immigration makes an ideal target for political forces that want to be seen as fighting against the rapacity of globalisation without ever being required to address its root causes.

## Global Agoraphobia

Neoliberal globalisation may well have succeeded in subjecting the entire planet to the imperative of profit. But success has yielded to economic shocks, viral gloom and ecological catastrophe, turning our seas into hosts for enormous plastic gyres and plunging the planet into the catastrophe of climate change. Contemporary political conflicts reflect the affliction engendered by the steamroller of globalisation and the way in which it has created a sense of dislocation and exposure. These strains have become more painful at a time when globalisation is on the retreat, and when the wounds that have been opened by global capital's outward expansion are now rubbed with the salt of economic implosion.

The present era of the Great Recoil corresponds to the 'second movement' socialist economic historian Karl Polanyi described in *The Great Transformation*, when phases of capitalist expansion recede and are met by 'societal responses'.[49] According to Polanyi, in phases of profound crisis like that opened by the 1929 Wall Street Crash, society tends to act defensively, erecting forms of social protection against a capitalist logic that has manifestly failed to deliver prosperity, yet becomes even more aggressive in its attempts to extract profit. During this moment, societies are involved in a process of 're-internalisation' that aims to 're-embed' the economy in society. On certain occasions, this second movement ultimately produces a reactionary drive, pacifying the conflict between capital and labour under the aegis of an authoritarian corporatist state, typified by the fascist movements of the 1920s and 1930s. But this is not the only possible conclusion. Roosevelt's New Deal in the United States and the French and Spanish popular-front governments represented the left's attempts to resolve the same quandaries in a progressive direction. This theory has become fashionable once again in recent years, numerous economists contending that what we are facing in the aftermath of the 2008 crash is in fact a new 'Polanyi moment'.[50]

Indeed, the present crisis of globalisation has many echoes in Polanyi's analysis, and his discussion of the sense of 'exposure' produced by capitalist rapacity. The push for externalisation of neoliberal capitalism, with its geo-economic dislocations and the flattening of barriers and regulative institutions, has exposed workers and citizens to a number of economic flows against which they feel they have little control, which breeds a perception that might be described as agoraphobia – a fear of open spaces. Agoraphobia as a psychiatric phenomenon has in fact become a clinical emergency, many citizens being seized with anxiety over their uncertain future and by fear of contact with others.[51]

---

49   Karl Polanyi, *The Great Transformation: The Political and Economic Origins of Our Time* (Boston: Beacon, 2014).

50   Joe Guinan and Thomas M. Hanna, 'Polanyi Against the Whirlwind', *Renewal: A Journal of Social Democracy* 25: 1 (2017).

51   Borwin Bandelow and Sophie Michaelis, 'Epidemiology of Anxiety Disorders in the 21st Century', *Dialogues in Clinical Neuroscience* 17: 3 (2015), 327.

Metaphorically, however, the term can be used to capture the anxieties related to our sense of finding ourselves caught in an open global space deprived of protection or control.

We live in an agoraphobic world because globalisation is no longer perceived as a sea of opportunities that any sane citizen should tap into with enthusiasm, where the best will be prized for their efforts. Rather, it is increasingly regarded as something akin to a lawless and tempestuous ocean inhabited by monsters and ravaged by corsair ships that launch frequent attacks on workers and local communities. Global flows of finance, trade, services, information and people, celebrated by neoliberals as sources of economic prosperity, are now often seen as scourges to be defended against. This sense of vulnerability also applies to other areas of our everyday experience, including social media, that have exposed us to public scrutiny, as well as to the unwitting extraction of our data, leading many to retreat from it therapeutically, either temporarily or for good. Even global travel, long celebrated as an opportunity for exploration and to develop business relationships, has now been reframed as a means of accelerating the spread of viruses, while global trade has spawned biosecurity threats brought by invasive non-native species, such as the Asian fruit flies that convey the pathogen *Xylella fastidiosa*, which has destroyed many olive trees in Europe, and the fall armyworm that has devastated sub-Saharan Africa.

This condition of exposure goes a long way towards explaining the logic of contemporary politics. Many of the political tendencies that typify the Great Recoil reflect an endopolitics – that is, a politics of the interior – that attempts to provide some relief from such exposure, to reassert autonomy and interiority, in a world where capitalist interconnectedness has bred a sense of restless impotence about the future. Global capitalism has ushered in a redoubled externalisation, heightened by the planetary scale of the contemporary market and the way in which virtually all aspects of our everyday life, our cities and our social relationships are becoming commodified: spare rooms rented out on Airbnb; hours of work on sale on Amazon Turk or in service to food delivery companies; our every behaviour on social media being tracked and repurposed as an opportunity to target our eyeballs; the blight of tourism selling an authenticity that is ever more manufactured.

Now facing the externalised reality of global capital, 'spirit at once recoils in horror from this abstract unity, from this *selfless* substantiality, and against it affirms individuality', to quote a famous passage of Hegel's *Phenomenology of the Spirit*.[52] The perception of systemic vulnerability engenders a push towards re-internalisation, which attempts to rebalance a world out of kilter. As we have seen in the course of the chapter, this moment of counter-thrust has a clear material and structural dimension and can be seen in the backward movement of economic growth and global trade, amid a growing perception of the saturation of markets and the impossibility of further economic expansion within the present regime of accumulation. But even more important for the purpose of our discussion are the psychological and ideological ramifications of the Great Recoil.

The images of a politics turning back to itself are manifold in the present conjuncture. Populism's soul-searching and sometimes chauvinistic politics; the anxieties created by impending environmental catastrophe; the emphasis on repair, rescue and recovering in policies by Joe Biden and other world leaders; the flourishing of the retro culture and nostalgia that pervades much of our politics; even the celebration of psychological introversion in a world dominated by extroverts[53] – all seem to bear the mark of Polanyi's second movement and Hegel's *Erinnerung*, of a moment in which society is caught in internal reconstruction. Post-neoliberal endopolitics and the emphasis on questions of sovereignty, protection and control that have emerged between the populism of the 2010s and the neo-statism of the early 2020s – need to be understood as attempts to re-internalise capital, to re-embed economic processes in social and political institutions and to reaffirm a sense of interiority, order and equilibrium as a means to confront and navigate a world marked by uncertainty and disruption. Having laid out the political and economic contours of the Great Recoil, in the chapters that follow I will explore in more detail its ideological contents, focusing on three key notions that crop up at every turn in contemporary political debates: sovereignty, protection and control.

---

52  G. W. F. Hegel, *Phenomenology of Spirit*, transl. A. V. Miller (Oxford: Oxford University Press, 1977), 318.

53  Hamja Ahsan, *Shy Radicals: The Antisystemic Politics of the Militant Introvert* (London: Book Works, 2019).

# 3
# Sovereignty

In understanding the endopolitics of the Great Recoil and the political responses engendered by the crisis of neoliberal globalisation, a key term is: sovereignty. Usually understood as the right of the state to assert uncontested power over a territory, sovereignty pops up in the most varied of contexts: in discussions about the rollback of the state, in debates about migration, in criticism of technological imperialism, or in conversations about the social and economic implications of the pandemic. It has even precipitated its own '-ism' – the ugly term 'sovereigntyism' – used in France and Italy particularly, to describe defenders of national sovereignty against anti-sovereigntyists, otherwise known as globalists.

In the news media, the resurgence of the term sovereignty has been strongly associated with the ascent of the nationalist right during the 2010s. Brexit was presented from the start as a fight for sovereignty, in which the 'exit' option would put an end to the delegation of power to a supranational, 'globalist' institutions represented by the EU, and reclaim sovereignty at the national level. As Philip Stephens noted in the *Financial Times*, 'the neuralgic word in the British debate about Europe is sovereignty'.[54] In the autumn of 2020, four years after the Brexit referendum and a few months before his resignation, Boris Johnson's chief adviser at Downing Street, and former Director of the 'Vote Leave'

---

54  Philip Stephens, 'Boris Johnson Is Wrong. Parliament Has the Ultimate Authority', *Financial Times*, 25 February 2016.

campaign, Dominic Cummings, argued that a No Deal outcome in the negotiations would be a 'pivot to sovereignty', allowing the UK government to pursue its vision of an activist state.[1] Donald Trump's successful 2016 campaign for the US presidency was also presented very much as a fight for sovereignty amid a situation in which US national interests had been overlooked, allowing China and its NATO allies to profit. In 2017, Trump argued at the UN General Assembly for the restoration of 'strong and independent nations that embrace their sovereignty to promote security, prosperity, and peace'.[2] In France in recent years, Marine Le Pen has pronounced the word *souveraineté* at every possible opportunity in her public tirades against the EU, as well as in her targeting of Muslim immigrants, portraying herself and her allies as defenders of national sovereignty fighting against the globalists at the helm of unaccountable supranational agencies.[3]

The term sovereignty, however, is more politically ambiguous than its use by the right, and the facile equation between sovereigntyists and nationalists, suggests. Italy's post-ideological and hyper-populist Five Star Movement has eagerly embraced the idea of sovereignty in its political discourse. One of its former leaders, self-styled *chavista* Alessandro Di Battista, has often repeated the republican slogan, 'Sovereignty belongs to the People', arguing that Italy should look after its national economic interests, and even presented the restoration of sovereignty as a condition for happiness.[4] On the resurgent radical left, sovereignty has also been widely debated by leaders such as Pablo Iglesias, Bernie Sanders and Jean-Luc Mélenchon. Iglesias has repeatedly argued for the importance of sovereignty as a condition for democracy. In a parliamentary speech in 2017, he insisted: 'The solution of the EU crisis will

---

1   Sam Lowe, 'Why Boris Johnson Is Considering a No-Deal Brexit for a Bruised Economy', *Financial Times*, 8 September 2020.

2   'Remarks by President Trump to the 72nd Session of the United Nations General Assembly', 19 September 2017, at whitehouse.gov.

3   For example, in September 2018, in an interview on BFMTV with Jean-Jacques Bourdin, she took aim at globalism as a 'doctrine that defends the circulation of goods, of people and of financial flows, and leads to the disappearance of nations, which need to be dispossessed of their sovereignty'. She added that 'Sovereigntyists think that nations need to conserve sovereignty, because democracy is in question'. 'Marine Le Pen face à Jean-Jacques Bourdin en direct – 17/09', 17 September 2019, at bfmtv.com.

4   Alessandro Di Battista, *A testa in su: investire in felicità per non essere sudditi* (New York: Rizzoli, 2016).

involve giving a new meaning to the word sovereignty.'[5] Opposing the Trans-Pacific Partnership trade treaty (TPP), Sanders said that it would 'undermine US sovereignty'. In France, Mélenchon has curtly replied to accusations of 'sovereigntyism' by tweeting that 'the word "sovereignty" comes from the political family to which I belong. The notion of "sovereignty of the people" was born in defiance of Louis XVI'.[6]

Significantly, a preoccupation with sovereignty has also surfaced in protest movements since the 2008 crash. In the 2011 occupations of town squares by the Spanish Indignados, the Greek Aganaktismenoi and Occupy Wall Street – and more recently in the activism of the French Gilets Jaunes – the ideal of democratic sovereignty was often deployed to criticise neoliberal elites. Indicative of this trend is the emergence in social movement discourse of a number of new sovereignty-related expressions, such as food sovereignty, technological sovereignty and energy sovereignty. Food sovereignty is a term used by the international peasant movement Via Campesina, which was an important part of the larger anti-globalisation movement. Technological sovereignty has become a catchword – a term popularised by, among others, Barcelona-based digital activists close to leftist mayor Ada Colau to express the embracing of open data standards and non-oligopolistic platforms. And energy sovereignty is used by anti-climate change activists to express the opportunity for greater local autonomy and self-reliance offered by renewable energy.[7]

These expressions show that sovereignty has become something like a master-signifier of post-neoliberal discourse: a 'quilting point', to use the image of psychoanalyst Jacques Lacan, around which manifold demands and sensibilities may be woven and temporarily stabilised.[8] But why has sovereignty – instead of many other possible notions – become so central in the present conjuncture? As this chapter will demonstrate, the revival

---

5    Aitor Riveiro, 'Pablo Iglesias pone en duda "la historia de éxito de la UE" y apuesta por más soberanía para superar la crisis', *El Diario*, 15 March 2017.

6    Mélenchon's tweet reads: 'Le mot "souveraineté" vient de la famille politique à laquelle j'appartiens. La notion de "souveraineté du peuple" est née face à Louis XVI. #EnTouteFranchise'. Jean-Luc Mélenchon, Twitter, 17 May 2020.

7    Raj Patel, 'Food Sovereignty', *Journal of Peasant Studies* 36: 3 (2009); Hug March and Ramon Ribera-Fumaz, 'Barcelona: From Corporate Smart City to Technological Sovereignty', in Andrew Karvonen, Federico Cugurullo and Federico Caprotti, *Inside Smart Cities* (London: Routledge, 2019), 227–42.

8    Jacques Lacan, *The Seminar of Jacques Lacan: The Psychoses, 1955–56*, ed. Jacques-Alain Miller, transl. Russell Grigg (London: Routledge, 1993), 268–70.

of sovereignty needs to be understood as a reaction to the ideological attack launched by neoliberalism upon the legitimacy of state power and the way it facilitated the practical erosion of national sovereignty in a globalised world. Friedrich Hayek, Ludwig von Mises, Milton Friedman, and other 'founding fathers' of neoliberalism all warned about the excessive intrusiveness of the state and its possible totalitarian perversions. This perspective provided ideological justification for the construction of the global market, which ushered in a transnational financial and trading system operating regardless of, and sometimes against, sovereign jurisdictions. Invocations of sovereignty seen most prominently on the right, but increasingly also on the left, aspire to reverse this state of affairs, reasserting the ability of territorially defined communities to act autonomously of the institutions and norms of neoliberal globalisation. Rather than being a unifying rallying point, however, the idea of sovereignty remains very contentious: while reactionary narratives emphasise the primacy of territorial sovereignty, progressive ones champion the democratic principle of popular sovereignty as a means to overcome political impotence and attack the entrenched power of economic oligarchies.

## The Invention of Sovereignty

The rise of sovereignty as a central question in contemporary politics is puzzling in many respects. This notion was, until recently, something fit only for the dusty shelves of university libraries, or in the buttoned-up context of diplomatic negotiations; not a word one would have expected to be thrown as a slogan in the heat of televised political debates and clashes on social media. It may be said that a preoccupation with sovereignty – in the sense of the nature and extent of political power and its relationship to place – is as old as human history. Classics of ancient philosophy such as Plato's *Republic*, Aristotle's *Politics* and Cicero's *On the Commonwealth* were fundamentally concerned with what would today be understood as questions of sovereignty.[9] Discussing how a

---

9   Plato, *Republic*, ed. and transl. Chris Emlyn-Jones and William Preddy, 2 vols (Cambridge, MA: Harvard University Press, 2013); Aristotle, *Politics*, transl. H. Rackham (Cambridge, MA: Harvard University Press, 1977); Marcus Tullius Cicero, *On the Commonwealth and On the Laws*, ed. and transl. James E. G. Zetzel (Cambridge: Cambridge University Press, 1999).

political community should be organised and ruled, they touched upon issues of territory, borders and political authority that have now become closely associated with the doctrine of sovereignty. But sovereignty in the proper sense is a quintessentially modern concept that emerged out of debates about political authority in the late Middle Ages, the Renaissance and the age of absolutism, coming to maturity only at the moment of the French Revolution.[10]

The coining of the term sovereignty is attributed to Jean Bodin, a sixteenth-century French jurist and political philosopher, who introduced it in his work *The Six Books of the Republic*.[11] Bodin described sovereignty as '*la puissance absolue et perpetuelle d'une République*' ('the absolute and perpetual power of a Republic'), and listed a number of principles underpinning it that every functioning modern polity now shares: a state with stable borders; exclusive jurisdiction over its territory; no power superior to that of the state. This claim marked a break with the political status quo. In Bodin's time, national kingdoms represented just one of several levels of sovereignty and had to contend with the power exercised by both the Empire and the Church from above, and by feudal lords with their seigneurial privileges from below, in a highly parcelised and layered system of power.[12] A member of the Parliament of Paris at the beginning of the French Wars of Religion between Catholics and Huguenots, Bodin's intention was to establish a framework for civil power to guard against a repetition of religious strife, which in his view had resulted from an intermixing of religious and political power. His solution was the nation-state, which should exert uncontested authority over a unified and homogeneous territory, under the control of a single centre of power: the national capital.[13]

---

10   A number of authors have analysed the transition from the sacred Roman Empire to nation-states. Personally, I find Schulze's work on state-building and Perry Anderson's analysis of the rise of the absolutist state the most important contributions to this discussion: Hagen Schulze with William E. Yuill, *States, Nations and Nationalism: From the Middle Ages to the Present* (Oxford: Blackwell, 1996); Perry Anderson, *Lineages of the Absolutist State* (London: Verso, 2013 [1974]).

11   Jean Bodin and Julian H. Franklin, *On Sovereignty: Four Chapters from the Six Books of the Commonwealth* (Cambridge: Cambridge University Press, 2010).

12   Anderson, *Lineages of the Absolutist State*.

13   Bodin and Franklin, *On Sovereignty*. Perry Anderson notes that one of the characteristics of the absolutist state is the way in which it is predicated on the notion of

Bodin's formulation of the question of sovereignty was the arrival point of a long process whose origins hark back to the late Roman Empire and the early Middle Ages, with the investiture controversy that brought Emperor and Pope into direct opposition. Scholastic authors and jurists including John of Salisbury and Thomas Aquinas discussed the nature and extent of political power, allocating ever greater freedom to cities and kingdoms vis-à-vis the emperor and the pope.[14] Building on these debates, Bodin coined *souveraineté* from the Latin word *superanus*, literally 'superior', to denote the idea not only of the superiority or *supremacy* of state power over imperial and papal power. For Bodin, the king was 'emperor in his own Kingdom', as medieval canon law had already come to accept; he flatly denied the legitimacy of any emperor above the state. Each kingdom had its own supreme ruler, with none above him, and no foreign power allowed to interfere.

Sovereignty thus became a key notion in political philosophy and practice. Seventy years after Bodin's work, in *Leviathan*, Thomas Hobbes would describe sovereignty as 'the public soul, giving life and motion to the Commonwealth', making this notion the core principle of the social contract between citizens and the ruler.[15] The Treaty of Westphalia of 1648, which ended the Thirty Years' War, adopted Bodin's blueprint, sanctioning the existence of a plurality of nation-states in Europe, each with its own people, its own confessional affiliation and its own stable borders; most importantly, each derived political legitimacy from itself, rather than from superior bodies such as the Holy Roman Empire or the Church. Sovereignty thus became synonymous with the absolutist state and its authoritarian centralism. But sovereignty would later also become something rather different: a term appropriated by revolutionary movements to affirm that political power should be in the hands of the people rather than the king, as expressed in the idea of popular sovereignty.

---

a homogeneous and mutually exclusive territory. See Anderson, *Lineages of the Absolutist State*, pp. 15–17.

14   Stuart Elden, *The Birth of Territory* (Chicago, IL: University of Chicago Press, 2013).

15   Thomas Hobbes, *Leviathan*, ed. J. C. A. Gaskin (Oxford: Oxford University Press, 2008), p. 221.

## Domination and Democracy

If sovereignty has become such a flashpoint in contemporary discussions, it is because it represents the point of collision of distinct historical and institutional trajectories. While sovereignty always implies state power and control over a territory, this meaning acquires different connotations in the competing notions of territorial sovereignty and popular sovereignty – sovereignty over a territory and sovereignty of the people. Territorial sovereignty implies domination by force within a nation's borders, often combined with an aggressive posture towards foreign powers, as well as an assertion of the supremacy of the native community and its rootedness in the land. The idea of popular sovereignty, strongly informed by the work of Genevan philosopher Jean-Jacques Rousseau, is instead concerned with democracy. It affirms the supremacy of the people and their institutions over private powers.

The most explicit theorisation of the idea of territorial sovereignty can be found in the work of Carl Schmitt, the political philosopher and jurist infamous for his association with the Nazi Third Reich. Schmitt first discussed sovereignty in his 1922 book *Political Theology*, in which he argued that political notions are the secularised counterparts of theological concepts.[16] It was in this text that Schmitt developed his view of the state of exception – what might be described as a 'temporal theory of sovereignty', given that it is concerned with the moment of decision. This is the theory that was famously taken up by the Italian philosopher Giorgio Agamben – who was heavily influenced by Foucault – to argue that the state of exception is the default mode of governance in contemporary society.[17] Equally important, however, is Schmitt's discussion of the spatial nature of sovereignty, developed in his 1950 book *Nomos of the Earth*.

Schmitt began from the common Greek roots *nomos* ('law') and *nemein* ('to take'), arguing that the law derives from the act of appropriating land.[18] 'The solid ground of the earth is delineated by fences,

---

16   Carl Schmitt, *Political Theology: Four Chapters on the Concept of Sovereignty* (Chicago, IL: University of Chicago Press, 2005).

17   Giorgio Agamben, *Homo Sacer: Sovereign Power and Bare Life* (Redwood City, CA: Stanford University Press, 1998).

18   Carl Schmitt and G. L. Ulmen, *The Nomos of the Earth in the International Law of the Jus Publicum Europaeum* (New York: Telos, 2006).

enclosures, boundaries, walls, houses, and other constructs', and it is through this structure of material demarcation that 'the orders and orientations of human social life become apparent'.[19] This approach echoed the insights of various thinkers who had already commented on the relationship between political power and territorial control. They include the early eighteenth-century Italian philosopher Giambattista Vico's discussion of spatial division and demarcation (*la divisione dei campi*) as an element of social order and Immanuel Kant's discussion of the 'supreme proprietorship of the soil', which he held to act as 'the main condition for the possibility of ownership and all further law'.[20] Schmitt pushed this idea further, framing land appropriation not merely as a precondition for the legal and social order, but as its underlying logic and the basis of an alternative theory of power. In this eminently 'foundationalist' perspective, all human institutions, including private property, involve an act of 'land-appropriation' that institutes the 'supreme ownership of the community as a whole'.[21] The territory, and thus its defence and aggrandisement, become ends in their own right, as in the reactionary fetishisation of borders evinced by Italian fascist Julius Evola, who celebrated the myth of Alexander erecting an iron wall against the uncivilised barbarians of Gog and Magog – a preoccupation reminiscent of the new obsession with border walls on the part of figures like Donald Trump and Viktor Orbán in their respective battles against immigration.

The view of popular sovereignty mobilised in recent years by protest movements and the radical left proceeds from a radically different direction. Sovereignty is not equated to domination, but understood as the

19  Ibid., p. 42
20  Giambattista Vico, *The New Science of Giambattista Vico*, transl. Thomas Goddard Bergin and Max Harold Fisch (Ithaca, NY: Cornell University Press, 1984); Immanuel Kant, *The Philosophy of Law: An Exposition of the Fundamental Principles of Jurisprudence as the Science of Right* (Clark, NJ: The Lawbook Exchange, 2001), p. 183: 'Of the Supreme Proprietor of the Land, it may be said that *he possesses nothing as his own*, except himself; for if he possessed things in the State alongside of others, dispute and litigation would be possible with these others regarding these things, and there would be no independent Judge to settle the cause. But it may be also said that *he possesses everything*; for he has the Supreme Right of Sovereignty over the whole People, to whom all external things severally (*divisim*) belong; and as such he assigns distributively to every one what is to be his.'
21  Ibid., pp. 80–108.

supremacy of the will of the people embodied in the laws and institutions of the state. The idea of popular sovereignty was famously introduced by Jean-Jacques Rousseau in his 1762 book *The Social Contract*.[22] For Rousseau, sovereignty, hitherto the privilege of the king or 'sovereign', should become an attribute of the people – namely, the totality of the citizens residing in a certain area.[23] This idea, informed by Rousseau's experience of assembly democracy in Geneva, inspired the French Revolution, which led to the decapitation of the incumbent sovereign and installed in his stead a bourgeois republic in which sovereignty belonged to the people – a principle that went on to inspire the struggles for national independence and democracy of the nineteenth century.[24]

More than 230 years after the French Revolution, popular sovereignty may seem to have become a stale institutional principle. In fact, the notion of sovereignty features in virtually all republican constitutions. The first article of the French constitution of 1848, for example, affirmed that 'sovereignty exists in the whole body of French citizens'.[25] Similarly, the third article of the constitution of the French Fifth Republic, adopted more than a century after in 1958, states that 'national sovereignty shall be vested in the people, who shall exercise it through their representatives and by means of referendum'.[26] Nonetheless, at a time when neoliberal globalisation has enfeebled the power of nation-states in which this principle was embodied, popular sovereignty has regained some of its revolutionary dimension. Popular sovereignty is predicated on two forms of supremacy: first the supremacy of the people as a whole over any specific sub-group or individual; and second, the supremacy of the state, ruled by the people, over private interests and economic powers. In this context, the state's control over its own territory, fetishised by the likes of Schmitt, is only a corollary; territorial domination is simply a means by which the popular will is enforced, because democracy cannot

22   Jean-Jacques Rousseau, *The Social Contract and Other Later Political Writings*, transl. Victor Gourevitch (Cambridge: Cambridge University Press, 2019).
23   Ibid.
24   Lucia Rubinelli, *Constituent Power: A History* (Cambridge: Cambridge University Press, 2020).
25   Karl Marx, 'The Constitution of the French Republic Adopted November 4, 1848', in Karl Marx and Friedrich Engels, *Collected Works, Volume 10: Marx and Engels, 1849–1851* (London: Lawrence & Wishart, 1975).
26   *The French Constitution of 1958* (New York: French Embassy, Press and Information Division, 1958).

exist without some notion of location, a specification of the territory over which popular power can assert its supremacy. In the present context, it is in particular the second form of supremacy invoked by popular sovereignty, that of the popular will over private interests that is in question, as a result of neoliberal policies that have affirmed the primacy of the oligarchic power of the wealthy and of corporations over democratic principles.

## Neoliberal Anti-Sovereigntyism

The return of sovereignty in this troubled era is to a great extent a return of the neoliberal repressed. No other term has attracted more polemical ferocity from the pens of pro-market ideologues than sovereignty. Reading the foundational texts of the neoliberal canon, starting with authors such as Friedrich Hayek, Ludwig von Mises and Karl Popper, one often finds explicit attacks on sovereignty, and in particular popular sovereignty, which are presented as the ultimate movers of a state power seen as threatening individual freedom and the spontaneous order of civil society. As Canadian historian Quinn Slobodian highlights, for neoliberals, 'commitments to national sovereignty and autonomy were dangerous if taken seriously. They were stalwart critics of national sovereignty, believing that after empires, nations must remain embedded in an international institutional order that safeguarded capital and protected its right to move throughout the world.'[27]

The enmity towards sovereignty was explicitly thematised in Hayek's seminal book *The Road to Serfdom*, published in 1944.[28] In this strong polemic against socialism and state planning, Hayek repeatedly attacked 'unfettered sovereignty in the economic sphere', 'unrestricted political sovereignty' and the boundless ambition of 'popular sovereignty and democratic government' to encroach upon ever-increasing areas of social life.[29] Hayek, who saw himself as an enemy of totalitarianism, was concerned about the rise of a 'megastate', which would turn its citizens

---

27   Quinn Slobodian, *Globalists: The End of Empire and the Birth of Neoliberalism* (Cambridge, MA: Harvard University Press, 2020), p. 9.

28   F. A. Hayek, *The Road to Serfdom: Text and Documents: The Definitive Edition* (London: Routledge, 2014).

29   Ibid., p. 238.

into automatons subject to the dictatorship of planning. In this view, Nazism was the all-too-predictable point of arrival of the sovereign national-popular state – or, to paraphrase Bertrand Russell, Hitler was the outcome of Rousseau. As for the Keynesian welfare state, it differed only in degree from Soviet totalitarianism.

The notion of sovereignty was also the target of attack in Hayek's second book, *The Constitution of Liberty* (1960).[30] In this volume, which Margaret Thatcher famously banged on a table at a Conservative Party policy meeting, shouting 'This is what we believe!', a specific subsection is dedicated to popular sovereignty and majority rule. Hayek describes sovereignty as the creed of the 'doctrinaire democrat' who believes that 'majority rule is unlimited and unlimitable'. Thus, 'the ideal of democracy, originally intended to prevent all arbitrary power . . . becomes the justification for a new arbitrary power'.[31] This, for Hayek was unacceptable, as he considered that the existence of a political community is premised on 'commonly held principles' that have primacy over any specific decision.[32] The rule of law should take precedence over the popular will and administrative courts should always be free to declare a government's decision void.[33] These days, we find this very logic realised through the enormous power acquired by corporate law firms and the system of international arbitration that often sidelines states, allowing corporations to make law and justice for their own convenience. In the terms introduced in Hayek's fourth book, comprising three volumes and titled *Law, Legislation and Liberty* (1973–9), sovereignty, with its hierarchical nature and top-down morphology, represents *taxis*, the artificial order of the state and organisations; this is opposed to *kosmos*, the spontaneous order of society and markets, of freedom, choice and openness.[34] For *kosmos* to be fully unleashed, the iron cage of *taxis* – the grip of state sovereignty – must be lifted.

Interestingly for our purposes, much of Hayek's criticism of sovereignty is developed through an attack on state *protection* and *control*,

---

30   F. A. Hayek, *The Constitution of Liberty: The Definitive Edition* (London: Routledge, 2011).

31   Ibid., p. 106.

32   Ibid., p. 107.

33   Ibid., pp. 199–202.

34   Friedrich A. Hayek, *Law, Legislation and Liberty, Volume 1: Rules and Order* (Chicago, IL: University of Chicago Press, 1973), p. 43–6.

which, as we shall see, are sovereignty's practical incarnations, its ends and means. Economic and social protection are seen as dangerous temptations leading down the path to inefficiency and ultimately slavery. Thus, in *The Road to Serfdom*, Hayek takes aim at various forms of social protection that were becoming established in the nation-states of his time. He blames trade protectionism for inefficiency and for having ushered in monopolies and cartels.[35] Furthermore, he denounces the rigidity of the British war economy and the laziness of 'the fortunate possessor of jobs for whom protection against competition has made it unnecessary to budge ever so little to make room for those without.'[36] For Hayek, workers harbour unrealistic demands for 'the protection of their "standard of life", of the "fair price", or the "professional income" to which they regard themselves as entitled.'[37] The only protection he could approve of was 'protection against the monster state,'[38] or 'protection of the private citizen against this tendency of an ever growing administrative machinery to engulf the private sphere.'[39]

Similarly, state control is seen as a bureaucratic interference that deprives individuals and firms of their economic freedom. For Hayek, 'it may become a real danger to liberty if too large a section of economic activity comes to be subject to the direct control of the state.'[40] The greatest horror, for Hayek, is the 'thicket of arbitrary controls' coming from the state, including control over housing and over monetary policy, 'price control' and 'location control' over the building of factories. This enmity towards state control was echoed by US neoliberal economist Milton Friedman, in his *Capitalism and Freedom*, published in 1962. The Chicago economist – who was awarded the Nobel Prize in Economics two years after Hayek – denounced all forms of government control, from 'controls on output' and 'rent controls' to the most worrying of all: 'control on money.'[41] All these forms of control were identified as constraints on freedom, the 'freedom to choose' – in other words,

---

35   Ibid., p. 48.
36   Ibid., p. 133.
37   Ibid.
38   Ibid., p. 223.
39   Hayek, *Constitution of Liberty*, p. 293.
40   Ibid., p. 196.
41   Milton Friedman, *Capitalism and Freedom* (Chicago, IL: University of Chicago Press, 2009).

individual market freedom – which, for neoliberals, was the sacrosanct value, to be defended at all costs.[42]

## Freedom and Power

Neoliberals conceived of sovereignty as a steel encasement suffocating the ability of individuals to determine their own preferred course of investment and consumption. Sovereignty was deemed the enemy of investor and consumer choice, and therefore the enemy of freedom. Indeed, neoliberals have often presented themselves as the champions of freedom against totalitarianism, as seen for example in the friendship between Hayek and Soviet dissident Alexandr Solzhenitsyn. But the freedom they advocate is a very narrow one, with no social or public dimension. It is a 'market freedom' predicated on the capacity to perform economic transactions without interference by state power: the greedy freedom of 'possessive individualism', which frames individuals as naturally egotistical agents.[43] Neoliberals effectively turned upside down the theory of the social contract of Hobbes and Rousseau, which had provided the conceptual pillar of modern republicanism. Painting sovereignty, rather than the state of nature, as a primeval and intolerable condition, they substituted the social contract with the commercial contract as the ideal basis of all human relationships, whereby *lex mercatoria* would become the supreme law.

In his 1944 book *Bureaucracy*, Ludwig von Mises went as far as to advocate the notions of 'sovereignty of the consumers' and 'sovereignty of investors' against the sovereignty of the state.[44] He cautioned that 'socialism means full government control of every sphere of the individual's life'. For von Mises, the 'unrestricted supremacy of the government in its capacity as central board of production' constitutes a mortal

---

42   Amartya Sen has analysed this centrality of choice in the neoliberal paradigm in his essay, 'Freedom of Choice: Concept and Content', *European Economic Review* 32: 2–3 (1988).

43   Jim McGuigan, 'The Neoliberal Self', *Culture Unbound* 6: 1 (2014).

44   Ludwig von Mises and Bettina Bien Greaves, *Bureaucracy* (New Haven, CT: Yale University Press, 1944). This idea of the sovereignty of the consumer comes close to the idea of the 'sovereign individual' propounded in James Dale Davidson and William Rees-Mogg, *The Sovereign Individual: The Coming Economic Revolution: How to Survive and Prosper in It* (London: Pan, 1998).

enemy of the freedom of individuals and companies.[45] Contrary to the heteronomy of socialist sovereignty, the ultimate decision about all economic processes should be given to consumers and investors, who are best placed to judge according to the neoliberal principle: 'markets know better than bureaucrats'.

A positive understanding of freedom directed towards the public good has instead been central to republican theory. According to this tradition, real freedom is possible only within a republic – a political community bound by the same laws. Niccolò Machiavelli famously asserted that democratic republics should aim for 'free life' (*vivere libero*), and that this depended on citizens' virtue – their participation in its decisions and collective actions.[46] Membership of a republic by definition involves some surrender of personal freedom, as obedience to its laws restricts the range of individual behaviour. However, Jean-Jacques Rousseau argued in *The Social Contract*, it is only through some suspension of individual freedom and acceptance of the sovereignty of the people that a community can assert its collective freedom – its capacity to control its own destiny.[47] This trade-off became very relevant during the Covid-19 pandemic, as large swathes of the right embraced a libertarian refusal to comply with anti-contagion rules such as social distancing and the wearing of masks, considering such protective measures as akin to 'communism'. The republican view of freedom as self-government implies that our rights are indivisibly related to our duties, deriving from an acceptance of the shared institutions of the state.[48] But this view is at odds with the possessive individualism propounded by neoliberals.

Neoliberalism has often been represented as an 'anti-statist' ideology; and to a great extent this is true. Eric Hobsbawm, for example, has argued that the doctrine of contemporary 'ultraliberalism' goes beyond the original laissez-faire liberal view propounded by Adam Smith, which accepted some degree of state interventionism.[49] Indeed,

45   Ludwig von Mises and Bettina Bien Greaves, *Bureaucracy*, p. 10.

46   Niccolò Machiavelli, *Discourses on Livy* (Chicago, IL: University of Chicago Press, 2009).

47   Rousseau, *Social Contract*.

48   Philip Pettit, *Republicanism: A Theory of Freedom and Government* (Oxford: Oxford University Press, 2010).

49   Eric Hobsbawm, 'The Future of the State', *Development and Change* 27: 2 (1996), 267–78.

neoliberal propaganda typically takes aim at the paternalism of the 'nanny state', bureaucratic 'red tape' and the public 'gravy train'. The state is represented as wasteful, meddlesome and overbearing – hence, neoliberals have traditionally advocated its 'rolling back'. US anti-tax activist Grover Norquist famously said, 'My goal is to cut government in half in twenty-five years, to get it down to the size where we can drown it in the bathtub.' He and other conservative activists even developed a 'starve the beast' strategy, geared at reducing government spending by cutting its revenue.[50] Similarly, Milton Friedman often insisted in his works and public speeches that the state only had to play the role of referee. The reality of the neoliberal approach to the state is, however, more complex than the idea of a shrinking of the state suggests. It is true that a strand of libertarian discourse that overlaps with neoliberalism, such as the solipsism of the likes of Ayn Rand and Robert Nozick, borders on anarcho-capitalism or 'minarchism', the view according to which government should be responsible only for security and defence, leaving everything else to the 'spontaneous' activity of society.[51] However, actually existing neoliberalism – the neoliberalism that came to fruition in policy-making – had a more pragmatic stance, acknowledging, that for markets to thrive, some degree of state mediation was necessary. As Quinn Slobodian argues, neoliberals were committed to 'redesigning states, laws and other institutions to protect the market' rather than merely doing away with government.[52]

This more constructivist view of the state as a guarantor and regulator of the market, rather than just a referee as proposed by Milton Friedman, is prominent in the neoliberal variant of 'ordoliberalism' developed in Germany under the aegis of thinkers like Walter Eucken and Franz Böhm.[53] As the etymology of ordoliberalism indicates, the freedom of the market is based on the presence of social order (Latin: ordo) guaranteed by the state. As Michel Foucault notes in The Birth of Biopolitics,

50  Michael J. New, 'Starve the Beast: A Further Examination', Cato Journal 29 (2009): 487.

51  Robert Nozick, Anarchy, State, and Utopia (New York: Basic, 1974).

52  Slobodian, Globalists, p. 6.

53  Walter Eucken and Franz Böhm are the two best-known theorists of ordoliberalism. Their defining works in German are, respectively, Walter Eucken, Grundsätze der wirtschaftspolitik (Tübingen: Mohr, 1955); Franz Böhm, Die Ordnung der Wirtschaft als geschichtliche Aufgabe und rechtsschöpferische Leistung (Stuttgart: W. Kohlhammer, 1937).

ordoliberals proposed that the state should be involved in the establishment and maintenance of the necessary conditions for markets to
thrive.[54] Crucially, the state has to devise regulations to ensure companies operate as rational economic agents. In this sense, deregulation –
that most familiar of neoliberal policies – is just another form of regulation: one that happens to favour business interests. Furthermore,
neoliberals in power have not shied away from using the state's repressive apparatus against citizens unconvinced of the wisdom of a market
society.

Besides this auxilary role, however, the state should abstain from any
positive interventionism, eschewing 'discretionary policies' such as
guaranteeing full employment, or launching a public works programme
for the public good. Its role should be limited to ensuring a fair degree
of competition and the stability of prices, and addressing exceptional
situations of 'market failure'. Neoliberals remained highly suspicious of
all proactive forms of state interventionism, behind which they saw the
risk of economic nationalism and the temptation to insulate countries
from the world economy. To this end, as Slobodian highlights, they
'proposed large but loose federations within which the constituent
nations would retain control over cultural policy, but be bound to maintain free trade and free capital movements between nations'.[55] Depriving
the state of its means of economic intervention and its control over
macroeconomic and industrial policy, neoliberals not only eroded the
ability of the state to control the economy; they also established the
structural conditions for political debates to be increasingly dominated
by all sorts of culture wars, which have become the favourite terrain of
the nationalist right to divert attention from economic conflicts.

## Openness in the Business Interest

Neoliberalism owes its success not only to its transformation of economic
doctrine, but also to its ability to present itself as an emancipatory

---

54 Michel Foucault, Arnold I. Davidson and Graham Burchell, *The Birth of Biopolitics: Lectures at the Collège de France, 1978–1979* (Berlin/Heidelberg: Springer, 2008).

55 Slobodian, *Globalists*, p. 95.

project: the struggle against the stifling fetters of state power, and thus against closure and intolerance. This moralising streak is visible in the works of numerous neoliberal thinkers, including Ayn Rand's celebration of entrepreneurial heroism and Hayek's pose as a freedom fighter arming himself against the oppression of totalitarian systems.[56] But it is in the anti-politics scepticism of British-Austrian philosopher Karl Popper that we find the boldest attempt to infuse the neoliberal project with an anti-authoritarian ethos. The equivalent in political philosophy of Hayek's and Friedman's defence of market individualism in economics, Karl Popper's *The Open Society* counterposed 'closed societies' – also described as tribal – to 'open societies'. He argued for the superiority of the latter, in which people are free to make personal decisions rather than being told what to do by others and by the state.[57]

With his resistance to illegitimate authority, Socrates is Popper's tragic hero of the open society – a conscionable citizen who dies at the hands of the state rather than renouncing his freedom of thought. The enemies of the open society, on the other hand, are major Western philosophers Popper sees as the intellectual fountainheads of collectivism and totalitarianism. The root of all political evil is found in Plato, who argued in *The Republic* and *The Laws* for the superiority of the collective over the individual.[58] According to Popper, this 'tribalism' of ancient political philosophy feeds into the thought of Hegel, who he considered guilty of hubris because of his assertion that history has a meaning, a 'spirit' and who he flatly derided as a charlatan. But the ultimate target of Popper's philosophical liberalism was most obviously Marx, who he accused of preaching a totalitarian view of history that allowed no place for individual choice.[59]

For Popper, politics should acknowledge that history is outside anyone's control, and that any plan or strategy to guide its course is dangerous for freedom. Abandoning any aspirations of radical social transformation, politicians should embrace 'fallibilism'. They should stoically accept that society cannot be steered nor guided and adopt a piecemeal rather than systemic approach to problems, cognisant of the

---

56   Ayn Rand, *Atlas Shrugged* (New York: Spark, 2014 [1957]).
57   Karl Popper, *The Open Society and Its Enemies* (London: Routledge, 2012).
58   Plato, *Republic*; Plato, *Euthyphro/Apology/Crito/Phaedo/Phaedrus*, transl. Harold North Fowler (Cambridge, MA: Harvard University Press, 1990 [1904]).
59   Popper, *The Open Society and Its Enemies*, pp. 368–77.

undesirability of top-down political interventions and their ineffective-
ness in complex societies. Popper's recommendations have become
mainstays of neoliberal political practice; fallibilism surfaces reliably
whenever Western politicians claim that social problems, including the
coronavirus pandemic, cannot be resolved but only managed, and it is
routinely asserted that civil society and philanthropy, rather than the
state, should take the lead in addressing social issues.

This view of the fallibility of politics informs Popper's furious polemic
against planning and social engineering – elements of socialism he sees
as inevitably leading towards authoritarianism.[60] 'Interventionism',
Popper cautions is 'extremely dangerous' because 'if we relax our watch-
fulness, and if we do not strengthen our democratic institutions while
giving more power to the state by interventionist "planning", then we
may lose our freedom'.[61] Counter to the stifling heteronomy he attributes
to socialism, which he views as a new tribalism, the open society would
be a dynamic one in which citizens would 'strive to rise socially, and to
take the places of other members'. This explains his hostility to Plato's
fear of commercialism; in Popper's view, commerce is a civilising force
prompting nations to be more open to one another and thus less
tribal.[62]

The edifying image of the open society has been frequently quoted by
neoliberal pundits to criticise their right-wing and left-wing opponents
of intolerable tribalism. Popper's book has given its name to George
Soros's Open Society, a foundation that promotes freedom and democracy, though with the proceeds of financial speculation. These days the
celebration of 'openness' in all its forms has become one of the central
tenets of neoliberal common sense, in which closure of any kind is
invariably deprecated. A variety of neoliberal ideological apparatuses,
from *Wired* magazine to the *Wall Street Journal*, and including the average TED talk, have proposed that openness, transparency and consensus are a good thing, and that their opposite – closure, opacity, secrecy,
rivalry – are to be disapproved of, regardless of their underlying motives.
In the economic field we are told that countries need to open up to
global trade and foreign investments if they want to thrive. In digital

---

60   Ibid., pp. 244–9.
61   Ibid., p. 338.
62   Ibid., p. 174.

culture, open-source and open-data standards are seen as enhancing accountability and social media invites us to 'open up' and reveal our inner selves. Popper's polemic has become a contemporary *doxa*.

Ideas of openness are also invoked in the context of cultural policy to defend tolerance in a multicultural society now endangered by the rise of an intolerant nativist right the world over. The idea of openness has become associated with what US political theorist and feminist Nancy Fraser calls 'progressive neoliberalism': an 'alliance of mainstream currents of new social movements (feminism, anti-racism, multiculturalism, and LGBTQ rights), on the one side, and high-end "symbolic" and service-based business sectors (Wall Street, Silicon Valley, and Hollywood), on the other.'[63] Blending together 'ideals of emancipation and lethal forms of financialization,'[64] progressive neoliberalism has attempted to appropriate minority rights and other civil rights and progressive causes. Many multinational corporations have presented themselves as committed to racial and sexual equality by celebrating parts of the calendar dedicated to LGBT and Black history, or championing these causes in their advertisements. This was seen in summer 2020, when celebrities, multinationals and the news media hypocritically jumped on the bandwagon of support for the Black Lives Matter protests in order to market themselves as morally principled actors.

While waxing lyrical about minority rights, neoliberalism has in fact traditionally had a very different kind of minority in mind: the 'minority of the opulent', US founding father and president James Madison noted, must be defended against the redistributive demands of the majority.[65] As Hayek asserted: 'If we recognize rights of minorities, this implies that the power of the majority ultimately derives from, and is limited by, the principles which the minorities also accept.'[66] This means no government should be authorised to push through measures strongly resented by a minority in society – in particular, by the minority of entrepreneurs, who would see their private power undercut by the political power of the majority. Hence, the disingenuous subtext of the edifying

63    Nancy Fraser, 'The End of Progressive Neoliberalism', *Dissent*, 2 January 2017.
64    Ibid.
65    James Madison, 'Suffrage and Majority Rule' in *Selected Writings of James Madison*, ed. Ralph Louis Ketcham (Indianapolis: Hackett Publishing, 2006).
66    Hayek, *Constitution of Liberty*, 107.

neoliberal discourse of openness and defence of minorities is the priming of private power and the freedom of enterprise over democracy.

## The Triumph of Market Freedom

Reading the works of Hayek, von Mises, Friedman and other neoliberals in the present era has a haunting effect: they read like blueprints that have largely been fulfilled. Neoliberal ideologues did not stop at the level of academic intervention, but consciously developed a hegemonic project in the 'trenches of civil society'. As proposed by US historian Philip Mirowski in his discussion of the Mont Pelerin Society as a 'neoliberal thought collective', the likes of Hayek and von Mises contributed to the construction of a sophisticated propaganda machine and the development of a body of intellectuals and cadres who went on to fill key posts in universities, pressure groups, state institutions and international agencies.[67] It would take many decades before neoliberal ideas, initially considered heretical and at odds with the received Keynesian wisdom, would become politically viable, transforming doctrine into practice. A series of economic crises and geopolitical shocks, including the 1973 oil crisis, the end of the gold standard and the intractability of stagflation – namely a combination of high inflation and high unemployment – within the Keynesian paradigm provided a window of opportunity for the neoliberal revolution to unfold.[68]

The political tipping point in neoliberalism's rise to hegemonic status was the election of Margaret Thatcher in 1979 and Ronald Reagan in 1980. These politicians radically overhauled the position of the Conservative and Republican parties, which until then had stuck to the consensus policy of the Fordist era of maintaining an alliance between labour and capital. They harshly attacked trade unions, which they denounced as distortive of market mechanisms, and began to chip away at welfare-state provisions that had been hard-won by workers' struggles during the 1960s and 1970s. Public assets such as housing were sold to

---

67  Philip Mirowski, *Never Let a Serious Crisis Go to Waste: How Neoliberalism Survived the Financial Meltdown* (London: Verso, 2013).

68  David Harvey, *A Brief History of Neoliberalism* (New York: Oxford University Press, 2007).

private companies and individuals, with the aim of transforming large sections of the population from workers into aspiring capitalists and creating a property owners' and small share-holders' democracy. The former council housing tenant, now turned into a home-owner as a result of the 'right to buy', would have a vested interest in the success of the market, while workers' demands for better wages would be pacified by access to credit.[69]

If, during the high point of the era of globalisation, neoliberalism became something akin to a *pensée unique*, adopted across the political spectrum, it was because it managed to shed its close association with the right, and progressively seep into the social-democratic field, where the superiority of the logic of the market found ever greater acceptance. Margaret Thatcher was right when she noted that New Labour's neoliberal platform was her greatest political achievement. Responding to the surge of the neoliberal right and the defeats of the labour movement, European social-democratic parties and the US Democratic Party abandoned many of their social pledges.

Anthony Giddens's idea of a 'Third Way' between capitalism and socialism – which informed the likes of Bill Clinton in the United States, Tony Blair in Britain, Gerhard Schröder in Germany and Romano Prodi in Italy – proposed to reconcile social democracy with the global free market.[70] In light of the failure of socialist governments, most notably Mitterrand's in France in the 1980s, to pursue a state-interventionist agenda, leaders and ideologues of the moderate left argued that the only realistic way to deliver prosperity in a globalised world was to find a compromise with financial markets, multinational corporations and international trade, in a neoliberal consensus far more skewed towards business than the social-democratic consensus had been.[71] Thus, Clinton supported NAFTA; Schröder in Germany reformed social security; Prodi's Ulivo centre-left coalition in Italy presided over the most sweeping privatisation programmes in the history of the country; and Tony Blair introduced the Private Finance

---

69   Grace Blakeley, *Stolen: How to Save the World from Financialisation* (London: Repeater, 2019).

70   Anthony Giddens, *The Third Way: The Renewal of Social Democracy* (Hoboken, NJ: John Wiley, 2013).

71   Daniel Singer, *Is Socialism Doomed? The Meaning of Mitterrand* (New York: Oxford University Press, 1988).

Initiative to pay for new public-sector buildings, while Gordon Brown, his chancellor and heir as prime minister, allowed the City to conduct its business unimpeded, with the justification that tax revenues from the financial sector could be used to subsidise disadvantaged communities in Labour heartlands. The centre-left pursued these policies with even more fanaticism than the right, in a sorry manifestation of the obtuse zeal of the newly converted.

Enjoying bipartisan support, pro-market policies devised by the likes of Hayek and Friedman have gone a long way to reshape the world economy. As we have seen in the preceding chapter, barriers to trade, capital and labour have been radically reduced with the aim of turning the planet into a 'smooth space' easily traversed by flows of capital, commodities and services. But the consequences have been hurtful for democracy and have resulted in social inequality in wealth, income and access to services.[72] Central to this project has been the effective emptying out of state sovereignty, and in particular of economic sovereignty, in line with the recommendations issued by neoliberal ideologues. As renowned sociologist of globalisation Saskia Sassen has argued, 'Governments used to have a whole array of policies to govern their national economies: policies on taxes, public spending, interest rates, credit controls, exchange rates, capital controls, and income. The global financial markets have affected all of these, some of them sharply.'[73]

Various pillars of national economic sovereignty, including monetary, fiscal, industrial and social policy, have thus been demolished by the wrecking ball of global markets. Financialisation and the rise of multinational corporations have severely diminished 'state capacity' – the effective ability of the state to steer the course of events and guarantee security for its citizens. Nation-states have handed financial markets and multinationals enormous blackmail power, which can keep any attempts at state intervention in check. For example, the rise of what German political economist Wolfgang Streeck has described as the 'debt state' – the dependence of governments on the international bond market for their financing – has severely limited the range

---

72   Branko Milanović, *Global Inequality: A New Approach for the Age of Globalization* (Cambridge, MA: Harvard University Press, 2016).

73   Saskia Sassen, *Losing Control? Sovereignty in the Age of Globalization* (New York: Columbia University Press, 1996), p. 22.

of discretionary economic policies.[74] By boycotting sales of public bonds and pushing up their yields, investors can compel governments to squeeze public spending if they are to avoid a downgrade to junk-bond status. Multinational corporations can exact adjustments on tax policies and environmental regulations by threatening to relocate their activity to a more 'business-friendly' regulatory environment. Similarly, participation in global trade, and WTO and EU restrictions on state aid, have limited the use of government subsidies, which are essential to fostering fledgling industries and protecting national champions. Finally, international capital mobility and the existence of tax havens have meant that the state has lost control over taxation: a rise in corporate or individual tax rates results in an outflow of wealth from the country. In the European Union, this trend has been compounded by the loss of monetary sovereignty: countries with different levels of debt, deficits, unemployment and growth must all dance to the same tune, sung by Eurotower technocrats who, in accordance with the ECB mandate, are primarily concerned about 'price stability', namely keeping inflation low.

This bulldozing of state capacity has resulted in a widespread perception of political impotence, which is extremely corrosive for democracy. When politicians curtly reply to their citizens' demands for more public services and employment opportunities by saying that their hands are tied by the need for fiscal prudence, or by parameters set by Brussels, it is obvious that disillusion about politics, and a sense of betrayal by the political class, will gain ground. Ultimately, this antidemocratic orientation is no mere accidental by-product of neoliberal 'reforms'. It accords entirely with the neoliberal scepticism towards mass democracy exhibited by the likes of Hayek and von Mises, and the constant search for external constraints that might limit the scope of popular sovereignty. The most shameful example of these anti-democratic attitudes has been the complicity of neoliberalism with dictatorships – most infamously, with Pinochet's authoritarian regime in Chile. Pinochet's coup and subsequent rule was supported by a group of Chilean economists trained by Milton Friedman and Arnold Harberger at the University of Chicago – the so-called Chicago Boys. But the enmity of neoliberals towards

---

74  Wolfgang Streeck, 'The Politics of Public Debt: Neoliberalism, Capitalist Development and the Restructuring of the State', *German Economic Review* 15: 1 (2014).

democracy has also shown itself in less violent yet more pervasive phenomena.

Neoliberalism has been the main driver of what English political scientist Colin Crouch has named 'post-democracy': a society in which, while the formal institutions of democracy are preserved, they are in effect hollowed out.[75] Over the last four decades, ever greater areas of political decision-making have been 'externalised' to entrepreneurs, brokers and experts of all sorts, and to unelected national authorities and international agencies, often deemed more enlightened and well-informed than politicians. Most indicative of this tendency was the famous assertion by former US Federal Reserve chair Alan Greenspan in a 2007 interview with Swiss newspaper *Tages-Anzeiger*: 'We are fortunate that, thanks to globalisation, policy decisions in the US have been largely replaced by global market forces. National security aside, it hardly makes any difference who will be the next president. The world is governed by market forces.'[76] For Crouch, this subordination of democracy leads to 'an atmosphere of cynicism about politics and politicians, [and] low expectations about their achievements'.[77]

Neoliberals have sacrificed mass democracy and its institutions on the altar of the global market and its promise of economic growth. But the collective prosperity that was supposed to be the reward in this devil's bargain never came to fruition. Since the 2008 crisis, GDP per capita has stagnated in countries such as the US, the UK and Germany and decreased in Italy, France, Greece, Brazil and Spain.[78] Furthermore, inequality, as measured by contrasting the income of the top 10 per cent and that of the bottom 50 per cent, has worsened not just in the West but also in China and India, which have otherwise experienced steady growth in GDP per capita. Furthermore, neoliberal deregulation and trade openness has meant growing labour precarity and exposure to international market competition.[79] In the aftermath of the 2008

---

75  Colin Crouch, *Post-Democracy* (Cambridge: Polity, 2004).

76  Interview with Alan Greenspan (19 September 2007), quoted in Adam Tooze, *Crashed: How a Decade of Financial Crises Changed the World* (London: Penguin, 2018), p. 443.

77  Crouch, *Post-Democracy*, p. 23.

78  World Bank, GDP per capita (current US$). Data 2019.

79  Albena Azmanova, *Capitalism on Edge: How Fighting Precarity Can Achieve Radical Change without Crisis or Utopia* (New York: Columbia University Press, 2020).

financial crash, and now of the coronavirus crisis, it should have become apparent even to the most distracted observer that the neoliberal promise of delivering individuals from the oppression of state power was merely an excuse for giving a free pass to the most rapacious capitalists. In our time, the gospel of free markets has become hard to preach, even for its most ardent supporters. Contemporary political reality points to a return of anti-market attitudes and state interventionism that are anathema to neoliberal ideologues. Even right-wing populists, still campaigning on a low-tax and pro-business platform, have started selectively chipping away at some neoliberal dogmas. Donald Trump has done much to undermine the sanctity of free trade, while Boris Johnson's declaration during the coronavirus emergency that 'there is such a thing as society' inverted Margaret Thatcher's most infamous dictum.[80] At the current historical moment, the bankruptcy of neoliberalism is widely seen as not only financial, but also moral. The question now, however, is what will emerge in neoliberalism's stead.[81]

## Reclaiming Popular Sovereignty

The attention paid to questions of sovereignty, and to its correlates of protection and control, in contemporary debates needs to be read as the political reaction to the failure of neoliberalism and the global system it has constructed. This setback is resurrecting neoliberalism's favourite fiend, the discretionary power of the national-popular state, and the principle of popular sovereignty it hails from. But, paradoxically, it is doing so precisely at a moment when the reality of national sovereignty is in question, global interconnectedness having upset many assumptions about the autonomy of nation-states. The present demand for the restoration of sovereignty – of the 'public soul of the commonwealth', to quote Hobbes – betokens a reaction to a world in which the lifting of state intervention on the market has sown the seeds of social instability and economic

80    Boris Johnson made this statement on 30 March 2020, to express the importance of collective effort against the virus. Some people saw it as a departure from Thatcherism. Robert Saunders, ' "There Is Such a Thing as Society". Has Boris Johnson Repudiated Thatcherism?' *New Statesman*, 31 March 2020.

81    Joseph E. Stiglitz, 'The End of Neoliberalism and the Rebirth of History', *Project Syndicate*, 4 November 2019, at project-syndicate.org

insecurity. Neoliberalism stands accused of an 'undoing of the demos', an erosion of the power of political communities.[82] Facing this situation, post-neoliberal endopolitics projects a recuperation of sovereignty as a means to respond to the agoraphobia engendered by neoliberal externalisation. It revolves around a reaffirmation of the principle of the authority of the state as a centre of political power against the centrifugal tendency of globalisation – but also a reclamation of the power of place as the pivot of collective attachments and the anchor of political communities.

While these general motives can be found on both the right and the left, the signifier of sovereignty is filled by a variety of signifieds and qualifications, which imply divergent political consequences. The main difference between progressive and reactionary approaches to sovereignty maps onto the opposition between the notions of territorial sovereignty and popular sovereignty, which we have discussed in the course of this chapter: sovereignty as territorial domination, or as democracy and self-government. In mobilising the notion of sovereignty, the right identifies the cause for the present political crisis in the way that globalisation has deprived the demos of its ethno-cultural coherence, and hence of social cohesion. Figures like Trump, Salvini and Bolsonaro have blamed a variety of representatives of globalism for this dilution of the demos and its identity: migrants accused of crime and terrorism; global financiers and capitalists pretending to be philanthropists; the officers of international organisations, including the World Health Organisation, wielding illegitimate power; and what they see as the perverse influence of progressive metropolitan intellectuals and their ideology of political correctness, 'gender theory' and 'cultural Marxism'.

What is at stake in this territorial framing of sovereignty is the supremacy of the native population and its control over its 'indigenous' territory. The proposed cure for global agoraphobia is rooted in a strong demarcation of borders separating the national territory from the outside, accompanied by the subjugation, if not outright extirpation, of all those inhabitants who are not seen as full citizens, and the insulation of the nation from extra-national interference. This posture leads to a fetishism of sovereignty betrayed by the very term 'sovereigntyism',

---

82   Wendy Brown, *Undoing the Demos: Neoliberalism's Stealth Revolution* (Boston, MA: MIT Press, 2015).

which suggests that sovereignty has become an end in itself. Ultimately, however, as the coronavirus emergency has revealed, this declared communitarianism is accompanied by a strong libertarian individualism. The nationalist right remains deeply imbued with neoliberal assumptions and often seems more concerned with the 'sovereign individual' than with the sovereign people.[83]

The prominence of this isolationist and egotistical sovereigntyism in contemporary debates is the reason why, for many on the left, any discussion of sovereignty seems to signify a lurch to the right. Such a knee-jerk reaction, however, overlooks the fact that, as Mélenchon and others have noted, it is in fact the left, starting with the Jacobins, that has historically affirmed sovereignty, in the specific sense of popular sovereignty, as a pillar of democratic politics. The view of sovereignty invoked by the new socialist left, from Podemos to Bernie Sanders, has a radically different, Rousseauean tinge from that of the right. For the left, it is the 'internal' aspect of sovereignty – the supremacy of political power over private powers – that counts.

On the left, sovereignty is deemed to have been lost because of the economic, rather than cultural or ethnic, subordination of the national-popular states to the global market. From this weakness derives the inability of the state to attend to popular demands – for example, to fight unemployment and poverty, and to deliver satisfactory public services. Those responsible for this trend are identified among corporate executives, bankers and billionaires – actors who threaten the well-being and security of the people as a whole. In response, a call is made to reassert state capacity, rehabilitating various forms of Keynesian state intervention and social protection, but also to broaden the possibilities of democratic control by citizens on decisions that affect them.

It is in this democratic perspective that we can understand new sovereignty-related terms, such as technological sovereignty and food sovereignty, that denote forms of collective power predicated on locality and proximity, against the power of multinationals and finance, often without invoking the mediation of state power. By all means, a progressive view of sovereignty should always approach this principle as a means to an end, avoiding its turning into an absolute end in its own right as supported by rightist 'sovereigntyism'. As this difference in

---

83   Davidson and Rees-Mogg, *Sovereign Individual.*

understandings shows, sovereignty reflects a social demand for security and order vis-à-vis the present condition of global agoraphobia to which different political responses can be given. What these might be will be explored in the following chapters, which examine two key ramifications of the politics of sovereignty: protection and control.

# 4
# Protection

On 19 March 2020, the Spanish deputy prime minister and Podemos leader Pablo Iglesias presented to the press a package of social measures to 'protect the most vulnerable categories in the face of coronavirus'. The programme, described as '*escudo social*' ('social shield') was predicated on the idea that 'the coronavirus crisis is not merely a health crisis, but also a social and economic crisis. To say that we fight this virus together is an empty phrase, unless it means that nobody is left alone in this situation'. Cautioning that politicians had to avoid a repetition of 'the mistakes of 2008 and guarantee that people approach this crisis with the maximum of security', he observed that 'security means also that the most vulnerable are not abandoned, that working people should not have to bet their health or that of their relatives, that they should be able to adapt their worktime to look after their relatives . . . that nobody's electricity supply . . . will be cut, and that nobody should be evicted from their homes'.[1]

The social shield introduced in Spain – like the measures adopted by other governments around the world – and the jargon of protection, security and care used by Pablo Iglesias in his speech, are a manifestation of the protectivism that has emerged as a key political trend in the era of the Great Recoil. The coronavirus crisis has mobilised a strong

---

1    Pablo Iglesias, Speech on the coronavirus emergency at Moncloa, 19 March 2020, at twitter.com. My translation.

discourse of protection, ranging from issues concerning PPE (personal protection equipment) to discussions about the need for support bubbles to sustain individuals during the crisis, calls to provide better pay for care workers, doctors and nurses working to protect the public, and the ubiquitous governmental advice to 'protect yourself and protect others'. But this emphasis on protection reaches well beyond the coronavirus emergency. We live in a period where the term protection – and associated notions such as safeguarding, security, care and safety – are invoked in response to a number of dangers that have become ever more alarming on the contemporary horizon – from the painful social aftermath of the 2008 economic crisis to the rising unemployment experienced during the coronavirus pandemic; from apocalyptic terrorism waged by groups like ISIS and white supremacists to the environmental crisis caused by runaway climate change; from mass migration to the loss of identity and social cohesion caused by the rise of globalisation. Despite their obvious differences, these issues are all presented in contemporary political discourse as existential threats against which society must be protected.

The discourse of protection punctuates the defining speeches and documents of contemporary politics, acquiring markedly reactionary connotations on the political right. Donald Trump has repeatedly asserted his role in guaranteeing the protection of Americans from foreign interests. He famously pledged to defend the nation's borders against an influx of migrants from south of the Rio Grande by building a border wall that was, however, never completed. In his 2020 State of the Union address, Trump said that one objective was paramount: to reverse bad trade deals, so as to 'defend our workers' and 'protect our intellectual property'.[2] Nigel Farage, British leader of UKIP and then of the Brexit Party, has often claimed that he wants to protect 'our precious independence', and afford special protections to fragile sectors of the British economy, including fisheries and manufacturing. Italy's Matteo Salvini, former deputy prime minister and federal secretary of the Lega party, has promised to 'protect Italian borders against the danger posed by illegal migration'. Salvini turned border defence into an almost sacred mandate, shutting down Italian ports to NGO ships rescuing migrants

---

2   Associated Press, 'Read the Full Text of Donald Trump's 2020 State of the Union', 6 February 2020, available at pbs.org.

at sea during his 2018–19 stint as interior minister. Furthermore, the nationalist right often promises to protect identity and tradition against the homogenising force of global multiculturalism. This discourse of protection also surfaces in right-wing conspiracy theories such as those circulated by QAnon, which argues that an alliance between the 'deep state' and Democrats is involved in a major paedophile ring. In one QAnon propaganda image, a man raises a shield against the 'Insurgency' in order to 'protect our children'.

On the left, the discourse of protection has been adopted in defence of social security, which Iglesias invokes in his speech, instead of police security. In June 2019, Bernie Sanders declared that 'freedom is possible only in a society that protects economic rights'.[3] During his tenure as Labour leader, Jeremy Corbyn repeatedly promised to protect jobs, health and social welfare. Representative Alexandria Ocasio-Cortez, Sanders's heir apparent as leader of the US left, declared in November 2019: 'I was sent here to safeguard and protect people', not the profits of private corporations. Even the EU, certainly not the most obvious flag-bearer for protectionism, has warmed to the discourse of protection, adopting the slogan 'A Europe that Protects', coined by French president Emmanuel Macron on the eve of the appointment of the new European Commission headed by Ursula von der Leyen, as a way to rekindle the loyalty of Europe's citizens towards Brussels institutions.[4]

These references to the protective role of the state highlight how protection, in all its many, often contradictory manifestations, is seen as a necessity for survival in a catastrophic world marked by ever-increasing social threats. As I will argue in this chapter, we live in an 'Age of the Pangolin' – a time when the demand for security and protection against danger has become dominant, displacing the seductive neoliberal discourse of aspiration, innovation and entrepreneurialism. Protection is a notion with a long tradition in political philosophy: since Plato, it has signified the defence of the community. Protection was understood by both Machiavelli and Hobbes as the 'bare minimum' of politics – that

---

3   Scotty Hendricks, 'Bernie Sanders: The US Already Has a Kind of Socialism – for the Rich', *Big Think*, 12 June 2019, at bigthink.com.

4   European Commission, 'Security Union – A Europe that Protects', 30 October 2019, at ec.europa.eu.

which allows the community's survival and reproduction in the face of threats of all kinds. Today, protection is demanded in response to the dislocation and externalisation produced by global capital, the exposure to the rapacious tendencies of an extractivist capitalism and the devastating ecological risks it has generated.[5]

## Under the City's Shield

Protection is a term that sounds somewhat alien to those who have spent most of their adult lives before the great crises of the early twenty-first century. During the period of triumphant neoliberalism, state protection – and in particular social protection and trade protectionism – was decried as paternalistic and as an obstacle to freedom and innovation. However, protection is central to politics. Following Thomas Hobbes, it may be said that security and protection are 'the very essence of Government'.[6] Military, health and economic protection guarantee the minimum condition of politics: the survival and reproduction of a society.

The question of 'protection' – from the Latin *protegere* (pro- + tegere – to cover the front) – has a long tradition in political theory. In Plato's *Republic*, the fountainhead of political thought in Western civilisation, rulers are called 'guardians' – *fýlakes* in ancient Greek. This is because, as implied by the root *fýlasso* – to watch, guard, protect, defend, but also to maintain, preserve, cherish – the role of political leaders is first of all 'preservation' and 'maintenance' of the polity. To paraphrase a famous Platonic dictum, if the shoemaker's art is the making of shoes, the politician's art is the protection of the polity against dangers – either external threats, such as wars or epidemics, or internal strife. In Book III of *The Republic*, Plato states that power-holders have to be 'protective of the city'.[7] This reflects the fact that the continued existence of the city is ultimately predicated on its ability to withstand dangers and preserve the health of its citizens. In the words of Cicero in *De Legibus*, a treatise

---

5   Karl Polanyi, *The Great Transformation: The Political and Economic Origins of Our Time* (Boston: Beacon, 2014), p. 167.

6   Ibid., p. 154.

7   Plato, *Republic*, ed. and transl. Chris Emlyn-Jones and William Preddy, 2 vols (Cambridge, MA: Harvard University Press, 2013), p. 109.

modelled after Plato's *Laws*, *salus populi suprema lex esto*: the welfare of the people shall be the supreme law.[8]

Protection is a good in itself, but also a necessary condition for social cohesion. Protection is what keeps the city together, what gives it a sense of purpose, what commits its citizens to the pursuit of a common mission. Protection, in this sense, is not just defensive; it is productive of the community. In fact, as Plato goes on to argue, the city's very solidarity rests on the recognition of the need for common forms of protection, on the fact that citizens know that 'the whole city protects each one of the private citizens', and that therefore, deprived of the protective shield of the city, they are left exposed to threats to their own physical survival.[9] This centrality of protection in the architecture of the city is revealed precisely in those moments when protection is lacking, with nefarious consequences for citizens.

Plato proposes the example of a 'man who had fifty slaves, or even more', and what would happen to him if he were thrown 'out of the city, him and his wife and his children, and [put], along with his servants and the rest of his property, in an isolated place where none of the free citizens could have any way to protect him'.[10] Regardless of one's wealth, outside the city, any citizen would find himself left exposed to all adversities. As the Greek practice of ostracism demonstrates, this was not just a fictional scenario. The expulsion of undesired citizens, sanctioned by a popular ballot, was so feared because it resulted in the condition of utter helplessness described by Plato. The city is thus imagined as a sort of protective womb; outside the city, there is only danger and fear, and life, to quote Hobbes's famous phrase is 'solitary, poor, nasty, brutish, and short'.[11]

This view of politics as protection was central to the two great political philosophers of the early modern era: Machiavelli and Hobbes. For Machiavelli, protection is central to political authority. Significantly, in *The Prince*, the measure of a principality's strength is 'whether the prince has so much power that he can (if necessary) stand up on his own, or

---

8    Marcus Tullius Cicero, *Cicero: On the Commonwealth and on the Laws*, ed. and transl. James E. G. Zetzel (Cambridge: Cambridge University Press, 2017).

9    Ibid., p. 277.

10    Ibid.

11    Thomas Hobbes, *Leviathan*, ed. J. C. A. Gaskin (Oxford: Oxford University Press, 2008), p. 84

whether he always needs the protection of others'.[12] The ability to protect oneself is the minimum condition for being an autonomous political actor. If one does not possess the means of protection, one should be resigned to the role of vassal of a stronger power, or to the humiliating yet relatively safe fate of living in a territory that has the status of a 'protectorate' – a place that falls under the protection of someone else. These days, many countries, while nominally sovereign, are under the de facto military authority of a suzerain, such as the United States, China or Russia, and the protection of its atomic 'umbrella'.

In *The Prince*, the protective function of the state is represented through a suggestive hydraulic metaphor. The Florentine diplomat argues that all princes should prepare for adverse circumstances and downturns in political fortune. He compares what he capitalises as Fortune 'to one of those destructive rivers that, when they become enraged, flood the plains, ruin the trees and buildings, raising the earth from one spot and dropping it onto another'.[13] A ruler should act as a wise engineer who prepares for bad weather. He will take 'precautions with dikes and dams when the weather is calm, so that when they rise up again either the waters will be channelled off or their force will be neither so damaging nor so out of control'.[14] As Cicero had already noted in *Commonwealth*, a fundamental quality of a good ruler should be prudence – literally looking forward (as implied in the Latin root *pro-videre*). The good ruler will always prepare for the multiple threats that arise out of the chaotic flow of worldly events, including wars, famines and epidemics. By planning defence against them, the prince will be able to control them, rather than being caught in their tempestuous tide.

## Divisive Fears

The demand for protection prevalent in our era springs from a sense of fear. Much has been said in recent years about our times as an 'age of

---

12  Niccolò Machiavelli, *The Prince*, ed. and transl. Peter Bondanella (Oxford: Oxford University Press, 2005), p. 38.

13  Ibid., p. 84.

14  Ibid.

fear' and the 'politics of fear' peddled by the nationalist right.[15] Often, however, the reason for this prominence of fear in contemporary society seems to be missed – especially among liberals, who take the influence of fear in politics as tantamount to barbarism. But it is impossible to understand the post-neoliberal politics of protection without considering its connection to fear. Hobbes is often considered as the philosopher of the politics of fear, and this is not altogether wrong. Fear was one of many emotions considered by Hobbes – others included hope and desire; but it was by far the most important, for its various political consequences. Fear was a very important category not only in Hobbes's writings, but also in his own upbringing. In his verse autobiography, originally written in Latin, he famously remarked, 'My mother gave birth to twins: myself and fear', since he was delivered at the time when the Spanish Armada of King Philip II was approaching the coast of England, in what was ultimately an unsuccessful attempt to force the English into submission.[16] Furthermore, his life was repeatedly in danger, such as after the 1666 plague, when he was lambasted for his atheism.

Fear infuses Hobbes's anthropological discussion of the state of nature, which preceded and informed Jean-Jacques Rousseau's own. Fear is what defines primitive society before the creation of political institutions – a condition marked by 'continual fear, and danger of violent death'. For Hobbes, fear, among other emotions, is what human beings share with animals, and is thus a manifestation of our irrational element: 'this perpetuall feare, always accompanying mankind in the ignorance of causes'.[17] Fear is an elemental force which only the presence of the state can channel in a productive way. The state, in this sense, is a response to human fear – an institution that serves to regulate and organise it so as to prevent its destruction of the fragile social bonds that sustain society. In Hobbes, fear constitutes the first mover of political action, much as desire acts as the dominant political motivation in the work of Spinoza and many philosophers under his influence, such as François Lyotard, Gilles Deleuze and Antonio Negri.

15   Molly Ball, 'Donald Trump and the Politics of Fear', *Atlantic*, 2 September 2016.

16   Thomas Hobbes, *The Life of Mr Thomas Hobbes of Malmesbury* (Exeter: The Rota at the University of Exeter, 1979).

17   Hobbes, *Leviathan*, p. 72.

This is why Hobbes has long been seen as a somewhat dismal philosopher, whose conclusions necessarily tended towards the authoritarian. But Hobbesian insights are returning with a vengeance in the late neoliberalism of the post-pandemic era, when fear pervades political affairs.

In the initial section of *Leviathan*, Hobbes catalogues various forms of fear. The list includes melancholy, terror, fear of death, fear of spirits, 'fear of Darknesse and Ghosts', fear of oppression, fear of poverty and calamity, fear of punishment – and also 'hydrophobia' and 'tyrannophobia'. This multiplicity of fear has important consequences for politics. From different kinds of fears stem different political reactions. Specifically, all fears fall into two categories: 'mutual fear' and 'common fear' – in other words, fear harboured by humans towards one another, and fear of common dangers or punishments affecting them all.[18] The most prevalent fear in Hobbes is mutual fear, which is dominant in the state of nature – a condition that resurfaces in civil wars such as the one that was raging in England precisely at the time he was writing *Leviathan*. The competitive spirit of individuals and their equality in natural endowments leads to diffidence; and diffidence – in other words, mutual suspicion – leads in turn to war, war between individuals and civil war, of 'every one against one another'.[19]

For Hobbes, only in the presence of a 'common power' able to 'overawe them' and 'keep them in quiet' through fear of punishment and death can this internecine struggle between people be suspended. It is impossible to 'bridle men's ambition, avarice, anger, and other passions, without the fear of some coercive power'.[20] This discussion may seem dubious or repulsive; but it is reminiscent of the way in which the weakening of the state has unleashed individual rapacity during the neoliberal era, in the economic war of all against all that has deeply divided society. The source of a common fear capable of uniting society is not only to be found in the power of the state. Interestingly, for a time like ours, marked by fear of coronavirus and climate change, common fear is also related to natural dangers, such as plagues, floods and earthquakes

---

18   Lars Svendsen, *A Philosophy of Fear* (London: Reaktion, 2008).
19   Hobbes, *Leviathan*, p. 83.
20   Ibid., p. 91.

– or thunderbolts attributed to the anger of the gods, as discussed by Giambattista Vico.[21]

This distinction between mutual fear and common fear, and their respective relationships with unity and division, provides a useful grid to make sense of the different 'uses of fear' that are now emerging in the post-neoliberal politics of protection. The nationalist right has often been accused of using fear as a means to divide the people. During the 2020 presidential campaign, Joe Biden paraphrased a New Testament passage: 'A house divided against itself cannot stand.' It was a comment on the divisiveness created by Trump's tenure as president, his antagonising of Black Lives Matter and his support for groups on the extreme right.[22] Similarly, Pope Francis clearly had the far right's politics of hate in mind when he attacked 'toxic Manichaeism' in his 2020 encyclical, titled 'Fratelli Tutti' ('All Brothers'). Indeed, the anxieties the right mobilises mostly correspond to the Hobbesian category of mutual fear, pitting different sections of the population – defined by race, gender or belief – or entire nations, against one another.

One typical example of this stoking of mutual fear is the right's use of the fear of crime, which is often tightly interwoven with fear of migrants and ethnic minorities. This is most evident in countries with appallingly high murder rates like the United States and Brazil. In 2018, Brazil had 57,000 violent deaths, compared to 20,000 in war-torn Syria. Jair Bolsonaro's promise to implement heavy-handed solutions, such as deregulating the purchase of weapons and sending military troops to the favelas, which are overwhelmingly inhabited by people of colour, was a winning card in his election as president in October 2018. In the United States, Donald Trump ran the 2016 and more explicitly the 2020 campaign on a law and order platform to defend America from criminals often strongly identified with immigrants and ethnic minorities. He branded the Black Lives Matter protests sparked by the killing of George Floyd as terrorism. Furthermore, he referred to the 'defund the police' slogan, issued by some activists during the demonstrations, and embraced by AOC, to argue that the Democratic Party was controlled by the 'radical left' and unable to guarantee protection for the citizenry.

---

21   Giambattista Vico, *The New Science of Giambattista Vico*, transl. Thomas Goddard Bergin and Max Harold Fisch (Ithaca, NY: Cornell University Press, 1984), p. 78.
22   Matthew 12:22–8.

The other great fear pandered to most crudely by the right is fear of foreign powers – a fear that has a long and infamous pedigree. The conflict between different polities and the need for protection that derives from it is, according to Plato, the original motivation for political organisation and the institution of guardians. In Ancient Greece, war between city-states was frequent and politics was intensely focused on the city's defence (viz. Themistocles). Stories of cities that had been sacked and their inhabitants sold into slavery were a stark reminder that entire peoples could be erased from history. Fear of annihilation continues to haunt contemporary politics. With the end of the Cold War and the collapse of the Soviet Union, the terrifying prospect of an all-out nuclear war had long seemed to be off the cards. But the growing rivalry between the United States and China and the violent conflicts in the Middle East during the 2010s shows that we are far from the global 'perpetual peace' imagined by Immanuel Kant.[23] In fact, as geostrategic competition escalates, we see the right wing in the United States and Europe beating the nationalist, Sinophobic drum. As the decline of the United States and the Western alliance deepens in the post-pandemic era, breeding a profound resentment and fear of the loss of status, we may well witness such chauvinism growing, amid an even more fear-driven politics than we have been used to in the first decades of the twenty-first century.

## The Politics of Care

The highly divisive fears mobilised by the nationalist right are not the only ones that inflect social demands for state protection. In contemporary politics we also find 'common fears' related to the destructive effect a destabilised environment and new illnesses will have on our survival, exemplified by climate change and the coronavirus crisis. These are common fears because they seem to pit humanity against external agents which, like the lightning described by Vico, strike fear into everyone and therefore can potentially act as a 'negativity' against which to construct a sense of unity and solidarity.

23   Immanuel Kant, *Perpetual Peace: A Philosophical Sketch* (Cambridge: Cambridge University Press, 1970).

At the same time, they are imbricated with social conflicts arising from the management of health and natural resources, which often pit workers and ordinary citizens against the interests of the wealthy, who oppose taxation, and environmentally damaging industries that refuse regulation.

The Covid-19 crisis has not only placed serious stress on countries' health systems, exposing their fragility to unforeseen shocks after two decades of underfunding and the privatisation of public health; it has also spawned deep worries and psychopathologies in the population. The quarantine imposed in many countries was observed strictly by the majority of citizens not only because of fear of legal consequences, but also for fear of infection and the recognition of the necessity of protective measures by the state. The disciplined response by the majority of citizens was welcomed from many quarters as a demonstration of the resurfacing of a sense of public duty and solidarity, based on an awareness that society could protect itself only if citizens protected one another. This reciprocity was well represented by the use of face masks, which, more than protecting the person wearing them, protect those in her vicinity; but if everyone wears a mask, this protection of the other also ends up being a protection of the self. This universalist framing of protection against the pandemic was heightened by declarations of a 'war against the virus', presented by many politicians as a mortal enemy of society.

The fear engendered by the pandemic did not seem to fit well the typical playbook of the nationalist right, which relies mostly on fears relating to immigration, crime and international rivalries and resentments. It involves a trust in science and scientific expertise, which contradicts the nationalist right's anti-intellectualism and anti-scientism. In fact, the right tried to redirect fear of the virus towards a number of obscure agents accused of using the emergency to manipulate public opinion. In the course of the pandemic, a number of anti-scientific conspiracy theories spread wildly, claiming all sorts of alternative interpretations of the events – suggesting the virus had been deliberately manufactured by Big Pharma – while many cast doubt on the efficacy of masking, social distancing and vaccines.

Conspiracy theories of this kind were mobilised by the so-called 'no-mask' movement and sometimes directly amplified, and retweeted, by leaders of the nationalist right such as Donald Trump. Even after being infected, Trump persisted in a stance of denial. Posing triumphantly on the balcony of the White House after his discharge from the Walter Reed Medical Center in October 2020, he was barely able to hide the fact that he was gasping for breath. Furthermore, the right tried to use the crisis to stoke resentment against China, whose reputation in fact suffered in the West amid the emergency. Trump made no apologies for calling Covid-19 'the China virus', while Steve Bannon claimed that it was a 'Chinese Communist Party virus', with allies in Italy, Brazil and Spain adopting a similar rhetoric.

On the socialist left, the onset of the pandemic led to discussions about a politics of care: an investment in health and the environment which could provide safety in the context of a widespread sense of fragility and insecurity.[24] Inspired by the role of health and other essential workers, scholars and activists have argued that care should become a lens through which to reorganise society, prioritising basic support mechanisms that everyone depends on. The politics of care implies a concern for basic needs – for fostering, curing and nurturing society and repairing a damaged natural environment. In practical terms, it calls for major investments in healthcare and education, social care and environmental protection, and good pay for care workers who too often are neglected. For instance, Joe Biden has pledged $400 billion for childcare and elderly care as part of his stimulus package, a choice his policy advisors defended in a telling manoeuvre by arguing that care is a fundamental element of infrastructure. A 'caring society' – a society in which everyone is assured of care and social protection – could defuse the fear of extinction stoked by the pandemic and create a renewed sense of security and hope for the future.

Despite the huge shock created by coronavirus, this emergency is dwarfed by incoming crises – in particular, climate change. Global warming has the potential to produce the greatest environmental catastrophe ever experienced by mankind. This issue poses an existential challenge to the stability of the biosphere, and no adequate response to it has so far been proposed. The warming of the planet is bound to lead to a number of destructive effects, especially if the rise in temperature is not kept beneath the 2° Celsius limit relative to the pre-industrial average temperature, which was identified in the 2015 Paris Accords as the

24  The Care Collective, *The Care Manifesto* (London: Verso, 2020).

necessary goal in order to avoid 'runaway climate change'. According to recent research, there is a chance that the symbolic boundary of 1.5 degrees might already be crossed in 2024.[25] Even with bold and rapid cuts in emissions of a kind that currently seems unlikely, the effects of global warming are bound to be very severe.[26]

As a consequence of climate change, the world will be faced with a treacherous rise in temperature and deadly heatwaves. A combination of high heat and humidity, already registered in the Persian Gulf, that can be lethal even for healthy people when in the open will become more common in the future.[27] Cities like New Delhi, Shanghai, Beijing and Los Angeles may be pushed beyond habitability before the end of the century.[28] Large stretches of coastline will face the risk of floods, with many coastal mega-cities threatened by sea-level rises projected to reach up to a metre by 2100 and much more in the following centuries.[29] A severe decline in agricultural yields amid rampant desertification and worsening water scarcity, will make it increasingly difficult to feed a growing world population.[30] Massive biodiversity loss is also expected, 50 per cent of species being likely to have been deprived of suitable climate conditions by the end of the century.[31] Furthermore, climate change will facilitate the spread of new diseases, including malaria, dengue and other tropical illnesses. It is also likely to contribute to the onset of new pandemics, due to the growing pressure of human communities on animal habitats and the higher likelihood of zoonotic transmission.[32] These catastrophic trends are bound to have enormous social consequences, millions of people being forced to move from areas that

25    Chelsea Harvey, 'Worrisome Signs Emerge for 1.5–Degree-C Climate Target', *Scientific American*, 10 July 2020.
26    David Wallace-Wells, *The Uninhabitable Earth: A Story of the Future* (London: Penguin, 2019).
27    Damian Carrington, 'Climate Change to Cause Humid Heatwaves That Will Kill Even Healthy People', *Guardian*, 2 August 2017.
28    Wallace-Wells, *The Uninhabitable Earth*, 44, 48.
29    Jonathan Watts, 'Sea Levels Could Rise More than a Metre by 2100, Experts Say', *Guardian*, 8 May 2020.
30    Wallace-Wells, *The Uninhabitable Earth*, 89.
31    Robin McKie, 'Biologists Think 50% of Species Will Be Facing Extinction by the End of the Century', *Guardian*, 25 February 2017.
32    Robin McKie, 'Rampant Destruction of Forests "Will Unleash More Pandemics"', *Guardian*, 30 August 2020.

have become impossible to live in.[33] Perhaps even more terrifying are the political consequences that the agoraphobia deriving from them might have. We have already experienced the capacity of a relatively modest economic downturn and the rise in immigration in the mid 2010s to stoke nationalist sentiment. What will happen to politics if a truly catastrophic decline brutally destroys people's livelihoods, sparking wars over water and food and creating enormous waves of refugees?

This calamitous prospect demonstrates the urgency of a politics of protection and care aimed at safeguarding the basic conditions for the continued existence of society. If environmental struggles have long been framed as 'protecting the environment', and preserving endangered species, such as the polar bears losing their habitat because of melting ice, it is now apparent that it has become a question of protecting humanity and the 'human habitat' itself – hence the broad resonance of the struggle against the prospect of extinction raised by the climate justice group Extinction Rebellion. While sometimes exaggerated, or even demotivating, in its apocalyptic tone, the rhetoric used by anti-climate change activists signals the urgent need for a massive effort to address this threat.

The fight against climate calls not only for measures that mitigate the greenhouse effect – namely, reductions in carbon emissions through the transition to renewable energies, an immediate halt to the extraction of fossil fuels and a radical overhaul of transport, energy, construction and food systems.[34] It also requires a number of 'climate adaptation' measures that involve protection vis-à-vis a destabilised natural environment. Rising sea levels will necessitate the improvement of coastal defences, including the reinforcement of coastal dunes, 'beach nourishment' efforts and the construction of sea walls and river dikes. Increasingly frequent flash floods will create a need for improved drainage infrastructures and urban planning measures to restrain excessive construction; creeping desertification will require transformations of agriculture, and in particular of the crops cultivated in each region; and extreme weather events will increase the need for protective technologies for buildings and infrastructures. Furthermore, this environmental crisis highlights the fact

---

33   Wallace-Wells, *The Uninhabitable Earth*, pp. 49–50.
34   Ann Pettifor, *The Case for the Green New Deal* (London: Verso, 2020).

that infinite growth is a mirage and our focus should instead be on consolidating and rebalancing an already highly technological society, focusing on repair and on qualitative improvement rather than unlimited quantitative expansion, as the discourse of 'sustainability', now widely accepted by the political mainstream, proposes.

These measures all cry out for a level of state intervention that far exceeds the light-touch, 'nudging' approach favoured by neoliberals. Breitbart and other right-wing media organisations stoke fears of an 'ecological Leninism' that would put the lives of ordinary people under intolerable levels of control. But the real risk that must be averted is rather that of eco-fascism, in which right-wing communitarianism is presented as the only possible response to averting social collapse amid an evermore inhospitable natural environment.

The prominence of all-too-motivated fears in contemporary politics is something that worries many on the left, given the perception that fear is a boon for the right. It is true that much right-wing politics has been built on fear – most notably fear of migrants and foreigners. Furthermore, a fear of losing social status has traditionally functioned as a major driver in the growth of fascist movements. However, a broad suspicion of fear as a political motivator seems inconsistent with the fact that, in present circumstances, there are numerous reasons for fear that are far from irrational or baseless. Fears need to be acknowledged and understood, rather than met with the contempt of those who are lucky enough to enjoy protection from danger. Only by addressing such fears head-on might it be possible to rekindle the emotion of hope that even the dismal Hobbes counted among the key drivers of politics – a hope that today is voiced by movements like Fridays for Future, whose concern for coming dangers is combined with the optimism that the struggle against difficult circumstances may usher in a better future.

## Fending Off Capital

The flood Machiavelli discusses in his work is the military danger represented by foreign forces threatening to overrun the territory of the state; the danger of Swiss, French and Spanish armies marauding over Italian soil in his own time. Today, however, the politics of protection are more concerned with the economy than with war – and in particular with the macroeconomic threats we have become familiar with in this age of depression. The destructive effects of stock crashes, capital flight and financial floods, combined with the threat of 'disruption' posed by digital businesses to retailers, taxi companies and other service providers are upsetting the fragile equilibria of local economies. Workers and citizens feel exposed to economic dangers that are upsetting their livelihoods and frustrating their desire for stability. But, faced with these threats, national governments often find themselves with few remedies. As we have seen in chapters 2 and 3, acceptance of the neoliberal dogma of 'openness' has entailed a renunciation of basic forms of economic protection (including tariffs, labour protections, social welfare, licensing powers, strong environmental regulations, and so on). Many states thus find themselves newly vulnerable – deprived of the dikes and canals that can channel and stem the tide of economic forces, imposing a degree of 'friction' on economic flows that might hinder some of the most rapacious enterprises and investments.

This situation of impotence and vulnerability goes a long way to explain why trade protectionism – that most disparaged of economic policies – has lately acquired new currency. This can be seen clearly in Donald Trump's withdrawal from the Trans-Pacific Partnership (TPP) trade treaty and subsequent initiation of a trade war with China. In recent years, the left – whose criticism of free trade had traditionally been limited to civil society practices such as fair trade – has also mobilised in support of moderate forms of commercial protectionism. Figures like Bernie Sanders and Jean-Luc Mélenchon have advocated the regulation of trade, foreign investment and capital flows as a means of protecting the environment and workers' rights. For example, in April 2019, Sanders, who opposed the NAFTA trade treaty, took aim at such treaties more broadly: 'Our trade deals were written by large multinational corporations for multinational corporations. Trade is a good thing. But we need a trade policy that works for working families, not just large corporations.' Similarly, the programme of Jean-Luc Mélenchon's La France Insoumise in the 2017 presidential elections pledged to 'refuse free trade, establish solidarity protectionism and economic cooperation.'[35]

---

35  Solidarity protectionism is the idea that lifting up social and environmental trade standards can foster solidarity between workers in different countries. Jean-Luc Mélenchon, *L'Avenir en commun. Le programme de la France insoumise et son candidat Jean-Luc Mélenchon* (Paris: Seuil, 2016), p. 91. My translation.

In the aftermath of the coronavirus crisis, even some centrist politicians have revised their views, admitting that global trade has been pushed to an extreme. This is reflected in the idea of 'European sovereignty' that Macron has in mind – according to which the European Union should speak with one mind on global trade issues, resorting to protectionist measures if trading partners do not play fair.[36] Protectionism – until recently having consistently negative connotations associated with fascist autarchy, as well as failed experiments in populist import-substitution and communist central planning – is now increasingly acceptable on the political scene, as we shall see in Chapter 9 when discussing the post-pandemic state.

What is at stake in post-pandemic politics is not just trade protectionism, but a more general approach to the politics of protection that I describe as 'protectivism'. Protectivism encompasses a greater variety of policies, including social welfare, workers' representation, environmental protection and other social support mechanisms whose urgent necessity has been demonstrated by the coronavirus crisis. Economic statism is evident in the fostering of fledgling industries in the digital and green-energy sectors, as well as in investment in essential public services such as health and education. This change of perspective reflects an environment in which the neoliberal promise of rapid growth, access to new foreign markets and widespread enrichment for a global middle class has been thoroughly discredited. The slogans invoking aspiration, entrepreneurialism, innovation and flexibility that imbued neoliberal possessive individualism ring increasingly hollow in the midst of recession. The political focus has instead shifted towards ideas of reconstruction and *consolidation*, to demands for the safeguarding of living conditions and the protection, and fair redistribution, of current levels of prosperity, against the prospect of catastrophic decline.

The obvious reference point for understanding this politics of economic protection is the work of Karl Polanyi – whose theory of the 'second movement' we have already introduced[37] – and in particular his discussion of the dialectic between inhabitation and improvement. For Polanyi, capitalism is a destabilising force that upsets society's balance.

36   Paolo Gerbaudo, 'Le nouveau protectionnisme', *Le Grand Continent*, 7 December 2020.

37   Chapter 2, above

Its promise of *improvement* is caught up in a fight to the death with society's struggle for *habitation*. 'Improvement' refers to capitalism's drive to optimise production: its emphasis on technological innovation to attain higher levels of productivity, and increased returns on investment. 'Habitation' refers to society's legitimate desire to enjoy some degree of stability and security – its fundamental instinct towards self-preservation.[38] This does not mean that economic activities and the market – which Polanyi carefully distinguishes from capitalism proper – are anti-social by nature. Rather, capitalism is a specific type of economy and property arrangement that revolves around a *disembedding* of the economy from society. In previous eras, economic activities were closely regimented by social relations and customs, as observed by many 'moral economists', including R. H. Tawney and E. P. Thompson, who advocated an economy based on mutuality and moral norms of fairness and justice. Medieval towns enforced strong protectionist measures through the creation of guilds and corporations that controlled access to the labour market; meanwhile 'mobile capital' was suspected of threatening 'to disintegrate the institutions of the town'.[39] Modern capitalism has, by and large, destroyed the social institutions that guaranteed social control over the economy, turning the market into a destructive force.

In the capitalist world of global finance and international trade, land, money and labour become mere commodities, and this creates a feeling Polanyi names as 'exposure' – a term that, as we have seen, well reflects neoliberal globalisation's drive towards externalisation, at the root of contemporary agoraphobia. Polanyi provides various examples of this exposure, including 'the exploitation of the physical strength of the worker, the destruction of family life, the devastation of neighbourhoods, the denudation of forests, the pollution of rivers, the deterioration of craft standards, the disruption of folkways and the general degradation of existence, including housing and arts'.[40] These tendencies become most apparent at moments of crisis, when people's livelihoods are turned upside down.

In response to this stress, societies have often exhibited practices of economic protection, which Polanyi discusses in Part II of *The Great*

---

38   Polanyi, *Great Transformation*, p. 36.
39   Ibid., p. 68.
40   Ibid., p. 139.

*Transformation* – suggestively titled 'Self-Protection of Society'.[41] Polanyi refers to the 'principle of social protection aiming at the conservation of man and nature as well as productive organization, relying on the varying support of those most immediately affected by the deleterious action of the market'.[42] Polanyi uses a number of related terms for protection: conservation, shelter, reaction, defence and attenuation – terms that seem eerily relevant to contemporary and future challenges. This phraseology conjures the idea of society as a reactive and defensive structure, which springs into action when subject to threats, whether of mass unemployment or pandemic disease.

For Polanyi, the social instinct for protection is not necessarily an irrational nor a conservative impulse, as liberals would have it. Rather, it proceeds from the desire to re-establish a measure of equilibrium and stability without which society cannot thrive. Although the term originates in the nationalist political economy of Friedrich List, economic protectionism cannot be reduced to a right-wing position. In fact, in his 1940 essay 'The Fascist Virus' Polanyi contrasts fascism's totalitarian politics of protection with the various '*protective interventions* on the part of society as a whole'[43] that have often been pursued by trade unions and socialist movements. These include 'factory laws, social insurance, municipal socialism, trade union activities and practices', all of which have been utilised in the attempt to reinsert social control and solidarity into the economy, and were 'socially necessary in order to prevent the destruction of the human substance through the blind action of the automatism of the market'.[44] Polanyi's analysis is highly relevant amid the fragility of the present. Only by constructing forms of economic and social protection adequate to confront the daunting challenges the future has in store for us can we hope to overcome the condition of naked exposure to market forces and regain some sense of economic and social security.

---

41    Polanyi, *The Great Transformation*, p. 251. Emphasis mine.
42    Ibid., p. 138.
43    Karl Polanyi, 'The Fascist Virus', in his *Economy and Society: Selected Writings*, ed. M. Cangiani and C. Thomasberger (Cambridge, MA: Polity Press, 2018), pp. 108–22.
44    Ibid., p. 109.

## Obedience for Protection

Protection often involves an act of subjugation, a domination of the powerful over the powerless, of the sovereign over the subject, of the protector over the protected. In the public imagination, protection is often associated with authoritarianism and paternalism, and resented by liberals, who consider protection as hostile to freedom. Furthermore, protection seems to connote the exclusion and expulsion of the unprotected, most vividly in the politics of borders and migration. But the politics of protection cannot be reduced to a conservative maintenance of the status quo. There are many forms of state protection that are essential to society's well-being, and that need to be urgently reinstated and expanded to confront the systemic crises of the twenty-first century; as proposed by Plato, these forms of collective protection are central to the bonds of solidarity at the heart of any polity.

Besides representing the ultimate objective of politics in the Hobbesian paradigm of sovereignty, protection also constitutes its basis of legitimacy: for political authority to be legitimate, it has to protect the people; if it stops protecting them, it becomes illegitimate. Protection is the object of the most important clause of the social contract – Hobbes's key conceptual invention. The social contract revolves around a very particular transaction: the exchange between protection and obedience; the citizen offers his obedience in exchange for the sovereign's protection. As Hobbes puts it, 'the end of Obedience is Protection'.[45] This exchange may sound like a rather brutal 'offer you can't refuse' of the kind that operates in the realm of mafia and prostitution rings. But it implies a fundamentally democratic corollary: obedience towards the sovereign – respect for laws, submission to the authority of the state, popular acceptance of civic duties – is not unconditional, but contingent on a credible offer of protection from the sovereign power.

When the state is incapable of guaranteeing protection to its subject, the social contract itself becomes void. As Hobbes phrases it, 'The obligation of subjects to the sovereign, is understood to last as long, and no longer, than the power lasteth, by which he is able to protect them.'[46] Everyone is thus authorised to look after their own life: 'for where there

---

45  Hobbes, *Leviathan*, p. 194.
46  Ibid., p. 147.

is no such Power, there is no protection to be had from the Law; and therefore every one may protect himself by his own power.[47] This suspension of the social contract because of the failure of the state to enforce social protection is reminiscent of the popular response to many great social and political calamities throughout history – such as following defeat in war, or when a country is hit by a major environmental crisis or famine.

Thus, Hobbes, generally considered the philosopher of law and order and an apologist of sovereign authority, does in fact have a theory of legitimate revolt against power. Rebellion is valid in those cases when the sovereign no longer provides the basic public good of protection. This seems to parallel the classic Confucian doctrine of authority in China, based on the notion of a celestial mandate assigned to the emperor. Also in this case, the mandate lasts only as long as the emperor demonstrates his ability to shield his own subjects from foreign or natural dangers – in circumstances when this does not apply, the people have the right to rise up. When authorities lose the ability to provide protection, it is their very existence that is at stake. When such crises reach a point of no return, as Hobbes's capitalisation insists, 'then is the Common-wealth DISSOLVED'.[48]

Today's rebellion of the people against the establishment is grounded precisely in the perception of their having been betrayed and deprived of the protection they were promised in exchange for their dutiful obedience. This grievance has been evident in the discourse of a number of recent popular protests, including France's Gilets Jaunes, the 2019 protests in Chile and Ecuador and the major wave of protest that is already emerging in response to the economic effects of the Covid-19 pandemic. These protests are infused with a sense of betrayal at the hands of state and economic systems that have shown themselves unable to defend the livelihood of citizens and workers. The reality of growing precarity, insecurity and depressed wages has revealed that the *neoliberal social contract* – entailing the promise of growth and opportunity – has been unilaterally breached by the capitalist class. In coming years, as the economic effects of the coronavirus crisis will affect basic conditions, governments will be under pressure to deliver social protection if

---

47   Ibid., p. 194.
48   Ibid.

they want to maintain the obedience of their citizens. However, we should be aware that, as Hobbes's argument about the correlation between obedience and protection implies, the additional state protection that many may welcome is bound to go hand-in-hand with demands for additional state control, which many resent. This 'price of protection' is bound to raise major dilemmas in Western capitalist democracies over the coming years.

## The Age of the Pangolin

The political challenges of the present resonate strongly with the leitmotiv of the politics of protection, which, as we have seen, is a key question in Western thought running from Plato through Machiavelli and Hobbes, to Karl Polanyi's discussion of society's response to the despoliation wrought by uncontrolled capitalism. In times when the trajectory of social and economic development seems to have reached a plateau, when ecological catastrophe is looming on the horizon, and when many people are worried about the bare minimum conditions of their existence and that of their children, it is not surprising that the demand for protection has moved once again into the foreground. In Polanyi's terms, the priority has become inhabitation rather than improvement, reconstruction and sustainability rather than acceleration. This attitude resonates with the declaration of Spanish prime minister Pedro Sánchez who, immediately after the beginning of the first lockdown, in March 2020, stated: 'Our society, which had grown used to changes that expand our possibilities of knowledge, health and life, now finds itself in a war to defend all we have taken for granted.'[49] The question is what a progressive politics of protection should amount to, and how to avoid an outcome in which a widespread sense of danger is used to feed political reaction.

The obvious risk is that the politics of protection will be exploited by the nationalist right, presenting migrants, ethnic minorities and foreign countries as existential threats to be defended against. To express the defensive character of societies reeling from the 1929 stock market

---

49   Pedro Sanchez, 'Speech on the Coronavirus Emergency', 14 March 2020. My translation.

crash, Polanyi used the image of a 'crustacean society' that pursued a 'sovereignty more jealous and absolute than anything known before'.[50] The image of a crustacean reveals some elements that lie at the heart of any politics of protection – in particular, the way in which the security of the 'inside' is predicated on insulation against, and often repulsion of, the 'outside', much as the suppleness of a lobster's meat is guaranteed by its leathery external shell. It is true that this defensive involution can provide shelter from external perils threatening society's survival. But this survival instinct can also engender a dangerous defensiveness, a jealous territoriality. This, incidentally, is also a characteristic of the ethology of the lobster, which – as argued by Jordan Peterson, the controversial conservative psychologist – often engages in violent dominance disputes in which it uses its claws to battle competitors.

A more endearing animal for illustrating the character of protectivism is the pangolin – the species initially blamed for the zoonotic jump that generated the Covid-19 pandemic. The insect-eating pangolin is the only mammal on the planet with scales. Like the armadillo, with which it is sometimes confused, it curls up into a ball when threatened – a tactic that allows it to survive encounters with much larger predators, including lions. Unlike the lobster, however, the pangolin is peaceful and shy, and is one of earth's most vulnerable animals. It has no teeth and lives a mostly solitary life, hiding in burrows and avoiding confrontation with other pangolins. It elicits sympathy precisely because, despite its investment in defence, it appears rather defenceless. Pangolins are poached in the tens of thousands every year because of the use of their scales in traditional Chinese medicine and because their meat is considered a delicacy. The respective postures of these two creatures – the aggressive territorial defensiveness of the lobster and the more good-natured defensive tactics of the pangolin – can be seen as metaphors for the different approaches to the politics of protection that are emerging on the right and the left.

On the nationalist right, the politics of protection is mostly associated with aggressiveness and a will to dominate. It is bent on sparking mutual fears – especially the fear of migrants, who it frames as aliens, but also mutual diffidence between nations. The prime protective function it assigns to the sovereign state is to protect 'natives', as well as their

---

50   Polanyi, *Great Transformation*, p. 211.

industry and property, against other nations and their economies, in a narrative in which capitalist competition is shrouded in the garb of competition between nations. This proprietorial protectionism claims to protect the community in its entirety and to deliver the physical security of law and order. But in fact, as will become more apparent in the discussion of class issues and economic policies that follows, behind these communitarian pretences hides a stubborn defence of special interests and established property relations.

This chapter has also explored the intimations of a progressive politics of protection. Social protectivism revolves around issues of social care and environmental repair. This approach focuses on the provision of basic economic security for everyone, guaranteeing universal standards of living to cure the worst forms of insecurity affecting workers and the most vulnerable. The fears that are dominant in this context are more economic than cultural in nature; the demand for protection is not motivated so much by fear of ethnic pollution as by a desire to denounce the social dissolution caused by the ravages of capitalism. In conclusion, protection has become the decisive question in post-neoliberal politics, the term that captures manifold anxieties that haunt our society. The struggle for political hegemony in the post-neoliberal era will be determined by which vision of protection gains more traction among electorates preoccupied by fear.

# 5

# Control

If protection is the ultimate end of state sovereignty, control is its practical means. In contemporary discourse, control invokes a variety of key functions of the state – such as capital controls, border controls, or environmental controls – many of which are deemed to have been weakened by neoliberal globalisation; more generally it alludes to the manifold mechanisms involved in translating political will into action. The recent popularisation of this notion is coloured strongly by politics. It stems from the 'take back control' slogan coined by the Leave campaign in the June 2016 Brexit referendum and was frequently mentioned on television programmes and in public speeches by Brexiteers, starting with the Leave campaign leader and current UK prime minister, Boris Johnson. Brexiteers argued that by leaving the European Union, Great Britain would be able to reassert democratic control over a number of important policy areas – migration, fisheries, trade, and so on – that were then unduly controlled by bureaucrats, or 'eurocrats' based in Brussels, putting ordinary British citizens at a disadvantage. Taking back control was seen as a token of sovereignty and ultimately democracy; though critics warned that, rather than delivering more control, it would simply increase the UK's international isolation.

The relevance of the question of control, however, reaches much further than the claim to sovereignty raised by the Brexit campaign. This notion is today being mobilised in the most disparate of circumstances: in discussions about the crisis of democracy and debates about pandemic measures; in policy proposals connected to ecological transition and discussions about global trade; in the revival of economic planning; in conspiracy theories and controversies about the relationship between science and politics. Control is a term that evokes questions of power, bureaucracy, coercion, state intervention and political intentionality – all of which were viewed with suspicion during the neoliberal era. It betokens a demand for political order, legibility and authority, amid a world in which neoliberal policies of deregulation have unleashed social and economic chaos. Furthermore, it is associated with calls for more democracy and civic participation, reversing the technocratic transformation of decision-making under neoliberalism. This breadth of meanings and applications explains why the notion of control has become the object of contention between the nationalist right and the socialist left, as each seeks to distance itself from the neoliberal centre and its suspicion of state control.

The mobilisation of the term control reaches well beyond the confines of the British Isles. On the right, it was often used during the 2010s in the context of claims to recover territorial control deemed to have been eroded by globalisation. In the United States, Donald Trump often used the imaginary and vocabulary of control as part of his chauvinistic rhetoric. For example, during the 2016 presidential campaign, he often described the situation at the southern border with Mexico as 'out of control' and took aim at the problem of 'uncontrolled migration'. In Italy, Matteo Salvini proposed in 2017, in framing his 'Italians First' discourse, that it was necessary to regain 'control of money, banks and borders', despite later reneging on his anti-euro commitment.[1] Similarly, Marine Le Pen often argued that France 'must control our borders', to stop 'massive migration', prevent terrorist attacks, and later to halt the spread of coronavirus.

On the left, the question of political control has also become the object of intense attention amid a growing preoccupation with the sorry state of democracy and citizenship, as well as demands for more bottom-up democratic control over decisions, and the perception of a crisis of state efficacy. In the aftermath of the Brexit referendum, some left groups even tried to appropriate the slogan of control for their camp. The Corbynite organisation Momentum launched a 'Take Back Control'

---

1  Lucia Annunziata, 'Mezz'ora in più', *Rai 3*, 24 March 2017.

tour affirming that 'people are sick and tired of having no control over the big decisions that affect their lives'.[2] In an interview with *Jacobin*, Jean-Luc Mélenchon argued that people were now demanding 'control over their personal lives and over their immediate and wider environment'.[3] In fact, the demand for a democratic recovery of control over the economy has been at the core of many recent protest movements and left campaigns: from demands for a 'real democracy' expressed by the 2011 movements of the squares to those of municipalist initiatives asserting control over the city, as well as broader demands for the economic oligarchy to be reined in and a public economy rebuilt.

The discourse of control has only intensified since the Covid-19 crisis began in early 2020. As the pandemic has raged, governments have competed to show that they had a firm grip on the reins of the country, while opponents have accused them of unleashing chaos. Unprecedented forms of control over the population have been enforced, from extensive lockdowns and quarantines to mass testing and tracking and the isolation of asymptomatic patients in so-called Noah's Arks. The health crisis sparked a heated debate on the political and ethical implications of the high level of state surveillance and enforcement during the pandemic. The way in which China effectively brought the coronavirus epidemic under control, while rich capitalist countries like the United States and the UK found themselves in deep trouble, has also raised the question of whether authoritarian states are more effective than liberal democracies in addressing emergencies.

Control thus represents a central question in understanding the endopolitics of the Great Recoil. It projects a reversal of the neoliberal imaginary, with its distaste for bureaucracy and authority. Whereas neoliberals have often railed against government controls of all sorts, which they consider an unnecessary interference with private freedom, a reaffirmation of political control is now deemed necessary to confront present and future catastrophes. As this chapter will show, the notion of control is closely connected to the rise of statecraft. In fact, sovereign states cannot exist without asserting what in today's political jargon we call 'control'. But there are various meanings of control, with

---

2   Julia Rampen, 'Momentum's The World Transformed to Launch "Take Back Control" Brexit Events', *New Statesman*, 25 November 2016.
3   Jean-Luc Mélenchon, 'A Future in Common', *Jacobin*, 27 August 2018.

contradictory political implications. In the course of this chapter, I will explore three: control as command, as direction and as autonomy. While control as command involves an authoritarian claim to power often backed by the threat of violence, control as direction revolves around decision-making, the ability of politics to shape the course of events, and who is responsible for guiding it. Finally, control as autonomy refers to the extent to which a polity can claim effective separation, or 'insulation', from the surrounding world. These different meanings are crucial in developing a vision of democratic control to counter the temptations of authoritarian control that are emerging in today's neo-statist landscape.

## Genealogies of Control

Control is a very common term, used in many different fields, from cybernetics to accounting, psychology (self-control), sociology (social control), military jargon (command, control and communication) and everyday language. Generally speaking, it can be defined as the ability to direct behaviour, individual or collective, as well as the specific operations and sanctions that derive from that ability. In psychology, control is mostly framed as self-control, the ability of a person to manage stress and achieve his or her goals.[4] We control things when we are confident that our plans are going to be fulfilled, that our thoughts will guide our actions to the desired result. Control as self-control and control over the environment are correlated with well-being and self-fulfilment, while lack of control has been clearly identified as a source of anxiety and the root of psychopathologies that have become more endemic in our era – especially since the onset of the coronavirus crisis and the collective trauma it has produced.[5] Thus, control is a virtue. No one wants to be 'out of control', except perhaps in certain transient moments in which suspension of control can result in a feeling of elation or euphoria.

In politics, control is equally central. In a general sense, it expresses

---

4   Ellen J. Langer and Robert P. Abelson, *The Psychology of Control* (Los Angeles, CA: Sage, 1983).

5   Michael W. Eysenck, Nazanin Derakshan, Rita Santos and Manuel G. Calvo, 'Anxiety and Cognitive Performance: Attentional Control Theory', *Emotion* 7: 2 (2007), p. 336.

the capacity of an actor – whether a leader, a party or a government – to assert its will. Control is correlated with power, authority, command, government, and ultimately sovereignty. Whoever is in control 'calls the shots', determining reality at his or her will. In the context of democratic politics, however, control does not just cascade down from the top, but also filters upwards. With the rise of mass democracies throughout the modern period, forms of top-down control have been progressively moderated by forms of citizen control over representatives – through periodic elections, through the monitoring effects of public opinion, and by virtue of the nature of the public sphere as a space of constant scrutiny of the actions of the powerful. Democracy thus involves a two-way flow of control, where those at the top control those at the bottom, who in turn control them. Much of political contention in democracies is staked on the question of who should be in control and by what right.

Political control is strongly interwoven with the state in its capacity as the most important structure of control over society, and indeed the model for most other forms of control. This is reflected in the very origin of the term control, which stems from the rise of statecraft during the late Middle Ages. The English term control originates from the medieval Latin term *contrarotulare*. The word was used to describe the action of an official who checked information against (*contra*) a roll (*rotula*).[6] In Anglo-Norman French, *contreroller* meant to keep a roll of accounts, a constantly updated 'scroll copy' against which all verbal and written testimonies had to be checked. It was in fact in the Norman courts in England and the Kingdom of Two Sicilies of the eleventh and twelfth centuries that the modern state took embryonic form, and the term control came to indicate practices of inspection, record-keeping and enforcement of state bureaucracy. The exercise of sovereign power required the development of extensive bureaucracies the likes of which had not been seen since the fall of the Roman Empire in Western Europe. Royal courts had to be capable of supervising large territories by gathering knowledge on subjects, harvests and cities, while sanctioning

---

6 'Late Middle English (as a verb in the sense "check or verify accounts", especially by referring to a duplicate register): from Anglo-Norman French *contreroller* "keep a copy of a roll of accounts", from medieval Latin *contrarotulare*, from *contrarotulus* "copy of a roll", from contra- "against" + rotulus "a roll". The noun is perhaps via French *contrôle*. Contrarotulare', G. W. S. Friedrichsen, R. W. Burchfield and C. T. Onions, *The Oxford Dictionary of English Etymology* (Wotton-under-Edge: Clarendon, 1966).

behaviour deemed injurious to the interests of the sovereign.[7] Think about the Domesday Book – the great survey of Britain and Wales completed in 1086 by order of William the Conqueror. Normans in Sicily created a similar document, called the *Catalogus Baronum* ('Catalogue of the Barons'). The primary purpose of these documents was to extend the control of the state, surveying the different properties and estates from which tax could be gathered to maintain its growing military and administrative apparatus.

In modern state politics, control is both abstract and concrete. At a more general level, the term designates the ability of sovereign power to be enacted – to dominate, restrain and direct. Control is the transmission belt between sovereignty, territory and population. This reality contradicts the assumptions of Gilles Deleuze and Michel Foucault, who see control as an alternative to sovereignty.[8] On the contrary, control is best understood as a fundamental component of sovereignty – the means to guarantee the effective exercise of political authority. At a concrete level, the term designates a number of specific state practices: police controls, border controls, fire-safety controls, capital controls, exchange controls, import controls, anti-corruption controls, custom controls, tax controls, alcoholic beverage control, health controls, environmental controls and many others. To these we can add the anti-pandemic controls that have become a familiar element of our lives since the beginning of 2020. Think, for example, of viral tests conducted by swabbing the inside of the nose or mouth, as well as discussions about a Covid-19 vaccine passport to allow people to board a plane. Practices of state control comprise four fundamental functions: inspection (in, for example, the revenue office controlling someone's tax return or the customs' agent inspecting a truck's cargo); information-gathering (a doctor testing whether someone is infected); verification (police establishing whether a person is who she purports to be by checking her ID card); and finally, enforcement and coercion (fining someone for a lockdown violation, or detaining someone for supermarket theft).

It is impossible to conceive of the state without control. But what are the ultimate motivations behind ideas of control in politics? And what

---

7   Perry Anderson, *Lineages of the Absolutist State* (London: Verso, 2013 [1974]).

8   Michel Foucault, *Security, Territory, Population: Lectures at the Collège de France, 1977–1978* (New York: Picador, 2007).

are the implications carried by different meanings attached to this notion? To explore the connection between control and statecraft, I will examine three types of state control and connected images that highlight different aspects of the notion: control as command (the fist); force and its relationship with authority; control as direction (the ship), namely the connection between decision and action; and control as autonomy (the island), which concerns the effective ability of societies to act as discrete units.

## Holding Power in One's Fist

The first form of control is command and domination: control as top-down authority. In politics, the most common use of control serves to describe the claim to power over an object, such as that of a leader over a movement or of a parley over a government. In Aristotle's *Politics*, the famous discussion about various constitutional arrangements – monarchy, aristocracy, democracy – invokes ideas of control.[9] The Greek term used here is *kyrion*, meaning supremacy and strength. This word, which straddles the ideas of sovereignty and power, is used to describe a relationship of inference between ruler and power. Hence, democracy is understood as control of the majority, monarchy as control by one king and oligarchy as control by the few. The form of the state, its institutional architecture, depends on who controls it: 'the one, the few, or the many'.[10]

Political control as domination is clothed in legitimacy and consensus. But it is not based simply on assent and peaceful obedience. It reflects an elemental aspect of state power – its reliance on force, because 'those who have the power of arms have the power to decide whether the constitution shall stand or fall', as Aristotle observes.[11] Control thus implies the possession of the means of coercion that provides the state with not only force, but also *enforcement*. A similar understanding of control as a correlate of force and command is evident in Machiavelli's *Prince*. In this book, the word *controllo* appears wherever power over

---

9    Aristotle, *Politics*, transl. H. Rackham (Cambridge, MA: Harvard University Press, 1977).
10    Ibid., p. 205.
11    Ibid., p. 577.

principalities is discussed. The term is frequently used to express the power of subjection exercised by the Prince over men and things, and the need to keep hold of territory once it has been conquered. Machiavelli stresses that 'laying a solid foundation is a crucial prerequisite for maintaining power', and that only 'defences that are under your *control* and based on your own ability are effective, certain and lasting'. He notes that 'a sensible man will base his power on what he *controls*, not on what others have freedom to choose.'[12]

Control thus involves both taking control, or conquest, and keeping control – maintaining mastery over territories that have recently been conquered, as expressed in the phrase *tenere in pugno*, 'holding something in one's fist'.[13] Machiavelli repeatedly laments that Italian princes have lost military control of their states, recommending a number of aggressive tactics to reassert their power. In fact, much of what today's nationalist leaders are concerned with corresponds with this Machiavellian view of control as command and domination. They promise to reassert the territorial hold of central government to keep at bay a nebulous enemy composed of migrants, foreign powers and the interests of global finance, all accused of interfering with the native community. This understanding of control as domination is thus closely related to the Schmittian conception of sovereignty (see Chapter 2, above); its prime image is that of a fist imposing its force over a territory.

The association between control and force is also apparent in the work of Hegel, who similarly addresses top-down control as a key correlate of hierarchy and domination. In the *Philosophy of Right*, he argues that '*Control* [of the state] is also necessary to diminish the danger of upheavals arising from clashing interests'.[14] The words used by Hegel in German to express control are *Gewalt*, a term that primarily means violence or force, and *Zwang*, which means coercion. This terminology makes it crystal clear that control involves a relationship of domination backed by the threat of force. Control is bound up with the manifold mechanisms through which the state asserts a 'legibility' over reality,

---

12   Niccolò Machiavelli, *The Prince*, ed. and transl. Peter Bondanella (Oxford: Oxford University Press, 2005), p. 84. Emphasis mine.

13   Ibid., p. 61.

14   G. W. F. Hegel, *Hegel's Philosophy of Right*, transl. T. M. Know (Oxford: Oxford University Press, 2015), p. 147. Emphasis mine.

often making use of practices of 'simplification' aimed at reducing reality to a few controllable factors.[15] However, equally important is the
enforceability of power. The moment a tax inspector, an immigration
official or doctor in a hazmat suit knocks at your door, the state ceases to
be an abstract or ideological concept and reveals its coercive underside
– the sword that is the natural accompaniment of the sceptre and the
scroll. Political control implies the 'monopoly of the legitimate use of
physical force in the enforcement of its order', which Weber famously
considered a prerogative of the state.[16] In other words, control is not just
the central logic of sovereignty, but also its demonic core – the means
through which the supremacy of state power is materially imposed over
a population and territory; and it is through such control that sovereignty is actualised.

## Beyond Statophobia

This relationship between control, force and domination raises burning
ethical and political questions that go a long way to explaining why
many on the left have misgivings about the necessity of control. State
control has long been associated with totalitarianism, a system that
exercises total control over private and public life. In one of the most
famous passages in *Nineteen Eighty-Four*, George Orwell famously laid
out the governing philosophy of the totalitarian party: 'Who controls
the past controls the future: who controls the present controls the past.'[17]
Many recent progressive social movements have developed a strong
criticism of top-down government control which they see, in Jürgen
Habermas's terms, as a colonisation of the life-world by the system.[18]
They have therefore adopted a strong anti-authoritarian discourse questioning the legitimacy of the state's top-down intervention.

The coronavirus crisis opened a lengthy debate about the risk posed

15   James C. Scott, *Seeing Like a State: How Certain Schemes to Improve the Human Condition Have Failed* (New Haven ,CT: Yale University Press, 2008).

16   Max Weber, *Economy and Society: An Outline of Interpretive Sociology*, vol. 1 (Berkeley, CA: University of California Press, 1978), p. 54.

17   George Orwell, *Nineteen Eighty-Four* (London: Penguin, 2019), p. 34.

18   Jürgen Habermas, *The Theory of Communicative Action: Lifeworld and Systems, A Critique of Functionalist Reason, Volume 2* (Hoboken, NJ: John Wiley, 1989).

by increases in surveillance to combat the pandemic, since the enforcement of quarantines requires compulsory testing and the use of tracing
apps that may infringe on individual privacy. The increasing scope of
state intervention has been met by many people, not with a recognition
of the necessity of control to ensure protection, but rather with an attitude of rejection bordering on paranoia. Some people have come to see
anti-contagion controls as authoritarian and illegitimate arms of a
'health dictatorship' or 'medicalisation of society'. Scepticism towards
state control has united people who otherwise seemed to have very little
in common, such as the alt-right and the anti-authoritarian left.

Protest squares in Berlin, Milan, Madrid and other cities witnessed
demonstrations of the so-called no-mask and no-vax movements,
bringing together a highly diverse crowd including far-right groups,
conspiracy theorists, supporters of the Great Barrington Declaration
issued by a group of lockdown sceptics, new-age cultists, and 'sovereigntyists' of all forms. Representative of this weird convergence were the
interventions of Giorgio Agamben, who supported the outlandish
notion that the pandemic was a pretext to impose an authoritarian
government. Echoing points made online by no-mask activists,
Agamben suggested it was 'almost as if with terrorism exhausted as a
cause for exceptional measures, the invention of an epidemic offered the
ideal pretext for scaling them up beyond any limitation', and proposed
that proximity and human contact had been unduly sacrificed in the
name of public health.[19]

Current political dilemmas require that this libertarian critique of
power, bordering on statophobia, be overcome. There is no way to
address present challenges without a recovery and democratisation of
top-down control. The socialist left has traditionally pursued the
construction of a democratic authority in the framework of a 'social
republic' – an authority whose top-down control would be checked by
bottom-up control exerted by the citizenry and workers; unlike anar-
chism, it does not demand the elimination of all forms of authority. The
customary definition of socialism is a system of 'workers' control over
the means of production'. Socialism saw state ownership of strategic
companies and hence control over economic structures, as the

---

19  Giorgio Agamben, 'L'invenzione di un'epidemia', *Quodlibet*, 26 February 2020,
at quodlibet.it.

necessary precondition for power, determining society's course and guiding it in an equal and just direction. Furthermore, socialist governments availed themselves of many levers of state power, such as labour regulation, industrial policy or state ownership of strategic companies through nationalisation.

While originating in the tragic history of the twentieth century, the equation of political control with totalitarianism has ended up legitimising familiar neoliberal nostrums. The anti-authoritarian criticism of power, strongly informed by the new social movements of the 1970s and 1980s, has ultimately proved to be a moralistic dead end.[20] This attitude has diverted attention from the need to chart a project of systemic transformation, deluding activists into believing that change should come exclusively from the bottom – from new practices of self-organisation in civil society, and from changes in lifestyle and consumption patterns. Amid the present crisis of neoliberalism, when evidence is clear of the nefarious effect of the dismantling of democratic forms of state control, it has become evident that no real solution to our predicament will result from a moralistic spurning of power. Any credible attempt to redress the present political and social crisis will have to proceed from a democratic re-appropriation and socialist reorientation of all those key state levers that are essential for controlling and shaping economic reality. To put it another way, political control should not be condemned, but reclaimed; its coercive underside should always be borne in mind, but so should the fact that eschewing control ultimately means renouncing power.

## The Ship of State

The second form of control is as direction and decision-making. Government has been conceived of since its inception as involving an act of control: the control exercised by a sea captain over a ship on an uncertain sea. The word 'government' in fact derives from the Greek *kybernetes* – a term that originally referred to the pilot of a ship; the same root that gave us both the Latin *gubernatio* and the term cybernetics, used to designate the study of control and communication. Both

---

20   John Holloway, *Change the World Without Taking Power: The Meaning of Revolution Today* (London: Pluto, 2019).

terms contain this nautical origin, designating the ability of steering, piloting and guiding a ship – the most primordial act of control by a thalassocratic power, such as Ancient Athens. This naval metaphor has informed our understanding of political leadership as an act of steering. Mao Zedong was famously known as the 'Great Helmsman'; in Italy, national-populist leader Matteo Salvini has earned the nickname 'the captain'. This trope bespeaks a view of control as an act of direction, which, unlike the framing of control as domination, is not concerned with the symbolism of the intimidating fist, but rather with the idea of charting a course within a space that is often unpredictable.

This imaginary of statecraft as seafaring, and of the ruler as helmsman, has been immortalised by the famous scene in Book VI of *The Republic*, which originated the phrase 'ship of state'.[21] On a ship, various characters are fighting for control. The ship's owner – probably a reference to the people – is good-natured and wise, but a little deaf and shortsighted, and is under pressure from a crew of despondent young sailors who want to take control without having the necessary ability. The sailors are 'wrangling with one another for control, each claiming that it is his right to steer though he has never learned the art'.[22] In the meantime, they drink and feast, depleting the ship's stores, and endangering its safety. The third character is the wise captain, who is educated and expert in all things related to seafaring, such as stargazing and reading the winds, but struggles to discipline the unruly crew, also because he considers that his clearly superior knowledge does not need any other form of legitimation, and he is not anxious to have to seize a power that he thinks belongs to him by right.

In this parable, we encounter a number of figures of great relevance for contemporary politics. The wise captain is the philosopher-king who, according to Plato, should rule the state. This character looks very similar to the neoliberal 'experts' who were so despised during the Brexit referendum, or the virologists and epidemiologists who were criticised by proponents of conspiracy theories during the coronavirus pandemic. The disobedient sailors entreating the ship-owner are populist politicians, like the Leave team that led Britain into a

---

21    Plato, *Republic*, ed. and transl. Chris Emlyn-Jones and William Preddy, 2 vols (Cambridge, MA: Harvard University Press, 2013), pp. 19–27.

22    Ibid., p. 19.

breakup with the EU on the basis of false arguments and without having a coherent implementation plan. And is the drunk ship-owner not a comment on how the people constituting the electorate often find themselves inebriated and led astray by false promises? Regardless of the exact roles to be assigned to each character – Plato experts continue to dispute this among themselves – what matters in this allegory is that the ship represents the state as a machinery over which a variety of political forces battle for power.

Plato's scene has been recapitulated several times in literature and philosophy. Perhaps the most famous case is Dante's variation on the same theme in Canto VI of *Purgatorio*. There, he describes Italy as a 'ship without pilot caught in a raging storm', lamenting the way in which division and strife among Italian states has left Italy in thrall to foreign domination.[23] This and similar representations of lack of control amid major emergencies seem to resonate with the condition of many polities today. Amid the combined health and economic shock of the coronavirus emergency, many states seem at risk of capsizing or foundering and are caught up in battles over political authority similar to those symbolised on Plato's ship.

Control has a clear technological dimension, already evident in its etymology. The ship became a metaphor of statecraft and political control because it was the first large machine constructed by human beings, dwarfing any other tool or object developed in ancient times. It might be compared to the enormous technological machinery that is the state – an 'artificial body' or 'mortal god', as the latter was famously described by Thomas Hobbes.[24] In light of this allegory, the state is imagined as a vehicle to be steered in a certain direction through unified command over a specific apparatus. Politics, ultimately, is not just an art, but also a *technique* – one that involves the control of various tools and apparatuses as well as access to the expertise required to use them. Government is, in a sense, not that different from a ship. Its ministries, agencies and administrative branches look like the various components of the ship: axle, spindle, barrel and rudder.

23    Dante Alighieri, *The Divine Comedy, Vol. 2: Purgatory*, transl. Mark Musa (London: Penguin, 1987), p. 59.
24    Thomas Hobbes, *Leviathan*, ed. J. C. A. Gaskin (Oxford: Oxford University Press, 2008), p. 114.

The technological aspect of control also has important implications for politics and power. Contra Foucault's view of power as diffused, political control is almost invariably centralised.[25] This is largely a function of the technological structure of power apparatuses, requiring that only one actor is at the helm at any given moment. Unity of command is in fact the most fundamental of all managerial principles.[26] There cannot be two steering wheels on a ship; and equally, there cannot be two governments in the same country in any normal situation, nor two brothers in power – as Hegel highlights in his commentary on Cain and Abel.[27] Similarly, two television remote controls in the hands of different family members are well known to cause a ruckus. It is true that, in mixed constitutional systems, power is divided between different branches (legislative, executive, judiciary) so as to guarantee checks and balances; but it is unified at any specific point. To return to the metaphor of the ship: unless the sailors were to agree on some form of coordination, and on a procedure for establishing who rules, we could imagine the ship moving in a haphazard way, zigzagging and eventually crashing against the shoals.

## Democratic Planning

The nexus between technology, technique and political control raises the obvious question of technocracy and its relationship with democracy. While the power of experts clearly predates neoliberalism, the control of technocrats over public policy has expanded in recent decades, amid the 'post-democratic' transformation of Western societies.[28] Populist movements often criticise the illegitimacy of technocratic power. Indeed, as Michael Young's dystopian scenario of the opposition between technocrats and populists in *The Rise of Meritocracy* explores, populism is by its nature sceptical of technical power.[29] This criticism

---

25   Foucault, *Security, Territory, Population.*

26   Henri Fayol, *General and Industrial Management* (Mansfield Center, CT: Martino, 2013).

27   G. W. F. Hegel, *Phenomenology of Spirit*, transl. A. V. Miller (Oxford: Oxford University Press, 1977), p. 188.

28   Colin Crouch, *Post-Democracy* (Cambridge: Polity, 2004).

29   Michael Dunlop Young, *The Rise of the Meritocracy* (Piscataway, NJ: Transaction, 1994).

rings particularly true during crises of authority, such as the one we are currently experiencing, when the loss of legitimacy of traditional parties, civil society organisations and the press is keenly visible. In this context, to return to Plato's metaphor, it is as if many populist leaders doubt whether the wise captain is really all that wise and raise the question of whether the drunken ship-owner representing the people is really as inebriated as the philosopher-expert claims.

These misgivings are not always a result of irrational opposition to intellectuals or science. They are also a function of the fact that experts, and in particular economists and journalists close to the neoliberal establishment, have often proved 'unwise captains' in a number of recent instances, from the 2008 economic crisis to the coronavirus crisis, both of which struck an unprepared political and technocratic class. Reclaiming the political nature of decision-making – the power of collective political choice rather than consumer choice – it should be affirmed that no decision, even the apparently more scientific and technical ones, such as the decisions connected with the 2020 Covid-19 crisis, the setting of climate-related targets or public investment plans such as the European Recovery Fund, should ever just be a matter of expertise; they should always be open to public scrutiny. But this approach, in turn, should not lead down the path, often taken by populist movements, of deriding any expertise, or to viewing state planning as inherently elitist and anti-democratic.

To reconcile expertise with democracy, it is necessary to adopt an approach that I describe as 'democratic planning'. As Chapter 3 explored, planning has been criticised by neoliberal ideologues as implying a dirigisme suffocating individual choice and social spontaneity. Yet, with the wisdom of hindsight after forty years of neoliberal hegemony, we can see that these criticisms were disingenuous. Neoliberals were opposed to planning in any form, because they saw in it an effective lever for the state to subject the economy and civil society to politics. Current emergencies – from coronavirus to climate change – are leading to a strong comeback in planning. Mandatory planning has been widely discredited by the failure of the Soviet economy, and by the way in which it was unresponsive to the needs of consumers. The likes of Hayek and Friedman were right to see mandatory planning as more inefficient than the market, particularly when the mass of information required to run the economy exceeds a certain threshold: the Soviet economy did not survive the computer age. But these failings should not be taken as an indictment of planning in any form.

Indicative planning was systematically adopted by market-based and mixed economies, including many Western countries, such as Italy, France and Japan, until recent decades. Indicative planning involves the setting of targets and the use of state subsidies, grants and taxation, instead of directive measures such as quotas. The economic crisis produced by the coronavirus pandemic has already led states to develop complex national economic plans. Meeting the targets of the climate transition, such as on the reduction of carbon emissions, will call for strong indicative planning, making use of subsidies, regulations and huge state investments to force a rapid change in the economic system. This return of indicative planning seems to offer the opportunity to reclaim a conception of politics as a project shaped actively and intentionally by citizens and their representatives, one which runs counter to the neoliberal cult of market spontaneity.

It should, however, not be overlooked how centralised planning can lead to new technocratic and oligarchic distortions and how it can be used to favour the interests of corporations and vested interests. To avoid these risks, it is essential that, as proposed by Grace Blakeley, economic planning is wrested from the hands of economic elites and the state bureaucrats at their service.[30] From local consultations to various forms of digital democracy and ongoing public debate, all the available channels should be explored in order to involve the citizenry in the discussion and evaluation of various possible courses of action. Obviously, given the technical character of many issues that are involved in economic planning, decisions can never be completely democratic; nor are citizens capable of understanding every detail of policy. But more scope for public discussion, and a more persuasive effort on the part of politicians to explain the motivations behind any specific plan, can go a long way towards dispelling popular suspicion of the state and bureaucracy. All major political decisions should be explained in accessible language, creating a civic literacy on the main questions at stake. Furthermore, the state technocracy should be democratised. It is neither possible nor desirable to eliminate

---

30  Grace Blakeley, *The Corona Crash: How the Pandemic Will Change Capitalism* (London: Verso, 2020), p. 77.

technocrats altogether. Some measures can be taken to bring state technocracy more in line with the priorities of ordinary citizens. Creating public schools for state technocrats, with scholarships targeted at students from disadvantaged backgrounds and providing clear channels for entry into the state administration are some examples of measures that could do much to overcome the elitist character of state technocracy and its alliance with economic oligarchies.

## Autonomy and Autarchy

The final aspect of state control that needs to be examined is control as autonomy, a question that is very relevant to some of the urges of the Great Recoil, and in particular the desire to recover a sense of political individuality and interiority. Autonomy, literally 'self-legislation', has been central to democratic and republican thought.[31] Autonomy is opposed to heteronomy – the ability of Others to control the Self, depriving the subject of its independence and freedom. In a positive sense, it expresses the capacity of communities to assert a degree of political independence – the ability to decide their course of action without interference by other states, institutions or private powers. This faculty is constitutive of any working political community, but has been called into doubt by the neoliberal emptying out of state authority and the dislocations produced by globalisation.

The relation between control and autonomy is famously developed in Aristotle's discussion of self-sufficiency, expressed in classical Greek by the word *autárkeia*, from which the modern term 'autarchy' derives. As Aristotle notes in his *Politics*, 'for the state is not any chance multitude of people but one self-sufficient for the needs of life'.[32] Self-sufficiency is, for Aristotle, 'an end and a chief good'.[33] It is the precondition for the good life of a polity – which, significantly, he describes as a 'full and independent life, which in our view constitutes a happy and noble life'.[34]

---

31   Philip Pettit, *Republicanism: A Theory of Freedom and Government* (Wotton-under-Edge: Clarendon, 1997).
32   Aristotle, *Politics*, transl. H. Rackham (Cambridge, MA: Harvard University Press, 1977), p. 573.
33   Ibid., p. 9.
34   Ibid., p. 219.

It is the factor that guarantees a polity its freedom, the condition for its effective independence, namely its ability to run its affairs without external meddling.

Aristotle's discussion of self-sufficiency takes account of economic factors that have become central to any understanding of political control in our time. True to the rational empiricism that made him so influential among early economists, the peripatetic philosopher emphasises that self-sufficiency is predicated on the ability to produce the goods necessary for the community's reproduction, avoiding dependence on other city-states. Thus, 'self-sufficiency means having a supply of everything and lacking nothing'.[35] To this end, Aristotle recommends a diversified economy, providing locally for all the necessities of life: 'A multitude of farmers to provide the food, craftsmen, soldiers, rich people, priests, and people to decide matters of necessity and benefit'.[36] He also prescribes that city-states should limit the number of foreign merchants residing within them, to prevent their own economic well-being becoming too dependent on what today we might call international trade. Here, Aristotle seems unambiguously to take the side of sovereigntyists against globalists. But some elements of his teaching are valid from a socialist standpoint, especially in light of the way the pervasive economic interdependency ushered in by neoliberal globalisation has resulted in political impotence.

British economist John Maynard Keynes had Aristotle's discussion of self-sufficiency in mind when writing his famous essay on national self-sufficiency.[37] Delivered as a lecture at University College Dublin on 19 April 1933, the text advocated the need to 'minimize ... economic entanglement among nations'. For Keynes, there were goods and services, such as '[i]deas, knowledge, science, hospitality [and] travel' that, by their nature, could not be brought under national control, though those that could be definitely should: '[L]et goods be homespun whenever it is reasonably and conveniently possible, and, above all, let finance be primarily national'.[38] He further proposed that the 'policy of an increased national self-sufficiency is to be considered, not as an ideal

---

35   Ibid., p. 559.
36   Ibid., p. 563.
37   Keynes, J. M. *Studies: An Irish Quarterly Review*, pp. 177–93.
38   Ibid., p. 181

in itself, but as directed to the creation of an environment in which other ideals can be safely and conveniently pursued'.[39] Thereby, economic self-sufficiency – only ever to be approximated in practice – would provide an ideal pathway for what Keynes described as 'our own favourite experiments towards the ideal social republic of the future'. In other words, the advantage of self-sufficiency lay in the fact that it would confer upon governments political control over their economy, allowing them to pursue policies deemed beneficial for their communities; if necessary at the cost of subordinating economic convenience to social priorities.

If the notion of self-sufficiency, with its uncanny implications of autarchic isolation, is worthy of discussion in the present conjuncture, it is because of the nefarious economic and social effects engendered by its polar opposite: the cult of openness preached by neoliberals. The exigencies of the so-called international division of labour – goods often being produced using components assembled in faraway countries – generate a system of global production and distribution that is the opposite of national self-sufficiency. Furthermore, global finance and the reliance of states on international investors to purchase their debt have eroded the effective economic independence of nations. When, for example, in order to stave off a sovereign debt crisis, contemporary Greece was forced to sign agreements with the Troika composed of the ECB, the IMF and the Eurogroup, the government in Athens was obliged to sell a number of key public assets. These included airports and railways, most of which were then acquired by German companies. What would Aristotle have thought of that?

## Osmotic Insulation

The key thesis running from Aristotle to Keynes is that self-sufficiency requires some form of isolation, or insulation, from the world. As these terms suggest, the narrative of political autonomy frames the space of control as an island, partly separate from the rest of the world. To invert John Donne's famous assertion that 'no man is an island', used frequently by British Remainers to argue that 'no country is an island', it might in fact be said that, in some sense, all countries are islands. The nature of

---

39   Ibid., p. 185

the nation as a discrete unit of social organisation with its own customs, language, currency, and so on, engenders a partial separation from the rest of the world. During the social-democratic era, this was compounded by all sorts of economic barriers with strong insulation effects: capital controls preventing capital flight; border and customs controls stemming the flow of goods and people; export and import tariffs attenuating the pressure of global trade on local industries. For Keynes, the need for such barriers, which besides being levers of control are also means of protection, becomes more important given the way in which technologies of transportation and communication have eroded the 'isolation effect' that was previously inherent in geographic distance. In other words, a condition of interconnectedness – which defines our social experience far more than it did in Keynes's day – calls not for indiscriminate openness, but for selective openness and closure.

This emphasis on the need for boundaries as a condition for control is well represented in the context of systems theory – for example, in the work of Niklas Luhman and Stafford Beer.[40] In the theory of thermodynamics, which provides the foundation for systems theory, a system is separated from the rest of the world, described as 'the surroundings', by the presence of a boundary. It is through boundaries that systems establish their perimeter of activity, and therefore the field or domain that is under their control.

The systemic necessity of boundaries raises evident ethical issues, given the association of borders with the politics of migration. Borders have been rightly denounced as having caused the deaths of tens of thousands of migrants attempting to cross the Mediterranean Sea and the border between the United States and Mexico. Even at the height of neoliberal globalisation – belying its gospel of openness and the erasure of all barriers – there was, if anything, an intensification of border controls and anti-migration barriers of all sorts. One should avoid falling into the contrarian trap represented by Régis Debray's 'eulogy for borders' or Angela Nagle's argument that closed borders can favour the working class.[41] As argued in Chapter 2, the severe policing of borders

---

40   Stafford Beer, *Decision and Control: The Meaning of Operational Research and Management Cybernetics* (Chichester: John Wiley, 1995).

41   Régis Debray, *Éloge des frontières* (Paris: Editions Gallimard, 2013). Angela Nagle, 'The Left Case against Open Borders', *American Affairs* 11: 4 (Winter 2018).

strongly supported by the right is implicated in the defence of inequality at the global level. However, the moral condemnation of borders often articulated by activists – a feature, for example, of the 'no borders' discourse adopted in campaigns against migration controls – leads to an equally untenable political position. The complete elimination of borders, by any definition, would mean the relinquishing of sovereignty over not only migration, but also trade, finance, environmental regulation and taxation.

Rather than placing extreme scenarios in opposition – a world of entrenched borders against one with no borders at all – we should approach the question of borders from a perspective of political realism. As systems theorists have observed, borders are not only barriers, but also crossing points and thresholds. They are best pictured as osmotic membranes – the means through which systems exchange work or energy. Completely closed systems are very rare. Not even North Korea, in spite of its moniker as the 'hermit state', is really autarchic; in fact, it survives because of strong support from China. In many circumstances, systems, from biology to telecommunications, actively foster inputs and outputs, since they are fundamental for their very survival. Thus, rather than implying closure, the bounded nature of all systems should be understood as a modulation of flows, of inputs and outputs, towards the aim of maintaining a state of approximate equilibrium.

From the perspective of complex systems theory, neither globalism nor sovereigntyism are tenable in reality. The radically open systems wished for by globalists would rapidly expire, dissolving into the surrounding environment, as their extreme porosity would not allow them any measure of self-regulation. Equally, however, the closed autarchic systems dreamed of by fanatical sovereigntyists would be consigned to 'heat death' according to thermodynamic theory. Thus, rather than embracing the absolutist narratives of globalism or sovereigntyism, what is really at stake amid the Great Recoil is the question of what limited degree of self-sufficiency and autonomy nation-states should realistically pursue in order to achieve some degree of 'buoyancy' – 'homeostatic equilibrium', to use a cybernetic metaphor – in a world marked by strong interconnectedness. The question, in other words, is not whether to be 'in' or 'out' of globalisation, but how to navigate global space without the ship of state being overwhelmed by internal or external pressures; how to establish *controls* and forms of economic friction that can moderate the speed of global flows and make openness, which many find desirable, sustainable: for example, through moderate tariffs and non-tariff measures, or by imposing a tax on transactions such as the Tobin tax. If, as Zygmunt Bauman puts it, contemporary capitalism is marked by an escapist impulse, governments should aim not to make such escape altogether impossible, which would not be realistic, but rather as slow and arduous as possible.

## Taking Democratic Control

As we have seen in the course of this chapter, control is the elementary logic of statecraft, and denotes a number of operations through which sovereign power is practically enacted. Throughout history, the notion of control has served to express a number of key capacities of statecraft: to assert command over a population and a territory; to chart a direction out of the chaotic flow of worldly events; to achieve a degree of autonomy for political communities from surrounding reality. Despite widespread anti-authoritarian reservations about power, the political dilemmas we now confront call for the rehabilitation of political control, and more specifically, for the construction of democratic forms of control that can reconcile respect for personal freedom and democracy with the hierarchical and coercive nature of state authority.

Demands for control have become so resonant today precisely because people feel that political control – something previously taken for granted – has been lost. The drive towards externalisation embodied by neoliberal globalisation has left us exposed to the action of forces that are beyond our individual and collective field of intervention. Governments appear in the guise of ships unable to chart a meaningful course in the tempestuous seas of the global economy. In this context, the demands for a restoration of control reflect all-too-real challenges. They respond to a condition of agoraphobia that, as we have seen, has become the dominant social anxiety of late neoliberalism, and to the legitimate desire for a return to order and stability amid a world caught in chaos.

The obvious risk of a politics of control is that of pushing things to the other extreme – moving away from agoraphobia only to fall prey to claustrophobia, or worse, adopting an obsessive view in which everything has to be made subject to control. Control mania is the opposite, but in a way also the complement, of anxiety about loss of control; they are two extremes that mirror each other, signalling the difficulty of achieving a workable equilibrium. Much of contemporary sovereigntyism contains an element of control mania. It peddles the dream of sealed systems impermeable to the world, unaware of the fact that complete closure is never possible, since all systems rely on communication with the outside. To go back to Machiavelli's metaphor of the flood, the control maniac is someone who toys with the dream of constructing a dam so high that the flow of water will be completely stemmed, rather than being more realistically guided by some lateral canals.

Control mania surfaces in numerous conspiracy theories that have a singular currency today. They can be seen as the cognitive response of those who feel without control in a world that seems as if it is constantly slipping out of their grasp. In a way, conspiracy theories could be read as a surrogate for class-struggle theory, but with an element of moral myth – a battle between Good and Evil that pits ordinary men willing to see the truth against apparently almighty elites constantly bent on thwarting their actions. Whether their protagonists are David Icke's reptilians, the Illuminati, or the obscure elites of the Pizzagate conspiracy and the QAnon insurgency, at their core these narratives portray an extremely powerful cabal pulling the strings of political reality. This perception of the almighty power of the elites is in fact no more than a reflection of the powerlessness of those who subscribe to conspiracy theories. Obviously, no such overwhelmingly powerful cabal exists; but the fantasy that it does paradoxically provides some hope of redemption. The fact that control is in fact being exercised by someone reassures believers that it might ultimately be reclaimed by the powerless, and that social problems that now appear intractable may finally be addressed.

For control mania, with its consequence of a paranoid style of politics, the necessary corrective is effective democratic control. Democratic control would acknowledge that power and control are not absolute, but always depend on the balance of forces between various actors, both internationally and within each country. It proceeds from the idea that authority should not be eliminated, but democratised. Further, it understands control not as the assertion of absolute domination over a territory viewed as completely insulated from the outside, but rather as the charting of a course within an environment that is always uncertain and, like a stormy sea, requires some effort of adaptation. Finally, the qualification 'democratic' denotes the fact that if we are serious about 'taking back control', this can only be the product of active popular participation. The many decisions that were externalised to experts, lobbyists and career politicians must be 're-internalised', brought back under public scrutiny. Only by reconceiving the mechanisms of articulation by which popular sovereignty exerts an influence on the state – whether in the realm of freedom of speech, the management of elections, popular protest, or autonomy in the workplace, home and neighbourhood – can we hope to overcome our sense of impotence and defeat the entrenched power of those who would rather leave us with no control at all.

# 6

# The New Social Blocs

Having explored endopolitics in the Great Recoil and the triad of sovereignty, protection and control at its heart, it is now time to map the support base of various political actors competing for post-neoliberal hegemony and to determine how different social groups and class interests are aligned in this new scenario. Class is a very contentious topic in contemporary debates, an yet unavoidable category in illuminating current political cleavages. During the neoliberal era many contended that class had become less relevant in guiding political and electoral behaviour.[1] The rise of populist movements on the right and the left during the 2010s has only amplified these beliefs. Populism, it is argued by Peter Mair, appeals to a mass of atomised individuals, rather than to members of socioeconomic classes.[2] Similarly, Ernesto Laclau and Chantal Mouffe have often presented populism as an alternative to class politics. This view of populism as disconnected from class has generated the false impression that emerging movements on the left and the right are a 'catch-all' phenomena with no class bias whatsoever. Strategically, this leads to a difficulty in identifying the sectors of the electorate that are most likely to respond positively to socialist appeals.

---

1   Jytte Klausen, 'The Breakdown of Class Politics: A Debate on Post-Industrial Stratification', *American Political Science Review* 96: 4 (2002), 846.

2   Peter Mair, 'Populist Democracy vs Party Democracy', in Yves Mény and Y. Surel, eds, *Democracies and the Populist Challenge* (London: Palgrave Macmillan, 2002).

It is true that class is not the only factor guiding electoral behaviour and that it is important to account for other socio-demographic trends. Scholars have highlighted the importance of a number of variables, including age, gender, ethnicity, cultural views and geographic location. Keir Milburn has spoken of a 'Generation Left' because of the disproportionate support given by millennials to Jeremy Corbyn and Bernie Sanders, while their elders turned to the right.[3] Others have emphasised instead the return of an urban–rural cleavage, and the importance of regional disparities in fuelling the populist explosion. Another line of interpretation has stressed the importance of the gulf between progressives and conservatives in terms of cultural values.[4] Finally, the role of ethnicity and gender has been widely debated in reference to the socio-demographic divide between Democrats and Republicans in the US, though the resistance of women and minorities to nationalist appeals has often been overestimated.

While a rounded understanding of political alignments needs to take into account all these factors, class continues to be central to an understanding of contemporary social blocs. The rise of populist movements and growing political polarisation are ultimately strongly interwoven with social discontent and class conflict in an era marked by deep economic crisis and widening inequality. Indeed, as we have argued, populism has a clear structural dimension, which reflects growing social inequality under late neoliberalism, and the attempt of both the nationalist right and socialist left to appeal to sections of society gripped by fear of poverty and exclusion. This implicit class dimension of populism has been particularly noted in reference to the populist right and the way it has appealed to so-called 'left behind' workers.

Alarms about the flight of the working-class vote towards right-wing populism have been sounded since the 1980s and 1990s. But they have only intensified since the 2008 crisis, amid evidence of growing right-wing penetration in working-class constituencies traditionally loyal to the left. Trump even came to the point of presenting himself as the leader of a 'workers' party', and in 2018, White House adviser Anthony Scaramucci affirmed that Trump was a 'blue-collar president'. Similarly,

---

3   Keir Milburn, *Generation Left* (Oxford: John Wiley, 2019).

4   Pippa Norris and Ronald Inglehart, *Cultural Backlash: Trump, Brexit and Authoritarian Populism* (Cambridge: Cambridge University Press, 2019); Arlie Russell Hochschild, *Strangers in Their Own Land: Anger and Mourning on the American Right* (New York: New Press, 2018).

in Italy, Matteo Salvini has claimed Lega as the true inheritor of the legacy of the Italian Communist Party and its leader Enrico Berlinguer. The posturing of the nationalist right as the 'workers' party' is evidently disingenuous. While enlisting growing support from the working class, the right continues to lean heavily on the sectors of the bourgeoisie traditionally loyal to the right, an 'old middle class' including entrepreneurs, foremen, technicians and business owners. In 2016, Trump voters' mean income was higher than that of Clinton's voters, and well above the national average, and this class bias was even more marked in 2020.[5] Similarly, it is not true that these days the left only represents the urban middle class as right-wing ideologues claim. In recent years it has earned growing support among the service precariat which experiences some of the most brutal conditions of exploitation. Thus, rather than reasoning in the simplistic terms of a complete identity between a specific class and a political force, we should explore the *social blocs* or class alliances supporting the left, right and centre and the way they group together different 'class fractions' within larger classes.[6]

The right's social bloc allies two constituencies: the old middle class and the old working class; insecure manufacturing workers and the middle stratum of technicians, supervisors and business owners. A significant proportion of these people live in peri-urban and ex-urban areas, heavily dependent on industry and logistics as a result of policies of internal 'de-localisation'. The left's new social bloc comprises not only the new middle class of government, culture and knowledge professionals, but also sections of the new working class or 'service precariat' consisting of shelf-fillers, cashiers, cleaners, drivers, delivery riders, and so on. This cohort, which unlike manufacturing workers is mostly concentrated in big and medium cities, has been growing steadily in recent years, and is affected by low pay and precarious working conditions. The neoliberal centre retains control over the upper strata of managers, wealthy pensioners and secure fractions of the other classes worried about political instability and the danger of opposed populisms.[7]

---

5   Christine and John Burn-Murdoch, 'By Numbers: How the US Voted in 2020', *Financial Times*, 7 November 2020.

6   The notion of class fraction was developed by Nicos Poulantzas to make sense of the complex internal behaviour of classes. See Nicos Poulantzas, *Political Power and Social Classes*, transl. Timothy O'Hagan (London: New Left Books, 1973).

7   Daniel Oesch, and Line Rennwald, 'Electoral Competition in Europe's New Tripolar Political Space: Class Voting for the Left, Centre-Right and Radical Right', *European Journal of Political Research* 57: 4 (2018), 783–807.

Figure 6.1    Social blocs in the Great Recoil

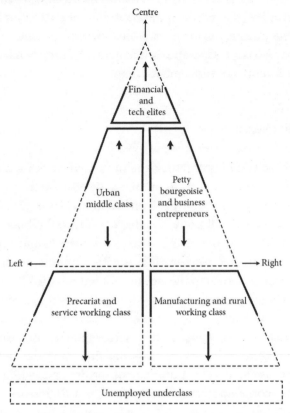

The class alliances supporting the socialist left and nationalist right draw from diverging fractions of the working class and middle class, with the neoliberal centre still enjoying the support of financial and tech elites and the upper stratum of the middle class.

The nature of these conflicting social blocs (see Figure 6.1) can better illuminate the alternative politics of protection and control offered by the socialist left and nationalist right. The constituencies they represent are concerned about different kinds of exposure and agoraphobia: blue-collar workers about international competition; service workers about precarious employment; shopkeepers about digital companies encroaching on their market; and the middle class about the devaluation of skills and the threat of automation. Hence, they are calling for quite different forms of protection: protection of property and status on the right; protection of jobs and public services on the left. In this scenario the strategic goal for the left is to overcome its overreliance on the educated middle class concentrated in large cities, prioritising efforts aimed at constructing alliances with workers in the hinterland. Furthermore, it needs to drive a wedge between the contradictory class interests represented by the prospectus of the populist right, exposing the fact that, behind its workerist proclamations, it conceals an agenda heavily skewed towards the interests of the capitalist class.

## The Populist Worker

Throughout the twentieth century, the industrial working class acted as the base of support for the left, as predicted by Marxist theory. Industrial workers constituted over 50 per cent of the electorate for left-wing parties across Western Europe, besides providing the bulk of socialist and communist party members.[8] This is why the twenty-first-century spectacle of industrial workers turning their backs on the left and moving in large numbers to the right – not only in the US rust belt and the industrial regions of the English Midlands, but in Picardy and Nord-Pas-de-Calais in France, and the old Industrial Triangle in northern Italy – is such a deeply disquieting phenomenon. But the narrative according to which the working class has now moved as a bloc to the populist right is clouded by a number of misunderstandings about the nature of the contemporary working class and its history of electoral behaviour.

Survey data provides a good starting point to explore the shift of the working-class electorate towards the nationalist right.[9] In their book on national-populism, Roger Eatwell and Matthew Goodwin argue that 60 per cent of working-class people and 70 per cent of working-class pensioners voted for Brexit.[10] In Italy, electoral studies registered significant workers' support for Lega. One quarter of production workers voted for Lega in the 2018 elections, and this share grew to 53 per cent

---

8    Stefano Bartolini, *The Political Mobilization of the European Left, 1860–1980: The Class Cleavage* (Cambridge: Cambridge University Press, 2007).

9    Daniel Oesch, 'Explaining workers' support for right-wing populist parties in Western Europe: Evidence from Austria, Belgium, France, Norway, and Switzerland', *International Political Science Review* 29: 3 (2008), 349–73.

10    Roger Eatwell and Matthew Goodwin, *National Populism: The Revolt against Liberal Democracy* (London: Penguin, 2018).

in 2019.[11] Among the occupations most likely to vote for Lega feature cooks, crop farm labourers, manufacturing labourers, freight handlers, and domestic helpers and cleaners.[12] In the United States, one marker of Donald Trump's ability to increase his share of the working-class vote was the fact that 43 per cent of union households voted for him in the 2016 presidential elections – 3 per cent more than for Romney in 2012.[13] In the United States, the occupational categories most supportive of Trump's campaign in 2016 and 2020 included typical working-class manual occupations: welders, cutters, machine operators, heavy-goods vehicle and tractor-trailer drivers, cooks, and industrial machinery mechanics.[14] In 2020, Biden managed to win back some of this working-class vote, as seen in his strong performance among less-educated workers. Similarly, in France, the electoral growth of Marine Le Pen's Front National has been premised on her ability to penetrate the working-class electorate; 39 per cent of workers voted for her in the first round of the 2017 presidential election, and her support ballooned in the second round, when 60 per cent of voters in this occupational category preferred her over Macron.[15]

This evidence of working-class support for the right is alarming. But it needs to be approached with some sense of perspective: it is not an altogether new phenomenon that a section of the working class should vote for the right. Even in the golden era of Fordist industrialism, when the working class voted for the left in large majorities, there always existed a right-wing portion of the working-class vote: the so-called 'working-class Tories' in the UK; 'Reagan Democrats' in the United States; and the industrial workers voting for Christian Democracy in Italy, in regions like Veneto and Lombardy. Rather than being pioneers in securing working-class votes for the right, as some sensationalist

11    Gianni Santamaria, 'Studio Ipsos. Gli operai hanno lasciato la sinistra', *Avvenire*, 8 March 2018; Caterina Spinelli, 'Sondaggio Swg, ribaltone leghista: "Il 53 per cento degli operai vota Lega." Schiaffo a Pd e M5s', *Libero*, 24 November 2019.

12    European Social Survey, 'ESS Round 9 Data', Norwegian Centre for Research Data, Norway, 2018, at europeansocialsurvey.org.

13    Philip Bump, 'Donald Trump Got Reagan-Like Support from Union Households', *Washington Post*, 10 November 2016.

14    Richard Florida, 'Why Is Your State Red or Blue? Look to the Dominant Occupational Class', Bloomberg City Lab, 28 November 2018, at bloomberg.com.

15    Jocelyn Evans and Gilles Ivaldi. "Présidentielle 2017: forces et faiblesses du Front national." (2017). *Revue Parlementaire*

representations would lead us to believe, the nationalist right has significantly expanded a trend that already existed. The emergence in the 1960s and 1970s of the so-called 'New Right' – the ideological and political ancestor of today's 'populist right' – relied on appealing to sectors of the working class disgruntled with the left, and exploiting the suspicion of some workers towards the causes of sexual and cultural emancipation that new social movements had embraced.

The textbook case of the right's conversion to a strategy of cultivating a working-class support base is offered by France's Front National. During the 1980s and 1990s, the party progressively abandoned some of their more elitist and quasi-fascist positions to adopt what Piketty has described as a 'social nativism',[16] denouncing poverty, low wages and cuts to public services while blaming immigrants and minorities for all of these ills, as we shall see in the next chapter. As Piketty argues, workers have become increasingly suspicious of a centre-left that has been complicit in policies of global economic integration and that seems to have little to offer to workers in terms of protection from international competition.[17] Furthermore, they have not found an alternative channel of representation for these issues within the radical left – which, especially before its populist mainstreaming in the 2010s, was focused on the grievances of the urban middle classes. If the working class is disaffected with the left, this does not mean that it has enthusiastically embraced the nationalist right, as seen in its high levels of abstention. Furthermore, the left has been making gains in emerging sectors of the working class, and in particular the service precariat, the occupational sector with the worst pay and working conditions.

## Blue-Collar and Pink-Collar Workers

Divergences in electoral behaviour within the working class map onto the key division between manufacturing and service. The manufacturing working class, often located in peripheral areas is increasingly siding with the right, while the 'service precariat' concentrated in large and

---

16   Thomas Piketty, *Capital and Ideology* (Cambridge, MA: Harvard University Press, 2020).

17   Piketty, *Capital and Ideology*, pp. 887–8.

medium-sized cities, is more inclined to vote for the left – which in recent years has focused its attention on the struggles of precarious workers at the very bottom of the social scale. To appreciate this divide it is necessary to reflect on how the working class, generally defined by manual rather than intellectual labour, has changed in recent decades. The industrial worker in blue overalls armed with a spanner in a large manufacturing plant was always a questionable metonymy: the use of one section of the working class to stand for the whole. The working class has traditionally encompassed a greater variety of manual occupations, including many outside the factory plant: porters, builders, truck and bus drivers, and so on. Only at the peak of the industrial era did manufacturing workers represent a majority of the working class. Their share of the overall workforce and of working-class occupations has declined significantly in recent decades. In the UK, manufacturing now accounts for around 10 per cent of the workforce, from a peak of around 30 per cent at the height of the industrial era.[18] At the same time, there has been rapid growth in the non-manufacturing working class. There are now far more manual workers in service occupations, defined as 'service and sales workers' in the International Labour Organization's International Standard Classification of Occupations (coded as ISCO 5) than there are industrial workers, defined as 'craft and related trades workers' (ISCO 7). Significantly, the most common occupation these days is sales assistant, rather than factory worker – a reflection of a consumerist society in which distribution and consumption have become more important in terms of value-generation than production.

This burgeoning new 'service precariat' tends to the consumption needs of the middle class. It is made up of cleaners tidying up the offices where professionals, technicians and managers work; waiters serving them coffee to maintain their focus on intense cognitive tasks; sales assistants tending to their often extravagant consumption habits; Amazon shelf-fillers handling their parcels; call centre workers dealing with their product returns or complaints; and riders performing meal deliveries to a creative class, apparently too busy with their professions to find time to cook, wash their dishes or do their laundry. This is also

---

18  Kiminori Matsuyama, 'Structural Change in an Interdependent World: A Global View of Manufacturing Decline', *Journal of the European Economic Association* 7: 2–3 (2009).

the class fraction that encompasses the workers who have come to be celebrated during the pandemic, such as carers and domestic cleaners; people who, while being described as 'essential workers', have to make do with very low wages that barely guarantee their day-to-day survival. This service precariat is the class depicted in Ken Loach's 2019 film *Sorry We Missed You*. Its two main characters are Ricky, working in the delivery sector, and his wife Abbie, who works as a home care nurse. In the film, the couple is driven to a nervous breakdown by a combination of work stress and family disarray.

This condition of precariousness and exhaustion is far from being just a matter of fiction. In fact, the service precariat is the most exploited and wronged category of all – one that, in terms of both wages and working conditions, lies near the very bottom of the social pyramid. This is why ISCO 5 occupations are often used as a baseline against which to measure the salaries and conditions of other categories of workers. The service precariat also tends to be poorly unionised compared with manufacturing workers, and to have weak rates of participation in elections compared to other classes. It is both the most underprivileged and most socially invisible of all class fractions, except for the underclass living off the informal economy.

This service precariat also differs from the industrial proletariat in terms of gender and race. While the manufacturing working class tends to be male, white and older on average than the service precariat, the latter is generally more multicultural, and has a strong female component. In fact, many service-proletariat jobs, such as nursing and other care-oriented occupations, are referred to as 'pink-collar' jobs, because they were traditionally associated with unpaid work conducted by women at home – such as cooking, washing and tending to the needs of the ill and the old – tasks that have been progressively integrated into the capitalist market. Furthermore, especially in large cities, service workers tend to form a highly multicultural workforce that includes a large number of immigrants and ethnic minorities. This is why people who belong to this class are often counted in the US under the category of 'minority vote' – as if their political preferences were governed by the colour of their skin rather than by their economic position.

The hardship experienced by the service precariat goes a long way to explaining why, in recent years, this category has become a focus of attention for left activists. The most notable union-organising drives in Europe and the United States in recent years have focused precisely on this fraction of the working class, as seen in the Justice for Janitors/Cleaners mobilisations and the successful US Fight for 15 campaign on behalf of fast-food workers. Furthermore, the plight of workers in the 'gig economy', such as Deliveroo riders, Uber drivers, Instacart shoppers and Amazon warehouse workers has been matched by the creation of new organisations and campaigns. While largely un-unionised, Amazon was forced to raise its US wage to $15 per hour, in response to an increasingly militant rank-and-file and labour shortages resulting from coronavirus-related peaks in demand and unsanitary working conditions at Amazon warehouses, and Whole Foods supermarkets.[19]

The portion of the service precariat that does vote is more favourable to the left than the equivalent share of the blue-collar proletariat.[20] In fact, service workers are increasingly seen by the left as a strategic electorate that may help compensate for its haemorrhaging of blue-collar votes. During the 2020 Democratic primary, Bernie Sanders often addressed the plight of service workers. One of the few successes of his second run at the party's nomination was winning the votes of Las Vegas workers employed in casinos and hotels. In the 2017 and 2019 UK elections, service workers were considerably more likely to vote for the Labour Party than blue-collar workers, both in urban and non-urban areas.[21] Similarly, Italy's Five Star Movement achieved a strong showing among waiters and shop assistants and has introduced measures to limit precariousness in the service sector.[22] It is true that attempts to boost the electoral turnout of this group have so far had limited success, reflecting the profound disempowerment experienced by workers, especially among the young and more precarious. Nonetheless, the rise in service-class support is a reason for hope in relation to the strategy of broadening the left's working-class base.

19   Whole Foods was acquired by Amazon in 2017.

20   Jane Gingrich, 'A New Progressive Coalition? The European Left in a Time of Change', *Political Quarterly* 88: 1 (2017), 39–51.

21   Jonathan Mellon, Geoffrey Evans, Edward Fieldhouse, et al., 'British Election Survey, 2019: Internet Panel Survey', July 2019.

22   European Social Survey, 'ESS Round 9 Data'.

## The Ruralisation of Manufacturing

When people think about industry and manufacturing, they probably picture the factories and smokestacks of early industrial cities such as Manchester, Paris, Chicago and Turin. These days, however, this image is anachronistic as a consequence of a long-standing process of 'ruralisation in manufacturing', the relocation of production plants from large cities to the hinterland that has profoundly transformed the identity of blue-collar workers. Beginning in the 1950s – though in the United States the process began at the time of Franklin Roosevelt's New Deal – companies started to decentralise production, moving their factories to medium-sized and small cities, profiting from better communication and transportation, as well as the lower wages and land costs of the exurbs.[23] This internal dynamic of de-localisation has only accelerated under neoliberalism, paralleling and complementing practices of offshoring, in a desperate search for a cheaper, more docile workforce.

As a consequence, many industrial workers live today in medium-sized and small population centres that are often far more dependent on manufacturing than larger urban centres, as political scientist Jonathan A. Rodden argues in *Why Cities Lose*.[24] In Europe, one is more likely to find blue-collar workers in places like Wolfsburg in Germany (100,000 inhabitants) or Sassuolo near Bergamo (40,000) than in larger cities like Milan, Bologna, Frankfurt and Munich. In the United States, places like Moraine in Ohio (6,400), the site of a glass factory recently acquired by Chinese firm Fuyao – as featured in the documentary *American Factory*[25] – and the small towns of North Dakota at the centre of the shale oil boom of the 2010s are more representative of today's industrial working-class settings than the old industrial centres, such as Pittsburgh, Chicago, Buffalo and New York. Similarly, in the UK, blue-collar workers make up a far larger share of the workforce in places like Boston – nicknamed 'Brexit-town' because of its record support for 'Leave' – and Hullavington in Wiltshire, the site of the main Dyson vacuum cleaner factory, than in London, Manchester, Liverpool or Edinburgh, the

---

23   Jonathan A. Rodden, *Why Cities Lose: The Deep Roots of the Urban-Rural Political Divide* (London: Hachette, 2019).

24   Ibid.

25   Steven Bognar and Julia Reichert (dir.), *American Factory* (Higher ground production / Participant Media, 2019).

hotspots of the first industrial revolution. Besides hosting the majority of manufacturing workers, these areas depend heavily on manufacturing for their income. Whereas in the US, in metropolitan counties only 25 per cent of income derives from manufacturing and 75 per cent from services, in non-metropolitan areas, the ratio is 50:50.[26]

Interestingly, nationalist-right electoral campaigning has often touched upon industrial towns. During the 2016 and 2020 US presidential campaigns, Trump visited many small towns in the Midwest. His first speech after the 2016 election was at a refrigerator factory in Huntington, Indiana (population: 17,000), where he promised manufacturing jobs would return. One of Marine Le Pen's media stunts during the 2017 French presidential campaign was to give a speech in front of the Alteo factory in Gardanne (20,000) in southern France, and the Whirlpool factory in Amiens (100,000) in northern France, which was threatened by de-localisation – though Le Pen lost the local election race. Matteo Salvini regularly tours smalltown Italy, hitting places like Fermo (37,000) in the Marche region, a town specialising in shoe production, and Legnago (25,000) in Veneto, a centre for the production of air-conditioning equipment, boilers and radiators; often he wore a customised sweatshirt bearing the name of the town concerned. For his part, Brexiter Nigel Farage has been photographed drinking pints of beer in towns like Seaham (20,000) and Hartlepool (92,000) – home, respectively, to a Huntsman titianium dioxide plant and a Tata steel factory.

Not only has the industrial working class become more geographically dispersed; its occupational experience bears only a slight resemblance to that of the mass worker of the Fordist era. Today, it is a smaller and more specialised workforce than it was fifty years ago. Contemporary factory workers are often highly skilled technicians rather than unskilled workers engaged in physically demanding work. Finally, they are far less unionised and politicised than they were in the past. In the US, union membership has fallen from 30 per cent to 12 per cent of the working population between 1960 and 2010 and many countries have experienced a similar trend. In the sprawling industrial zones of Western Europe and the US, the industrial plant is not part of a broader social and political assemblage, as it was at the height of the Fordist era, but just the location of a job like

---

26   Rodden, *Why Cities Lose*, p. 89.

any other. Often working in smaller firms that are integrated into complex supply chains, in which they rub shoulders with their boss and feel under constant threat of being laid off, workers are not ideally positioned to develop a strong class consciousness. This identity vacuum is ripe for exploitation by nativist appeals from the right.[27]

The exposure of manufacturing in the West to Asian competition explains the sympathy of many industrial workers for protectionist demands voiced by right-wing leaders like Trump, who promised to bring back jobs shipped overseas and punish unfair Chinese and other foreign competition. The case is quite different for the service industry. Service is not as exposed to international competition as the manufacturing sector; most jobs in food, retail and services have a strong relational and physical component, which means they cannot be easily offshored or automated. The real challenge they face instead is the downward pressure on wages, which is very strong in the service sector because there is less room for productivity gains, and because of the risk that, if the costs of services rise too high, customers may dispense with them altogether.[28] Despite the rather different circumstances of blue-collar and pink-collar workers, what they share is a painful perception of a decline in their living conditions and future prospects. To win the hearts and minds of this disgruntled working class, the left must take heed of its demand for protection and an economy more anchored to the needs, and under the control of local communities.

## Middle-Class Fragility

Donald Trump may claim to have been a workers' president, but the middle class were the group that voted for him in the highest numbers in 2016 and 2020, and his tax cuts favoured rentiers. Marine Le Pen may well have lured workers in the rust belt of Picardy and Nord-Pas-de-Calais, but her core support comes from wealthy voters in Provence and Côte d'Azur, where Rassemblement National has several mayors. Finally,

27   Nonna Mayer, 'The Radical Right in France', in Jens Rydgren, ed., *The Oxford Handbook of the Radical Right* (Oxford: Oxford University Press, 2018).

28   William J. Baumol, *The Cost Disease: Why Computers Get Cheaper and Health Care Doesn't* (New Haven, CT: Yale University Press, 2012).

fans of Matteo Salvini are to be found as much on the factory floor as among professional technicians and on company boards, where his flat-tax policy is wildly popular. Significantly, the most representative figure in Salvini's electoral base is not the factory worker but the accountant.[29] Similarly, to understand the social composition of the left's electorate, we cannot stop with the service precariat; we need to appreciate the enthusiastic support left parties have secured among the new middle class of social and intellectual workers. Having discussed working-class electoral behaviour it is now time to turn to the middle class.

According to the OECD, in the West, 61 per cent of citizens declare they belong to the middle class.[30] This contains an element of aspirational projection, meaning that the real figure is probably closer to 50 per cent. In any case the middle class is electorally decisive – especially given its higher-than-average rate of electoral participation. The middle class has traditionally been seen as adhering to moderate positions, and in the post-war period it was hoped its presence would act as an antidote against social strife and left radicalism, but also against the reactionary right. During the neoliberal era, it was the most courted of all sections of the electorate. Entrepreneurs and capitalist evangelists would wax lyrical about the middle-class contribution to the economy. It is the middle class that most fervently espoused the neoliberal gospel of careerism and possessive individualism, providing a consumer pool for an ever-growing gamut of global products. But large sections of the middle class in Western countries now feel betrayed, life-long toil having secured a modest retirement for its older members, while its active adults are struggling and its younger members are in despair about their likely downward social mobility in the future.

It is true that, during the crisis of the 2010s, not only the super-wealthy and financial elites that Joseph Stiglitz and Occupy Wall Street together characterised as 'the 1 per cent' but also the upper middle class – what Richard Reeves, in his book *Dream Hoarders*, describes as the 20 per cent – saw their incomes and wealth rise.[31] This upper middle class is

---

29   European Social Survey, Round 9, (2018).

30   OECD. *Under Pressure: The Squeezed Middle Class.* (Paris: OECD Publishing, 2019), p. 18

31   Richard V. Reeves, *Dream Hoarders: How the American Upper Middle Class Is Leaving Everyone Else in the Dust, Why That Is a Problem, and What to Do about It* (Washington, DC: Brookings Institution, 2018).

incidentally also the stratum most enthusiastically supporting the neoliberal centre, whose social bloc includes relatively well-to-do fractions of other classes who still favour the pursuit of neoliberal policies. Nonetheless, the remaining members of the middle class in the West, what we could refer to as the 'middling class' due to the precarity of their position, are facing the prospect of proletarianisation, or *déclassement* – being progressively stripped of the traditional tokens of middle-class status, such as home ownership, savings and a good salary following a good education.[32] Indeed, the question of the crisis of the middle class was openly discussed at the 2018 and 2019 Davos meeting, while the OECD has dedicated several reports to the new pressures to which the middle class is now subjected.

This 'middling class', those fractions of the middle class that do not belong to the 20 per cent of the well-to-do, is now gripped with a profound status anxiety. It is becoming ever more difficult to maintain middle-class membership. As reported by the OECD, 'Since the baby boomers generation, each new generation has seen its chances of belonging to the middle-income class fall.'[33] This fragility constitutes a more general character of middle-class experience that extends beyond periods of economic crisis. As Nicos Poulantzas notes, for a class in the middle, both upward and downward social mobility are possible, engendering fears about loss of position at least as much as desire of upward mobility.[34] Particularly exposed are small entrepreneurs and shopkeepers. Because of its access to credit and market revenues, the petty bourgeoisie is, on average, richer than the working class; but it is also more exposed to the vagaries of the market and to the risk of bankruptcy during economic downturns. During the 2010s Great Recession, the 'grand bourgeoisie' devoured the petty bourgeoisie and precarised the new middle class both increasingly thrown into the precariat, subject to uncertain incomes and welfare dependency. In the aftermath of the coronavirus crisis, the threat of proletarianisation is even more severe, in particular for shopkeepers and restaurant owners, whose establishments were forced to close for many months,

---

32   Teresa A. Sullivan, Elizabeth Warren and Jay Lawrence Westbrook, *The Fragile Middle Class: Americans in Debt* (New Haven, CT: Yale University Press, 2020).

33   Ibid., p. 26

34   Nicos Poulantzas, *Political Power and Social Classes* (London: New Left Books, 1975).

and whose market has been eaten up by Amazon and other digital platforms.

This crisis of the middle class is a worrying sign for society's stability. As Joseph Schumpeter noted, the middle class comprises 'protective strata', which act as a sort of social ballast to absorb shocks.[35] According to Schumpeter, these strata are always under threat, since the profiteering drive of capitalism pushes towards 'the crumbling of the protecting walls'. In so doing, however, capitalism ultimately undermines the social fabric that guarantees society's own reproduction, and hence also the long-term viability of a profit-driven economy.[36] The way in which neoliberal policies of privatisation and austerity eroded public services, including health and education – key social support structures – and the manner in which digital companies have eaten up many small businesses are examples of this ultimately self-destructive drive of capitalism. It is no surprise then that under such circumstances, middle-class strata usually suspicious of government intervention are now also demanding state protection.

## Managers versus Designers

'Middle class' is, if anything, an even more problematic umbrella term than 'working class'. It encompasses a great variety of professional figures, working conditions and levels of income and wealth, making it difficult to speak of it as a coherent electoral group. Despite this complexity it is possible to divide the middle class along one dominant cleavage – namely, between the new and old petty bourgeoisies described by Poulantzas; or the 'old middle class' and 'new middle class' discussed by Hanspeter Kriesi and Daniel Oesch.[37] Following Kriesi's categorisation, the old middle class comprises managers, technicians, and office workers. To this we can add employers and small business owners who share

---

35 Joseph A. Schumpeter, *Capitalism, Socialism and Democracy* (London: Routledge, 2013 [1942]).

36 Ibid.

37 Hanspeter Kriesi, 'New Social Movements and the New Class in the Netherlands', *American Journal of Sociology* 94: 5 (1989), 1078–116. See also Anthony Giddens, 'The Growth of the New Middle Class' in *The Class Structure of the Advanced Societies* (London: Hutchinson, 1973).

similar patterns of electoral behaviour. Conversely, the new middle class comprises socio-cultural professionals and skilled service workers.[38] While these two sections – old middle class and new middle class – share a nominal 'middle-class' status, they are in certain respects further apart in living conditions, expectations and values than the industrial proletariat and the service working class are. Furthermore, they tend to exhibit divergent electoral behaviour: the old middle class typically votes for the right or the centre (especially managers and some small business owners), while the new middle class tends to vote for the left.[39]

This divergence in political preference is expressed by Thomas Piketty in *Capital and Ideology* by opposing a 'Brahmin left' and a 'Merchant right': the first is supported by the class of highly educated administrators and intellectuals, the second by the commercial class of financial managers and business owners: 'The Brahmin left values scholastic success, intellectual work, and the acquisition of diplomas and knowledge; the merchant right emphasizes professional motivation, a flair for business, and negotiating skills.'[40] This close association of the left with the intelligentsia points to a reversal in educational alignments. The left now appeals to the more educated sections of the population, rather than to the uneducated masses of the traditional industrial working-class, who had only their labour-power to sell. This shift is a worrying indication of the left's *embourgeoisement*, which is the counterpart to the lurch of the industrial working class to the right. Yet, the section of the middle class gravitating towards the left tends to have lower income than the old middle class supporting the right. As Piketty himself notes, the right continues to command the support of most high-income voters – the more so as their wealth increases.

Traditionally, the section of the bourgeoisie that was identified as closest to the nationalist right was the old petty bourgeoisie, made up of small business owners and artisans. These were the figures who were mobilised in the 1950s and 1960s by French right-wing populist Pierre

---

38   Silja Häusermann and Hanspeter Kriesi, 'What Do Voters Want? Dimensions and Configurations in Individual-Level Preferences and Party Choice', *The Politics of Advanced Capitalism* (2015), 202–30.

39   Daniel Oesch and Line Rennwald, 'Electoral Competition in Europe's New Tripolar Political Space: Class Voting for the Left, Centre-Right and Radical Right', *European Journal of Political Research* 57: 4 (2018), 783–807.

40   Piketty, *Capital and Ideology*, p. 766.

Poujade and the Defence Union of Shopkeepers and Craftsmen to protest against taxation. This was also, incidentally, the class that lent strong support to fascist movements. Hannah Arendt famously described Nazism as stemming from a rebellion of the disgruntled petty bourgeoisie.[41] As Poulantzas shows in *Fascism and Dictatorship*, fascist movements enlisted shopkeepers and small entrepreneurs, as well as policemen and other public officials who feared a loss of economic status.[42] Today, however, within the right's social bloc the small business owner is complemented by other figures, and in particular by highly paid technicians and associate professionals, including accountants, estate agents and sales representatives – while managers, mostly continue to support the neoliberal centre. One group that typifies the ethos of the right-wing middle-class electorate are 'middle-class anti-elitists', in the words of the *Financial Times*'s Simon Kuper. These are people who live mostly in suburban areas of metropolises or in medium-sized cities, in exurbs like those in 'New Jersey and Long Island, around the English south-east, the Milan agglomeration and the quiet suburbs of Rotterdam', and who harbour strong suspicion towards 'big city figures and experts' – part of the intelligentsia they see as a threat to their wealth and position. It is a class whose members consider themselves the 'makers' and 'job creators'; those who work hardest and have to make difficult choices about the bottom line.

The new middle class that is the main pillar of support for the left has a very different nature. It is a class fraction that was very small in the past, but which has grown significantly in the course of the transformation towards a 'knowledge economy', which has called for highly educated experts capable of skilled work, including complex analytical and communicative tasks that are in high demand in a digital economy.[43] The most representative figures of this new middle class are the so-called 'socio-cultural professionals', who include teachers, journalists, librarians, university lecturers and researchers, as well as the

---

41    Hannah Arendt, *The Origins of Totalitarianism* (Boston, MA: Houghton Mifflin Harcourt, 1973), pp. 36–7.

42    As Poulantzas notes, fascist movements had a strong petty-bourgeois base of support. Nicos Poulantzas, *Fascism and Dictatorship: The Third International and the Problem of Fascism* (London: Verso, 2019).

43    Hanspeter Kriesi, 'New Social Movements and the New Class in the Netherlands', *American Journal of Sociology* 94: 5 (1989).

creative class of designers, programmers and marketers.[44] Since the 1970s, this has traditionally been considered a highly progressive constituency. In terms of political attitudes, the new middle class combines support for social-democratic redistributive policies with socially liberal values that include an emphasis on personal freedom, and the protection of the rights of sexual, ethnic and religious minorities.

The new middle class is not an exclusive monopoly of the left. Rather, it is a terrain of competition between the centre-left and the radical left, with some sections also supporting more centrist candidates. For example, in 2016 Hillary Clinton's electorate featured typical new middle-class figures, such as medical scientists, preschool teachers and market-research analysts.[45] However, large sections of the new middle class are strongly supportive of the redistributive and socially progressive policies of the socialist left. Socio-cultural professionals were by far the most important group supporting the rise of Podemos in Spain and of Jean-Luc Mélenchon's La France Insoumise, and an important component of the electorate of Bernie Sanders and Labour under Jeremy Corbyn. In the 2019 Spanish election, Podemos carried 26.9 per cent of the upper-middle-class vote and 26.2 per cent of that of the new middle class – both well above its average vote.[46]

The support of the new middle class for the left is coloured not only by progressive idealism but also by the serious economic hurdles placed before the more precarious and younger section of this group. As Sciences Po researcher Luc Rouban argues, the bulk of Mélenchon's supporters consists of people who are at the same time *diplômés* and *déclassés*, similar to the 'graduates without a future', identified by Paul Mason as the initiators of the 2011 protest movements.[47] The growing number of college graduates in a shrinking economy has led to a

44   Daniel Oesch and Line Rennwald, 'The Class Basis of Switzerland's Cleavage Between the New Left and the Populist Right', *Swiss Political Science Review* 16: 3 (2010); Richard Florida, *The Rise of the Creative Class* (New York: Basic, 2019).

45   Richard Florida, 'Why Is Your State Red or Blue? Look to the Dominant Occupational Class', *Bloomberg*, 28 November 2018.

46   European Social Survey, 'ESS Round 9 Data'.

47   Luc Rouban, 'Le peuple qui vote Mélenchon est-il le peuple?', *The Conversation*, 1 October 2017, at theconversation.com; Paul Mason, *Why It's Still Kicking Off Everywhere: The New Global Revolutions* (London: Verso, 2013), p. 72.

devaluation of university degrees and a widespread condition of precarity for intellectual workers. Furthermore, the professional class faces high costs of living in urban centres where its job opportunities are concentrated. High rents make it increasingly difficult to save money for a mortgage deposit making it hard to get on the property-ladder, that key, yet ever more difficult to attain, definer of middle-class status.

Many young members of the new middle class – including designers, IT specialists, programmers and researchers – are 'connected outsiders'.[48] While being highly educated and often proficient in foreign languages and the use of digital technology they face a situation of economic insecurity and decreasing expectations compared to their parents.[49] Furthermore, being the 'dominated dominant' class, to use Pierre Bourdieu's term, the intellectual section of the middle class does not only have a lower income compared to the commercial section, but often feels deprived of control over its work. It operates in workplaces in which decisions about strategy, responsibilities, time-table, division of labour and so on are decided by managers and technical professionals. This sense of *lack of control* often extends to society as a whole, due to the way in which, as discussed in Chapter 4, the technocratic nature of many decisions has moved important political decisions beyond public scrutiny. It is not by chance that it is from this new middle class that demands for forms of participatory democracy both online and offline have often been voiced. The middle class is thus pulled in two different directions, with the old and new middle class drawn into an internal conflict over authority, over social values and over the distribution of stagnating income. The fear of economic and social decline experienced by a majority of the middle class means that those who were once considered the bedrock of stability for Western capitalist democracies have themselves been polarised politically.

---

48   Paolo Gerbaudo, *The Digital Party: Political Organisation and Online Democracy* (London: Pluto Press, 2019), pp. 52–4.

49   Paolo Gerbaudo, *The Digital Party: Political Organisation and Online Democracy* (London: Pluto, 2019), pp. 45–8.

## The New Organic Intellectual

Having reconstructed the current social blocs of the nationalist right and socialist left, what is essential is devising strategies through which the left can strengthen and broaden its electoral support. What is evident is that the contemporary class structure is marked by fragmentation, which makes it difficult to construct coherent class alliances. Furthermore, the present weakness of trade unions, as seen in low membership numbers, means that the left lacks a strong pillar of organised support in the labour movement. It is true that we are currently experiencing a revival of unionism, especially in the service sector and the gig economy, and that Biden's pledge to support organised labour may herald an inversion of this tendency. But Amazon has so far managed to thwart unionisation and the $15 minimum wage has been struck down by conservative Democrats. So for the time being, socialist formations have to deal with a high degree of social dispersion within their potential electorate. In such challenging conditions it is essential to carefully consider how socialists can broaden their electoral support among the working class.

As Thomas Piketty suggests, the left's main problem is its excessive dependence on 'Brahmins', i.e. the new middle class of socio-cultural professionals and skilled service workers. It is often argued that this orientation of the left towards the urban middle class skews its agenda, making it unattractive to the working class. The disruptive role of the middle class in the construction of a socialist alliance was already a concern for German socialist writer August Bebel who, proud of his working-class upbringing, at the International Socialist Congress of 1904 spurned Frenchman Jean Jaurés's proposal of an alliance between the proletariat and the middle class. Robert Michels argued that middle-class participation was detrimental to the working-class movement, given that it led to the subordination of working-class interests to middle-class priorities; and fellow syndicalist Georges Sorel, in his book *Reflections on Violence*, saw the middle class as a traitor to the proletariat.[50] Similar in spirit were the scathing remarks made by George Orwell

---

50   Robert Michels, *Political Parties: A Sociological Study of the Oligarchical Tendencies of Modern Democracy*, transl. Eden Paul and Cedar Paul (New York: Hearst's International Library Company, 1915); Georges Sorel, *Reflections on Violence*, ed. Jeremy Jennings (Cambridge: Cambridge University Press, 1999).

in his chronicle of the Great Depression, *The Road to Wigan Pier*, where he contrasted the 'typical working-class Socialist' directly affected by economic injustice and poverty and the 'book-trained Socialist', campaigning merely out of moral motives.[51]

Obviously, given the current class composition of Western societies, in which around half of the population belongs to the middle class, and in which the middle class has higher-than-average rates of electoral participation, ostracising this category would be suicidal for any political movement aiming for power. However much they may have presented themselves as class parties (in the sense of working-class parties), communist and socialist parties have always had a significant middle-class component, appealing also to artisans, public employees, teachers, doctors and other professionals.[52] The construction of a 'popular bloc', consisting of an alliance between the organised working class, rural labourers and sections of the urban middle classes, has been the default left strategy since the times of Lenin and Gramsci. Thus, the question for socialist parties is not to do away with the middle-class vote. Rather, the aim should be, on the one hand, to avoid over-reliance on this electorate to achieve a greater diversification in support, and on the other hand, to make sure that the active section of the movement (overwhelmingly recruited from the middle class) does not fall prey to an obsession with cultural wars at the expense of the centrality of socio-economic cleavages. To achieve this goal, it is necessary to reflect on the role of organic intellectuals and the relationship between activists and the social bases they intend to organise and represent.[53]

For Gramsci, organic intellectuals were those active and organising components that emerged out of each major class and performed key directive functions. In the case of the working class, these were most notably trade union and party organisers, whose historical mission was to make the working class aware of its own potential. Some of them, like Bebel, hailed from the working class itself, thanks to the educational opportunities that socialist movements offered; but many others were 'borrowed' from the radical middle class. What

51   George Orwell, *The Road to Wigan Pier* (London: Penguin, 2001 [1937]).

52   Stefano Bartolini, *The Political Mobilization of the European Left, 1860–1980: The Class Cleavage* (Cambridge: Cambridge University Press, 2007).

53   Antonio Gramsci, *Selections from the Prison Notebooks*, ed. and transl. Quintin Hoare and Geoffrey Nowell Smith (London: Lawrence & Wishart, 1971), pp. 3–6.

made them 'organic', besides their class origins, was their rootedness in the popular classes – the fact that they were made to confront the life experience of the subaltern. The contemporary progressive intelligentsia often appears to lack any 'organic' rootedness in working-class communities, in terms of either its social background or experience.

Within the socialist movement, the presence of middle-class intellectuals was tempered by an ethos of commitment to popular mobilisation sometimes combined with an attitude of self-flagellation. Middle-class activists were forced to renounce the most conspicuous elements of their social status. They were sometimes expected to spend time working in factories, or living in working-class neighbourhoods – a tradition initiated by the Russian populists of the nineteenth century, who sent the idealistic intelligentsia into the countryside to live with peasants in order to rid them of their bourgeois affectations; though, needless to say, the peasants were often not too impressed. While such practices of middle-class penance may look anachronistic to us, the risks of middle-class self-centredness continues to be relevant in the present day and age and a major obstacle to the construction of an inclusive and diverse popular bloc. It is essential that activists, overwhelmingly hailing from the middle class, regain a sense of their privileged class position and their duty towards others less fortunate.

This necessity of appealing beyond the confines of the progressive urban middle class does not mean that the left needs to renege on its commitments to universalism, human rights and multicultural tolerance – as those preaching a 'conservative socialism' would contend. Many battles middle-class activists have embraced – from the defence of minorities including gay, lesbian and trans people to environmental priorities – have in fact by now become majoritarian in many Western countries, forcing the right to adapt its discourse too. Yet, it is true that the working class, both old and new, tends to be more conservative in terms of value and worldview and more suspicious of immigration. At times when the culture war over values and civil rights or on immigration becomes particularly polarised, there is a risk that the difference in ethical worldviews between the new middle class and working class may become an obstacle in cementing their class alliance. A unifying focus on economic demands for jobs and public services may win back to the left, workers who are relatively more socially conservative than the urban middle class but who were part of progressive coalitions in the past, as they prized welfare and full-employment policies.

For the left to regain a strong footing in the working class and fend off right-wing nationalism, it should eschew the flawed premise that the drifting away of the manufacturing working class from the left is exclusively a function of cultural factors. The causes of workers' discontent are primarily economic, stemming from the decline of labour revenues under neoliberalism – a direct consequence of free market deregulation and exposure to international competition in a globalised economy. Most importantly, it should be recognised that the class alliance between sections of the working class and the commercial middle class supporting the nationalist right is highly unstable.

As Piketty has noted, while highly critical of the European Union and global capitalism, 'social nativists' like Marine Le Pen are not keen to pursue redistributive measures that will attend to the real needs of the working class, as these are not in the interest of their middle-class voters or their patrons among the wealthy.[54] They try to deflect such demands, and to preserve the illusion that the interests of workers are close to their heart, by blaming supra-national institutions, foreign countries and immigrants for the lack of resources. Donald Trump's trade war against China, accompanied by tax cuts to the rich that delivered little for workers, is an example of this dishonesty.

The social protection workers demand cannot be satisfied for much longer under the present conditions. The socialist left needs to drive a wedge between the working-class and middle-class bases of the right. Progressives should denounce the profiteering behaviour of the new nationalists – in particular, their complicity with policies of privatisation of public services, and their hypocritical intimacy with global financial networks. For this narrative to be convincing, however, it is also necessary to overcome the perception of the left as distant and aloof. The left's ability to regain a stronger footing among blue-collar workers and consolidate its support among service workers will depend heavily on its capacity to develop an economic vision that appeals to

---

54   Piketty, *Capital and Ideology*, pp. 887–8.

voters beyond its metropolitan strongholds. Only by prioritising bread-and-butter issues such as jobs, healthcare and education, and protecting manufacturing, will the left be able to present itself plausibly as a force that can protect workers from the inequality and insecurity produced by a failing neoliberal order.

# 7

# Enemies of the People

Given the emphasis of contemporary politics on protection and security, clarifying who are the figures that are seen as embodying social dangers can help us better understand contemporary political alignments. The construction of the enemy is a fundamental aspect of all politics. Carl Schmitt famously proposed that politics always entails an enemy/friend distinction that divides the political field into two opposing camps.[1] It is sufficient to watch a political talk show or parliamentary debate in any Western democracy to see fiery accusations flying. In spite of the Kantian ideal embraced by many liberals, which views politics as a space of rational discussion and consensus, politics is first and foremost a space of conflict, in line with Mao Zedong's inversion of Clausewitz's famous dictum, in which 'politics is the continuation of war without bloodshed'.[2] The construction of the enemy is particularly important in times of populism. Political theorist Chantal Mouffe has argued that populism relies on the presence of a 'constitutive outside', in which enmity against the Other simultaneously provides an anchoring point for self-identity.[3] Strong antagonism – an intensification of the us-versus-them posture – acts as a partial substitute for the affirmation

---

1  Carl Schmitt, *The Concept of the Political: Expanded Edition* (Chicago, IL: University of Chicago Press, 2007), p. 26

2  Mao Zedong, *Problems of Strategy in China's Revolutionary War* (Beijing: Foreign Language Press, 1965), p. 180; Carl von Clausewitz, *On War* (London: Penguin, 1982).

3  Chantal Mouffe, *The Democratic Paradox* (London: Verso, 2000), p. 12.

of a well-defined positive identity, and a buttress for otherwise brittle social blocs. Thus, in examining the 'enemies of the people' prevalent in the politics of the Great Recoil, we may draw some lessons about what kind of 'people' contemporary movements seek to invoke and better understand the content of the politics of protection and control they put forward.

Different underclass and overclass targets feature prominently in contemporary politics: immigrants, the rich, and political and intellectual elites. The nationalist right typically focuses anger on immigrants, as well as ethnic minorities, pictured as a dangerous underclass threatening the security and well-being of the people. The right represents immigrants as a threat to cultural integrity and ethnic homogeneity by virtue of their increased demographic presence. Furthermore, it accuses them of suppressing wages by creating a 'reserve army of labour' at the disposal of capitalists.

The left points the finger instead at socioeconomic class enemies, such as wealthy bankers and greedy oligopolists. The rich stand accused both of depriving workers and citizens of social protection, and of frustrating the popular desire for democratic control. They are seen as enemies of collective prosperity and security who have attacked wages, working conditions and public services, while taking their companies and wealth offshore to avoid the taxes that normal citizens have to pay. Thus, while the nationalist right scapegoats those at the bottom of society, including the newly arrived, who are seen as harbingers of social disintegration, the socialist left focuses its invective against those at the top, whom it accuses of avarice and arrogance. A further enemy featuring prominently in the contemporary political drama is 'the establishment' or 'the caste' (a term popularised by the Five Star Movement), made up of politicians and state bureaucrats accused of operating in opaque ways and of favouring vested interests while depriving citizens of democratic control. Parallel to this runs the right's enmity against the intellectual elites suspected of substituting tradition with globalist and liberal worldviews. The differences between these enemies go a long way to illuminating the various conflicts about economic resources, culture and authority that have emerged in the present moment and the existence of radically different understandings of the causes of global agoraphobia.

## Bash the Immigrants

'Let's be straightforward with each other: Hungary is going to be condemned because the Hungarian people have decided that this country is not going to be a country of migrants.' Thus spoke Hungarian prime minister Viktor Orbán in September 2018, after the European Parliament adopted a resolution endorsing a report, authored by Dutch MEP Judith Sargentini, on the Hungarian treatment of migrants – among many other issues including corruption, freedom of the press and the integrity of the electoral system. Since his return to power, after a landslide victory in 2010 against a discredited Socialist Party, Orbán and his party, Fidesz – formally a member of the Christian-democratic European People's Party – have adopted an openly xenophobic discourse particularly targeting Roma and Muslims. During the 2015 migration crisis, Orbán refused to accept a quota of refugees, and even built a fence along the border with Croatia and Serbia.

Orbán, it turns out, was a forerunner of the mainstreaming of the kind of xenophobic populism that has rocked the world since the mid 2010s. Trump famously rode to victory by promising to halt immigration. At the launch of his presidential campaign, held at Trump Tower in New York on 16 June 2015, the hotel mogul and TV personality famously attacked Mexican immigrants in a wholesale fashion: 'They're bringing crime. They're rapists. And some, I assume, are good people.'[4] In spite of this, he still managed to win 29 per cent of the Latino vote in 2016, increasing the share to 32 per cent in 2020. In 2019 he enraged many people when he attacked the so-called Squad of progressive congresswomen comprising Alexandria Ocasio-Cortez, Ilhan Omar, Rashida Tlaib and Ayanna Presley, saying they should go back to where they came from, implying that minorities were non-nationals. Alt-right pundits such as Richard Spencer and Stefan Molyneux have popularised white supremacist ideas and virulently attacked liberal values of tolerance and inclusion, often taking aim at immigrants.[5]

In France, Marine Le Pen has presented migrants as the flagbearers of a 'rampant globalisation', damaging people's neighbourhoods, villages,

---

4 'Here's Donald Trump's Presidential Announcement Speech', 16 June 2015, *Time*.
5 Gavin Evans, 'The Unwelcome Revival of "Race Science"', *Guardian*, 2 March 2018.

schools and wages.[6] In one of the last campaign rallies of the 2017 presidential elections held in Paris she promised to end all immigration and 'put our borders back in place'. She emphatically closed the speech by saying 'I will *protect* you'.[7] In Italy, Matteo Salvini's rise since he became the leader of Lega in 2013 was predicated on his tough line on immigration. Salvini has often deployed the spectre of an 'invasion' from Africa;[8] during his one-year spell as interior minister he closed Italian ports to NGO ships rescuing boats of refugees from Libya and the rest of North Africa. 'Closed ports' (*porti chiusi*) – an assertion of decisiveness and intransigence – became his favourite slogan.[9] He also went on to propose a crackdown on 'little ethnic shops', such as convenience stores owned and run by Bangladeshis.[10] In the UK, Nigel Farage argued that migration had 'left many people in our towns and cities frankly finding it difficult to recognise the place being the same as it was ten to fifteen years ago'.[11] His attacks on migrants intensified in the course of the 2015 refugee crisis, and featured the infamous 'Breaking Point' poster ahead of the Brexit referendum, picturing a long queue of migrants, which strikingly resembled the imagery adopted in Nazi propaganda. Attacks against immigrants have been compounded by enmity towards already established ethnic minorities. The hard line taken by Donald Trump against the Black Lives Matter movement and his dalliance with white supremacist groups have highlighted that racial hatred remains a live issue.

To understand how this enmity against immigrants and minorities fits in with the right's politics of protection and control, we need to consider the historical origins of contemporary national-populism and its relationship to racial discrimination. Modern racism has a

---

6    Angelique Chrisafis, 'Marine Le Pen Rails against Rampant Globalisation after Election Success', *Guardian*, 24 April 2017.

7    ' "I will protect you!" Marine Le Pen Vows to End all Immigration to France', *Telegraph*, 18 April 2017.

8    Rachel Donadio, 'Salvini Puts Italy on a Collision Course with Europe', *Atlantic*, 9 August 2019 .

9    Silvia Sciorilli Borrelli, 'Matteo Salvini: Italy's Ports Are Closed to Migrant Vessels', *Politico*, 16 June 2018.

10    Nick Squires, 'Italy's Hardline Deputy PM Matteo Salvini Says "Little Ethnic Shops" Must Close by 9pm', *Telegraph*, 12 October 2019.

11    Rowena Mason, 'Nigel Farage: Immigration Has Left Britain Almost Unrecognisable', *Guardian*, 31 March 2015.

long history that can be traced back to slavery and imperialism. It was ideologically abetted by social Darwinism and the work of nineteenth-century French count Arthur de Gobineau, who theorised the existence of an Aryan master race which inspired Adolf Hitler.[12] The defeat of the Nazis and fascists during World War II, the victory of the US Civil Rights movement in the 1960s, the end of apartheid in South Africa in the 1990s, and finally the election of the first black president in US history in 2008 were all celebrated as milestones on an irreversible journey towards a 'post-racial society'. Far from having disappeared, however, xenophobia is rearing its head amid widespread fears of social decline that haunt the landscape of the Great Recoil.

In Europe, the first post-war party to attract votes for its racism was the Front National, which was founded and led for thirty years by Jean-Marie Le Pen. A former parachutist who had supported the failed Algerian coup against the French Republic in 1961, Le Pen proceeded to demolish many of the anti-fascist red lines in the political discourse of the French Fifth Republic. He strongly antagonised Muslim migrants coming from the Maghreb and French-speaking West Africa, insisting that they were ruining the French nation: '*Les français d'abord!*' ('French first!') was his rallying cry.[13] His support reached double digits as early as 1988 – his voters apparently able to ignore shameful remarks including the claim that the gas chambers were a 'detail of history'.[14]

The model established by Le Pen was quickly taken up around Western Europe by ambitious new right-wing leaders. In the 1980s, the Lega Nord, a federation of several autonomist groups in the north of Italy, likewise wielded racism in response to the first significant wave of foreign immigration into the country, as well as at internal migrants – the *terroni* from the Italian Mezzogiorno – who came to work in Lombardy and Veneto. In Austria in the 1990s, Jörg Haider's Freedom Party won support by presenting foreigners as scroungers and criminals, while portraying Islam as incompatible with Western values.

---

12  Michael Denis Biddiss, *Father of Racist Ideology: The Social and Political Thought of Count Gobineau* (New York: Weybright and Talley, 1970).

13  Catherine Fieschi, *Populocracy: The Tyranny of Authenticity and the Rise of Populism* (Newcastle upon Tyne: Agenda Publishing, 2019).

14  Ibid.

Xenophobic parties soon emerged in other European countries, from Great Britain, where UKIP was founded in 1993, to the Netherlands, where the Pim Fortuyn List was active in the early 2000s and Geert Wilders's Party for Freedom was founded in 2006, to end with the Kaczyński brothers' Law and Justice party in Poland and the transformation of Orbán's Fidesz from a Christian-democrat to a national conservative party.

While early right-wing populist movements were on the margins of the political arena, they have progressively become part of the political mainstream.[15] On the back of strong coverage from mainstream news media and the tabloid press focusing obsessively on immigration and crime, these parties have experienced strong electoral growth which has sometimes led them into government coalitions. Furthermore, right-wing populists have managed to exert a strong influence on mainstream conservative parties that have progressively adopted strict anti-immigration positions of their own to avoid being outflanked in the battle for consensus. The British Conservative Party moved swiftly to the right in response to pressure from the UKIP and Brexit parties, while Donald Trump's populist takeover of the Republican Party has completely transformed the identity of the party founded by Abraham Lincoln.

Growing anxiety about immigration is, to some extent, a function of the growth in the number of immigrants in Western countries. High levels of immigration into Europe and the United States at the high point of neoliberal capitalism, during the 1990s and the 2000s, have contributed to the growing political contentiousness of this issue. The refugee crisis of 2015 caused by the civil war in Syria was a key turning point. In Europe, immigration rose from 1 million per year in 2013 to 2.2 million in 2015. In its aftermath, immigration became a top political concern for most Europeans.[16] Numerous surveys have shown that many citizens in the United States and Europe believe that immigration has undermined conditions for ordinary people, as well as having

---

15    Aurelien Mondon and Aaron Winter, *Reactionary Democracy: How Racism and the Populist Far Right Became Mainstream* (London: Verso Books, 2020).

16    Daniel Stockemer, Arne Niemann, Doris Unger and Johanna Speyer, 'The "Refugee Crisis," Immigration Attitudes, and Euroscepticism', *International Migration Review* 54: 3 (2020), 883–912.

negative effects on security and national culture.[17] This perception is particularly strong among the rural blue-collar workers who have become a key electoral target for figures like Trump and Salvini.

It is true that, in recent years, immigration has declined and the coronavirus crisis has brought it to a temporary halt. Furthermore, according to the OECD 2020 Immigration Outlook, there are different signs international mobility will remain low in coming years as a consequence of 'weaker labour demand, persistent severe travel restrictions as well as the widespread use of teleworking among high-skilled workers and remote learning by students'.[18] However, population growth in Latin America and, especially, in sub-Saharan Africa, coupled with the effects of global warming in those regions, will ensure that, in the coming decades, immigration to the US and Europe will continue to be a major trend. Furthermore, it is delusional to think that, given that anti-immigration sentiment is nursed mostly by older people, it will ultimately disappear, as more open-minded later generations come to dominate. Right-wing xenophobia has demonstrated remarkable adaptability, and it can easily shift its target from newly arrived immigrants to well-established minority communities, cast in the role of the 'enemy within', and find ways to appeal also to people of more liberal leanings who may be alienated by overtly racist appeals.

## Immigration as Unifying Threat

Until the Great Recession of the 2010s, immigration was mostly perceived as a secondary issue, bound to appeal only to specific sections of the electorate – typically, the unemployed working class in areas with a high proportion of immigrants. But this question has now transcended the narrow confines of discussion on migration policies, quotas and integration. It has become a 'master issue' around which the right's protectionist discourse is organised, the lens through which the entire present social situation is read.

---

17   Phillip Connor and Jens Manuel Krogstad, 'Many worldwide oppose more migration–both into and out of their countries', *Pew Research* (2018).
18   OECD, *International Migration Outlook*, (OECD Publishing: 2020).

There is almost no social problem for which migrants and ethnic minorities are not blamed by right-wing populists. From unemployment to the erosion of public services, rising crime, the burden of high taxation and the perception of cultural decline – all these issues are now approached by the right in the ready-made language of the culture war on immigration. Crime is alleged to result from the fact that immigrants become foot-soldiers for criminal gangs. Unemployment is blamed on immigrants, who are denounced as a 'reserve army labour' who drive down wages by being willing to work for a pittance. Immigrants also stand accused of making native people feel like aliens in their own land, producing crises of identity and culture. Meanwhile, the deterioration of public services is put down to the 'swamping' of queues for public housing and welfare benefits by immigrants, rather than to cuts to public spending. Demographic crisis in the West is attributed to the politicians' preference for importing a docile labour force, rather than supporting native families' ability to have children. During the Covid-19 crisis, immigrants have also been accused by Trump and his allies of bringing the virus into the country, despite the fact that it was far more likely to be spread by frequent-flying managers and tourists. The immigrant is thus cast in the role of universal culprit, responsible for everything that is wrong with society. This figure has become the point of condensation of a wide array of fears and anxieties of the late neoliberal era: fears of economic decline, of identity loss, of demographic inundation, of multiplying threats to security.

Dominant explanations of anti-immigration sentiment argue that it is a cultural question in two ways. First, immigrants are often understood as a cultural threat, as agents who are bringing into the country customs, language, religion and attitudes seen as incompatible with the culture of 'indigenous' inhabitants. Nationalists have often argued that migrants endanger 'our way of life' and disrespect 'our values'. Marine Le Pen has attacked Muslims for offending against the French culture of secularism in the context of debates on the use of the veil in public spaces, while Viktor Orbán has presented them as a threat to Christianity.[19] Some nationalist leaders, such as

---

19   Shaun Walker, 'Orbán Deploys Christianity with a Twist to Tighten Grip in Hungary', *Guardian*, 14 July 2019.

Pim Fortuyn in the Netherlands, have even blamed Muslims for sexism and homophobia,[20] despite the nationalist right's long-standing opposition to gender equality. Second, anti-immigration sentiment is seen as a cultural question because it is an attitude to which citizens with low levels of education are deemed to be particularly susceptible.[21] But hatred towards immigrants is far from being simply a 'cultural' phenomenon.

What makes the immigrant such a perfect hate figure at moments when there is a crisis of national sovereignty is that this category represents the outsider par excellence: someone who, while inhabiting the territory of a given demos, does not share with it either lineage, culture or citizenship. In relation to a native community often fictitiously imagined as ethno-culturally uniform, the immigrant is seen as diminishing its homogeneity, and thus – so the argument runs – also its individuality and social cohesion.[22] If only there were no immigrants, the right suggests, the people would rediscover their fundamental unity, reclaim their authentic roots and overcome their frivolous internal conflicts. Indeed, there is some truth in this narrative. It has been repeatedly demonstrated that hate towards the outside can serve to defuse internal conflict and create a bogus sense of national unity. Matteo Salvini, for example – who, just a few years ago, was ranting against Neapolitans – has now, as one comic strip put it, managed to unite northern and southern Italians in their shared hatred of foreigners.

The role of immigrants as the quintessential Other in the 'exclusionary populism' of the right is particularly evident in the framing of immigrants and ethnic minorities as criminals posing a security threat.[23] In Italy, Salvini has often taken aim at 'Tunisian pushers' and 'Nigerian

20   Ruud Koopmans and Jasper Muis, 'The rise of right-wing populist Pim Fortuyn in the Netherlands: A discursive opportunity approach', *European Journal of Political Research* 48: 5 (2009), 642–64.

21   Daniel K. Pryce, 'US Citizens' Current Attitudes Toward Immigrants and Immigration: A Study from the General Social Survey', *Social Science Quarterly* 99: 4 (2018), 1467–83.

22   Nicholas De Genova, 'Rebordering "the People" Notes on Theorizing Populism', *South Atlantic Quarterly* 117: 2 (2018), 357–74.

23   Cas Mudde and Cristóbal Rovira Kaltwasser, 'Exclusionary vs. Inclusionary Populism: Comparing Contemporary Europe and Latin America', *Government and Opposition* 48: 2 (2013), 147–74.

prostitution rings',[24] associating particular ethnic groups with given criminal activities; in France, Le Pen has repeatedly branded ethnic-minority citizens living in the *banlieues* as 'scum' produced by immigration.[25] This propaganda has been boosted by a tabloid press in the hands of billionaire media moguls, which has strongly contributed to the stigmatisation of immigrants and ethnic minorities as inherently criminal. The disparagement of the immigrant population has in recent years been reinforced by the association of immigrants with terrorism. Since al-Qaeda burst into popular consciousness with a series of acts of terror, and especially in the wake of the mass slaughter perpetrated by ISIS, Muslim residents of Western countries have increasingly come under popular suspicion, while right-wing politicians have accused them of being a jihadist Fifth Column.[26]

It is often said that anti-migration sentiment aims at fuelling a war of the poor against the poor. Indeed, the priming of immigration reflects national-populists' duplicitous intention to gather popular support while at the same time deflecting economic elites (which they defend in spite of their supposed populism) from social anger and redistributive demands. Pitting the 'left-behind' working class against migrant workers, anti-migration discourse acts as an effective diversion tactic. But this ruse works because there are material interests anti-migration discourse can latch onto. Immigrants fill the most physically arduous and low-status jobs in the service precariat, as cleaners, care workers and shelf-fillers, as fruit-pickers, or in the informal economy. Due to their recent arrival, they are forced to climb their way up the social pyramid – an upward momentum that is naturally resented by those who feel exposed by the insecurity of their work.

Migrants are typically blamed both for 'stealing our jobs' and for being 'benefit scroungers'. The idea that immigrants steal employment opportunities has a long history on the populist right. In 1976, Jean-Pierre Stirbois, the strategist behind one of the first electoral

---

24    Marcello Maneri, ' "Vengono per delinquere": logiche e cicli di criminalizzazione dell'immigrazione', *La rivista delle politiche sociali* 2 (2019), 63–84.

25    Johannès Franck, 'Marine Le Pen met l'immigration au cœur de sa campagne des municipales', *Le Monde*, 7 March 2020.

26    Viktor Orbán has portrayed refugees from the Syrian civil war as potential terrorists, arguing in 2015 that 'all the terrorists are basically migrants'. Matthew Kaminski, 'All the Terrorists Are Migrants', *Politico*, 23 November 2015.

breakthroughs of the Front National, was already asserting: 'One million jobless are one million immigrants too many'. Today, this labour-protectionism is recycled in the representation of migrants as a 'reserve army of labour', as proposed by French New Right thinker Alain de Benoist and parroted by Italian far-right philosopher Diego Fusaro.[27] This theory was also touted by Boris Johnson, when he proclaimed that the reason corporations held wages down was that 'they have had access to unlimited pools of labour from other countries'.[28] The same narrative was also used against Polish construction workers and plumbers in the UK accused of undercutting wages during the Brexit campaign. There is lots of debate among scholars as to whether immigration exerts a downward pressure on wages.[29] In a deregulated labour market, it is easy to see how wage competition can pitch immigrants against natives in unskilled jobs. But attacking immigrants, forced to take any job, rather than the entrepreneurs exploiting them is a demonstration of cowardice and cruelty. The demand for 'local jobs for local people' goes hand in hand with what is described as 'welfare chauvinism', which wants to exclude immigrants considered as scroungers from access to benefits. This despite the fact that, far from constituting a 'welfare burden', migrants typically make a greater contribution to public coffers than they receive in benefits.[30]

The immigrant makes for an ideal sacrificial lamb, offered on the altar of the unholy nationalist alliance between sections of the working class, their bosses, provincial shopkeepers and well-paid technical professionals. For native blue-collar workers, blaming the current economic disarray on migrants allows them to validate themselves as part of the 'deserving working class' under threat from the informal economy. Opposition to immigrants assuages workers' fear of falling through the cracks of society, turning from respectable producers

27  Alain de Benoist, 'Immigration: The Reserve Army of Capital', transl. Tomislav Sunic, *Occidental Observer* 23 (2011); Diego Fusaro, *Storia e coscienza del precariato: servi e signori della globalizzazione*, (Milano: Bompiani, 2018).

28  Henry Zeffman, 'Brexit: Boris Johnson Takes Bid for Top Job to the Workers', *The Times*, 18 January 2019.

29  Martin Ruhs and Carlos Vargas-Silva, 'The Labour Market Effects of Immigration', *Migration Observatory* (2015).

30  Dorte Sindbjerg Martinsen and Gabriel Pons Rotger, 'The Fiscal Impact of EU Immigration on the Tax-Financed Welfare State: Testing the "Welfare Burden" Thesis', *European Union Politics* 18: 4 (2017), 620–39.

into a despicable underclass of 'takers'. From the perspective of managers, business owners and market professionals, the targeting of immigrants provides a means to channel popular anger downwards, thus diverting it from those at the top of the social pyramid. Furthermore, an intimidated migrant is much less likely to unionise, or defend his or her rights by other means, which makes for a conveniently docile employee.

Resentment towards immigrants is also related to fears of demographic substitution. The distress that besets many right-wing voters is that they are not only becoming economically superfluous, given that they depend on activities that are heavily exposed to international competition, but also that they will eventually be biologically replaced by more fertile foreigners. Across Western Europe and the United States, the birth rate has dropped to around 1.5 children – well below the global average. In his book *Whiteshift*, Eric Kaufmann argues that the white majorities of many Western societies are now realising that they will soon live in 'minority-majority' societies no longer dominated by the original ethnic 'stock'.[31] This fear of substitution is echoed in the language of 'invasion', or 'substitution' or even 'white genocide', used by the nationalist right. In May 2017, Matteo Salvini spoke darkly of an 'attempt to ethnically replace peoples with other peoples: it is simply an economic and commercial operation financed by people like Soros'.[32] Such claims evoke conspiracy theories wildly popular in alt-right online subcultures, such as the so-called Kalergi Plan, and the 'great replacement' proposed by French far-right author Renaud Camus. [33]

Much of the anti-immigration discourse of the right is reminiscent of fascism. But, despite its toxicity, its subtext is not the elimination of immigrants, but their control and exploitation. Consider, for example, the fact that Salvini was elected as senator in Rosarno, in Calabria, a location infested by the local 'Ndrangheta mafia. The town thrives on the exploitation of the cheap migrant workforce in agriculture; workers are sometimes paid as little as €2 per hour, and

31    Eric Kaufmann, *Whiteshift: Populism, Immigration and the Future of White Majorities* (London: Penguin, 2018).

32    Ansa, 'Salvini, fuorilegge Ong pagate da Soros', 2 May 2017.

33    Renaud Camus, *Le grand remplacement* (Paris: David Reinhar, 2015).

agricultural entrepreneurs who employ the migrant workforce over-whelmingly vote for Lega. Forcing immigrants into a subaltern position allows the lumpen-bourgeoisie that supports nationalist leaders to treat them like slaves and to pay both them and native workers miserly wages. In the US, the Immigration and Customs Enforcement (ICE), under the US Department of Homeland Security has deported hundreds of thousands of illegal migrants while spreading fear among millions of others, thus making them easier for rogue entrepreneurs to exploit.

Anti-immigration discourse is therefore fundamentally a discourse of demarcation that draws boundaries between an inside and an outside, between the native community and the migrants. This demarcation pushes the left onto uncomfortable terrain. Morally outraged by the toxic rhetoric of the right, the left is compelled to position itself as external to the 'threatened demos' and on the side of immigrants – who, unlike the local population, often have no right to vote, and therefore little power to shield themselves from such attacks.

This task of demarcation now encompasses architecture designed to restrain and control immigrants. The most famous example of this is Trump's pledge to build a wall on the border with Mexico, which provided the flagship policy of his 2016 campaign, but was repeatedly delayed by its huge price tag and the difficulty of acquiring the necessary land. Such barriers to migration also reveal the inconsistencies of nationalist discourse. As political philosopher Wendy Brown has argued, the chauvinistic politics of borders and the construction of new walls are not the expression of a triumphant national sovereignty.[34] They merely offer a powerful delusion of control over territory; a symbolic compensation for the loss of state power. Given that economic sovereignty has generally been weakened by global economic integration, coercion – over which the state still has a functioning monopoly – becomes the easiest way for politicians to advertise that they are still in control and able to protect the national community.

---

34   Wendy Brown, *Walled States, Waning Sovereignty* (Princeton, NJ: Princeton University Press, 2010).

Table 7.1   Elite enemies

|  | Cultural elite | Economic elite | Political elite |
|---|---|---|---|
| **Main antagonist** | *Populist right* | *Populist left* | *Populist centre* |
| **Examples** | Academics; journalists; people in showbusiness; NGOs; the creative class; scientists; doctors; news and digital media | The wealthy; entrepreneurs; bankers; brokers; landlords; managers and highly paid technicians/lawyers etc | Politicians; bureaucrats; civil servants; technocrats; supranational institutions; government consultants/experts |
| **Reasons for enmity** | A perceived betrayal of tradition and popular sentiments; imposition of cosmopolitan and liberal worldview | Exploitation of workers; tax avoidance; environmental degradation; interference with political decisions | Corruption; lack of transparency; laziness and wastefulness; distortion of the popular will; vote rigging |

## Soak the Rich

'Billionaires should not exist' – so proclaimed Bernie Sanders in September 2019, unveiling a proposal for a wealth tax on the richest Americans. In February 2020, he returned to the issue after his primary win in New Hampshire: 'We're taking on billionaires and we're taking on candidates funded by billionaires.' Sanders's enmity towards the super-rich, which largely defined his 2016 and 2020 presidential campaign runs, is the manifestation of a strong anti-plutocratic discourse that has become one of the defining characteristics of the socialist left that has emerged out of the populist moment. Where attacks against migrants take aim at the underclass, the rich are one of three elite or 'overclass' enemies that have been targeted by populist movements, the others being the political class and the intelligentsia (see Table 7.1.). Leaders like Jeremy Corbyn, Jean-Luc Mélenchon, Pablo Iglesias and Alexandria Ocasio-Cortez have often taken aim at the wealthy: Jeff Bezos, Mark Zuckerberg, Elon Musk and the Koch brothers in the United States; Philip Green and Richard Branson in the UK; Bernard Arnault in France; the Benetton family in Italy; and Amancio Ortega in Spain – all have become familiar targets.

This 'soak the rich' sentiment that re-emerged in the aftermath of the 2008 crisis has only intensified in recent years. In January 2019, the new firebrand Democratic congresswoman Alexandria Ocasio-Cortez proposed a top tax rate of 70 per cent, for those earning more than US$3 million, as one way of combating social inequality. The proposal attracted widespread media criticism, but surveys showed it commanded the support of a large majority of Americans, and even of Republican voters.[35] Dan Riffle, a senior counsel and policy adviser to AOC, created an uproar in the mainstream media in July 2019 when he coined the slogan 'Every Billionaire Is a Policy Failure'. He explained: 'The bigger Jeff Bezos and Bill Gates's slices of the pie are, the smaller everybody else's are going to be.'[36] In France, Jean-Luc Mélenchon has often fulminated against the super-rich, accusing them of narcissism and irresponsibility.[37] In June 2019 he said, 'the rich are too expensive', and suggested it was 'time for the rich to be altruistic'.[38] A propaganda videogame titled *Fiscal Kombat* launched during the 2017 campaign featured Mélenchon shaking money out of the deep pockets of rich entrepreneurs and financiers involved in tax avoidance.[39]

Pablo Iglesias has regularly taken aim at the Spanish rich, including Inditex owner Amancio Ortega who, for a brief time in 2015, was the richest person in the world, when his net worth peaked at $80 billion. He has also aimed his fire at the owner of the retail chain Mercadona, Juan Roig, and the owner of clothing company Mango, Isak Andic. In May 2020, during the Covid-19 crisis, Iglesias proposed a solidarity tax on the rich – a 2 per cent levy on net fortunes of €1 million or higher, progressively rising to 2.5 per cent on €10 million, 3 per cent on €50 million, and 3.5 per cent on €100 million, which was eventually approved in a watered-down version. He appealed to the 'fiscal patriotism' of the rich, adding that he was convinced that 'the majority of those with wealth above 1 million euros will wish to show solidarity with their

---

35    Eric Levitz, 'Poll: Majority Backs AOC's 70 Percent Top Marginal Tax Rate', *New York Magazine*, 15 January 2019.

36    Dylan Matthews, 'AOC's Policy Adviser Makes the Case for Abolishing Billionaires', *Vox*, 9 July 2019.

37    Jean-Luc Melénchon, 'Le president de riches', 9 November 2017, at melenchon.fr. My translation.

38    Jean-Luc Melénchon, 'Les riches coutent trop cher', at melenchon.fr.

39    fiscalkombat.eu. My translation.

compatriots'.[40] Similarly, during his tenure as Labour leader in the UK, Jeremy Corbyn often called for a redistribution of wealth and was accused by the press of 'demonising the rich'.[41] As *New Statesman* economic commentator Grace Blakeley noted, 'After decades of stagnation caused by the financial crisis, the financial elite centred in the City of London is the natural villain in any leftist populist narrative'.[42]

These attacks reflect a profound shift in public opinion at the time of the Great Recoil: the fattening of the wealthy elites and the huge inequalities that have resulted have attracted widespread popular outrage. This sentiment was perhaps best captured by Todd Phillips's film *Joker*, which depicts Gotham City's corrupt moneyed elites, attacked by protestors using the blunt slogan 'Kill the Rich', inspired by the bloody deeds of Arthur Fleck – the failed stand-up comedian who becomes the Joker. The reason why the film struck a chord in the public imagination and became an icon of protest was its unmasking of the callousness of inequality. Like other recent films, such as the Korean *Parasite* and the Spanish *The Platform*, it reflects growing popular unease at the concentration of wealth. Some enlightened members of the billionaire class, such as Warren Buffett, have long admitted the enormous scale of the imbalance in wealth, famously saying in 2006: 'There's class warfare, all right, but it's my class, the rich class, that's making war, and we're winning'.[43] In recent years skyrocketing inequality has become ever more an object of embarrassment. It even started to find its way onto the stage at the annual World Economic Forum in Davos, where, in 2019, Dutch economic historian Rutger Bregman ridiculed regular Davos-attendees, such as the singer Bono, for supporting what he termed 'bullshit' philanthropy schemes, claiming that the only solution to inequality was taxation. In March 2019, registering this shift in public opinion, a *Washington Post* article asked: 'Why does everybody suddenly hate billionaires?'[44]

40   Inés Santaeulalia, 'Iglesias dice que las grandes fortunas están "deseando" hacer un ejercicio de "patriotismo fiscal" ', *El País*, 14 May 2020. My translation.
41   Madison Marriage, 'Why the UK's Uber-wealthy Voters Fear a Corbyn-Led Government', *Financial Times*, 6 October 2018.
42   Grace Blakeley, *Stolen: How to Save the World from Financialisation* (London: Repeater, 2019), p. 231.
43   Ben Stein, 'In Class Warfare, Guess Which Class Is Winning', *New York Times*, 26 November 2006.
44   Roxanne Roberts, 'Why Does Everybody Suddenly Hate Billionaires? Because They've Made It Easy', *Washington Post*, 13 March 2019.

The growing resentment towards the rich reflects the grotesque enrichment of the wealthy. In the US, almost the entire burden of the 2008 financial crisis fell on workers and the middle class, while growth was siphoned off to affluent families.[45] In the three years after the crisis, the top 1 per cent captured 91 per cent of all real income. The same cohort saw a 34.7 per cent growth in income, while the bottom 99 per cent saw a miserly 0.8 per cent gain.[46] While wages remained stagnant, and residential real estate prices dropped, the stock market ballooned, feeding shareholder dividends. This injustice is well represented by the growing gap between CEO and average worker compensation. In 2019, the ratio between the two was 320 according to a report by the Economic Policy Institute, well above pre-2008 levels.[47] It was estimated that the average Amazon worker would need to work for eight weeks to earn the same money Bezos makes in a second.[48]

This outrageous gap in income and wealth explains why taxation has become the chief flashpoint in this fight against the wealthy. Public anger has focused on tax-avoidance practices and on the tax havens through which the wealthy manage to avoid paying their dues. While, since the 1980s, financial orthodoxy has decreed a reduction in progressive taxation – in accordance with the so-called Laffer curve, purporting to show that more government revenue is generated by lower tax regimes – a fiscal revolt has spread more recently throughout the middle classes. Demands are now frequently made to increase taxation on billionaire wealth and executive compensation in order to reverse inequality and fund public services. Economists including Joseph Stiglitz and Paul Krugman have often attacked the reluctance

---

45   Adam Tooze, *Crashed: How a Decade of Financial Crises Changed the World*, (London: Penguin, 2018).

46   Emmanuel Saez, 'Striking It Richer: The Evolution of Top Incomes in the United States (Updated with 2012 Preliminary Estimates)' (Berkeley: University of California, Department of Economics, 2013).

47   Lawrence Mishel and Jori Kandra, 'CEO Compensation Surged 14% in 2019 to $21.3 million', *Economic Policy Institute*, 18 August 2020: 'CEO compensation grew 105.1% from 2009 to 2019, the period capturing the recovery from the Great Recession; in that period granted CEO compensation grew 35.7%. In contrast, typical workers in these large firms saw their average annual compensation grow by just 7.6% over the last 10 years.'

48   Kate Ng, 'It Takes Eight Weeks for an Amazon Warehouse Worker to Earn What Jeff Bezos Makes in a Second, Says Union', *Independent*, 21 December 2020.

of the rich to pay taxes, and denounced their overweening influence on politics, which allows them to avoid taxation.[49] Movements of the early 2010s such as UK Uncut, which have taken aim at the tax-evasion activities of large firms and wealthy individuals have highlighted the unfairness of a system in which workers have to pay while the rich can simply decide not to. Outrage at this state of affairs has only grown in recent years. In 2018, it was reported that pop singer Ed Sheeran had paid more tax in the UK than online retail giant Amazon, thanks to the tax-accounting tricks used by Bezos's company.[50] In the European Union, tax-haven countries such as the Netherlands, Luxembourg and Ireland have become the target of growing criticism, in particular during the negotiations over the EU recovery fund in July 2020, when the Dutch government was accused of unjustifiably taking the moral high ground.[51]

The degree to which inequality is perceived as unjust is always a function of the general conditions of society and the number of people who enjoy decent levels of income and wealth. During the 1990s and early 2000s, the period of steady economic growth under neoliberalism, the gospel of 'trickle-down' economics and entrepreneurialism may have sounded somewhat plausible. Amid the current stagnation and economic contraction, however, extreme disparities in wealth have come to be perceived more widely as objectionable.[52] The growing gulf between the large majority, whose economic prospects are in decline, and the minority of the rich and wealthy, whose fortunes continue to grow unimpeded, has resulted in a growing perception of the rich as a threat, as a category to be protected from, rather than a condition any ordinary person can realistically aspire to.

49   Joseph E. Stiglitz, *The Price of Inequality: How Today's Divided Society Endangers Our Future* (New York: W.W. Norton, 2012); Paul Krugman, *Arguing with Zombies: Economics, Politics, and the Fight for a Better Future* (New York: W. W. Norton, 2020).

50   Georgina Littlejohn, 'Ed Sheeran Paid More in Tax Last Year Than Both Starbucks and Amazon', *Inews*, 10 October 2018.

51   Toby Sterling, 'Mr. No, No, No – Why Dutch PM Rutte Plays Role of EU Bogeyman', *Reuters*, 19 July 2020.

52   'Majority Say Wealthy Americans, Corporations Taxed Too Little', *Gallup*, 19 April 2017, at news.gallup.com.

## Capitalist Vampires

The targeting of the rich by the socialist left presupposes a radically different 'topology of enmity' from the one mobilised by the right. Where the right directs anger towards those at the bottom of the socio-economic ladder – at the underclass and at immigrants in particular – the left does the opposite. Unlike immigrants, whom the right frames as aliens who have forced their way into the community from the outside, the rich are portrayed by the left more like agents who exist within and above the demos, relentlessly feeding on its labour. They are seen as predatory forces against which society has to be protected, and oligarchs, who by dint of their wealth are stealing away our democracy and depriving people of control.

At first sight, the framing of the rich as enemies of the people may not seem too dissimilar from the traditional anti-capitalist rhetoric that has long been a mainstay of the radical left. 'Eat the rich' – a slogan still popular among anti-capitalists – harks back to Jean-Jacques Rousseau, who said that, when the poor have nothing to eat, they end up eating the rich. The main distinctive aspect of the contemporary populist framing of the rich, compared with the orthodox Marxist view of the capitalist as 'merely capital personified', lies in the moralistic framing of the issue.[53] Rich people are referred to today using terms that imply strong moral condemnation: the banksters (a term that became popular in the aftermath of the 2008 crash), the filthy rich, or the mafia capitalists. This view of the rich as criminals which ordinary citizens need to be protected from was exemplified by Bernie Sanders's claim, in the aftermath of the 2008 crash, that 'what Wall Street and credit card companies are doing is really not much different from what gangsters and loan sharks do who make predatory loans'.[54] Capitalists are sometimes even depicted as vultures or bloodsuckers – people belonging to a different species. Peter Thiel and members of the 'PayPal Mafia', according to a paranoid trope, are injecting themselves with young people's blood as part of a life-extension therapy.

The rich are represented as people who have placed themselves morally beyond the pale of society, deserting fundamental duties

---

53   Karl Marx, *Capital: Volume III* (London: Penguin, 1992), p. 558.
54   Bernie Sanders, 'Stop Wall Street Loan-Sharking', *The Hill*, 16 March 2009.

towards their fellow human beings. While owing their disproportionate wealth to everyone's efforts, they do all they can to avoid taxation, accumulating financial assets thanks to quantitative easing and government subsidies. In popular online memes, the rich are pictured sipping cocktails on palm-lined beaches in the Bahamas and the Cayman Islands, or enjoying life on their yachts and golf courses, removed from the crowds of ordinary people to whom they pay paltry wages. This arrogance is made all the more intolerable by the fact that the rich are a very tiny, yet incredibly powerful, minority, as popularised by Occupy Wall Street's references to the super-rich 1 per cent. In October 2018, the Anticapitalistas minority current within Podemos launched a campaign against the rich, arguing that they were 'the only dangerous minority'. Ironically, the status of the rich as a minority, however peculiar, was used by the liberal press to argue that the socialist left was just as intolerant as the nationalist right, only targeting the rich instead of immigrants – as if xenophobia had its natural counterpart in a new mysterious illness known as 'plutophobia'.

Hatred for the rich plays a similar unifying role to the one performed by the immigrant as the Other of the nationalist social bloc. It is the pivot of a class alliance comprising the service precariat and the downwardly mobile urban middle class, united in their hatred of the capitalist class.

The service precariat has good reasons to hate the rich when they compare their own meagre hourly wages with the vast incomes and wealth of the affluent class. Furthermore, it is the workforce that must cater to the narcissistic desires of the rich – serving their wine and expensive meals, cleaning their offices, taking care of their health. As in Bong Joon Ho's film *Parasite*, direct contact of the lower classes with the rich – experience of their obtuseness, cruelty and arrogance – only enhances hostility towards them. However, the transformation of the experience of workers in the time of the 'gig economy' seems to pose a serious paradox for antagonism in the workplace. In digital capitalism, the relations of production tend to be impersonal, and often mediated by an app – hence the expression 'Your boss is an algorithm', used to refer to the way in which Amazon workers and Uber drivers take their orders from software. Behind the software, however, there is an organisation, and real people who reap the benefits of exploitation. Besides algorithms, workers in the gig economy often interact with various corporate functionaries who act as supervisors and local enforcers. One fictional example is offered by the character of Maloney in Ken Loach's *Sorry We Missed You*, who constantly shouts orders such as, 'Let's get the cardboard off the concrete!' He sees himself as a worker, someone toiling as hard as anybody else; yet he is complicit in the vicious profit-driven exploitation of the people working for him. Low-level agents of exploitation like Maloney offer the opportunity to visualise the enemy in a position where he does not appear unreachable, and thus untouchable. The new middle class also bears many grudges against the rich, whose reluctance to pay taxes they themselves are forced to pay and whose squeezing of labour costs are seen as intolerable injustices. Furthermore, it is outraged at the way the concentration of wealth in the hands of a few people, as well as the ability of the rich to monopolise the media and lobby politicians to exert enormous influence on decisions that affect the living conditions of ordinary people.

The right is not entirely foreign to such attacks on the rich. On various occasions, it has tried to present itself as an enemy of global finance, to support its claim to be on the side of workers. A privileged target of attack in Europe has been the Hungarian-American financier George Soros – a major funder of progressive causes particularly hated by alt-right supporters for his Jewish identity, and represented in online memes as a lizard overlord engaged in blood libel and child abuse. Needless to say, this very narrow attack against one member of the international financial elite is not a stand against the class of the rich as such. This discourse corresponds to the classic form of 'status quo anti-capitalism' that, as Poulantzas noted, has often been historically mobilised by the far right – one that attempts to offer some reassurance to the middle and lower tiers of the bourgeoisie that they will be protected against the predations of big capital, and often dabbles in anti Semitic motives.[55]

The right cannot however fully claim ownership of anti-rich sentiment. First, it benefits from those upper middle-class sections which have moved from supporting the neoliberal centre to favouring

---

55  Nicos Poulantzas, *Fascism and Dictatorship: The Third International and the Problem of Fascism* (London: Verso, 2019), p. 242.

nationalists.[56] Furthermore, its political personnel, beginning with Donald Trump himself, are part and parcel of these strata, to the point where right-wing populism has sometimes been described as 'pluto-populism'.[57] Figures like Steve Bannon may well claim that Trump's Republican Party is a workers' party; but they can hardly shed the impression left by the fact that so many of its senior functionaries are former Goldman Sachs employees. Finally, the nationalist right's record in government has demonstrated where its interests really lie. Trump's government cut taxes for corporations and the wealthy, but failed to pass basic measures that might have won working-class support, such as an infrastructure bill, which would have been widely popular among trade unions. These contradictions between, on one hand, the right's moralistic anti-capitalism and bogus 'workerist' discourse and, on the other, its practical alliance with the super-rich, betray a weak link in its electoral coalition. This presents an opportunity for the left to expose the fraudulent deal offered to workers by nationalists.

## Down with the Establishment

Besides the rich, two other elite groups feature prominently in contemporary politics: the political class and the intelligentsia. The political class, which is deemed to have deprived ordinary people of democratic control, has frequently ended up in the crosshairs of populist movements. Adopting the term 'caste' to attack the corrupt political class, the Five Star Movement has been the most explicit in pursuing this motive.[58] It has accused politicians of seeing politics as a career that offers an opportunity to pilfer public resources and highlighted the need for public probity. Honesty (onestà) has long been the Five Star Movement's most repeated catchword. This attitude reflects what has been described as an anti-politics sentiment, which reflects the deep-seated popular

---

56    Michela Tindera, 'Here Are the Billionaires Backing Donald Trump's Campaign', Forbes, 17 April 2020.

57    Martin Wolf, 'Trump's Pluto-Populism Laid Bare', Financial Times, 2 May 2017.

58    John Foot, 'Beppe Grillo: A Comedian to Be Taken Seriously', Guardian, 30 October 2012.

resentment and suspicion of many citizens towards the political class, as signalled by approval ratings for politicians and institutions that stand at historical lows.[59]

The left has partly appropriated this anti-establishment narrative in the context of attacks against economic injustice. Books such as Owen Jones's *The Establishment* have homed in on the alliance between the business class and the political class, while new parties and leaders have harshly criticised the careerist behaviour of politicians of the neoliberal centre.[60] Podemos has adopted the Five Star Movement's jargon of 'the caste', and subsequently the term 'plot' (*trama*) to denounce the entanglement of political and economic interests. Despite their long service as career politicians, Jean-Luc Mélenchon, Jeremy Corbyn and Bernie Sanders have often condemned the political class and its unwillingness to listen to citizens' demands, while casting themselves as servants of the public interest, new tribunes of the people.

On the right, Donald Trump has made this anti-elite spirit a key component of his rhetoric. In the 2016 election, he challenged the establishment of the Republican Party, starting with the Bush family – in particular, former Florida governor Jeb Bush – and came out victorious. During his term as president, he promised to 'drain the swamp' of Washington in order to fix problems in the federal government. He alluded darkly to obscure forces both within and around the White House who were hindering his agenda, and lent support to conspiracy theories such as those circulated by QAnon. In Italy, Matteo Salvini, a career politician who became active at the age of twenty, has cleverly adopted the Five Star Movement's tirades against the political class. He has often ranted against the *governo delle poltrone* – literally the 'government of armchairs' – to denounce the obsession of the Five Star Movement and Italian Democratic Party with staying in power above all else. In the UK, Boris Johnson turned the 2019 general election into a 'people vs. parliament' contest, while tirades against experts by Leave supporters during the Brexit campaign had a similar

---

59   Éric Bélanger, 'Political Trust and Voting Behaviour', in Sonja Zmerli and Tom W. G. Van der Meer, *Handbook on Political Trust* (Cheltenham: Edward Elgar, 2017).

60   Owen Jones, *The Establishment: And How They Get Away with It* (New York: Melville House, 2015).

anti-politics orientation, betokening a deep suspicion of political institutions.[61]

Attacks on the political class are mirrored by tirades against the cultural elites – the 'professors', intellectuals and activists who are seen as being out of touch with ordinary people. The right has often denounced the left as avatars of 'radical chic', the 'metropolitan left', or out-of-touch intellectuals. Intellectuals are represented as condescending figures peddling a dangerous mix of 'cultural Marxism', derived from the authors of the Frankfurt School, and queer politics that is corrupting the demos, destroying traditional culture and contributing to low fertility rates. Furthermore, the intelligentsia is lambasted for the fact that its concern for immigrants apparently exceeds its sympathy for fellow citizens. What intellectuals stand accused of, in other words, is a mixture of sanctimony, lack of patriotism, hypocrisy and sheer venality – since they are sometimes even charged with being agents of a conspiracy of global finance. During the coronavirus crisis, this attitude has been compounded by aspersions aimed at doctors, virologists and epidemiologists, accused by groups on the far right of creating an atmosphere of excessive fear and paternalism, and of being in cahoots with pharmaceutical corporations. This narrative is particularly effective due to the resentment large sections of the working class harbour towards the intellectual elites, which they sometimes see as an even more exclusive category than the rich.[62]

The success of anti-politics discourse reflects a perception that the state's malfunctions are a consequence not of austerity policies and cuts to public spending, but of politicians' habit of diverting public funds for their own personal use – something that is particularly intolerable for citizens who are concerned about high taxation and rely heavily on shrinking public services. While political corruption is a major problem, unremitting criticism of politics and politicians risks reinforcing the neoliberal view of the state as inherently wasteful while detracting attention from corporate corruption. Furthermore,

---

61   George Parker and Laura Hughes, 'Boris Johnson Lays Ground for "People Vs Parliament", Election', *Financial Times*, 26 September 2019.

62   David Graeber, *Revolutions in Reverse* (London: Minor Compositions, 2011), p. 8.

measures informed by this perspective paradoxically risk exacerbating the corruptibility of the political class. For example, the Five Star Movement's battle against the power of money in politics has led to the withdrawal of public financing for political parties, thus making politicians heavily reliant on rich donors, while the reduction in the number of MPs promoted by the movement founded by Grillo has been strongly criticised for its weakening of parliament. Finally, the attitude of disdain towards the political class can lead to the opposite of the ethic of virtue and responsibility recommended by republicanism, enabling citizens to imagine themselves as blameless in comparison with irredeemable politicians. Rather than a recuperation of democratic control, the battle against the political elites risks turning into a nihilist stance that does little to move the balance of power in favour of ordinary citizens.

Having reconstructed the various enmities that organise the battlefield of contemporary politics, we can now assess how effective they have been in mobilising public opinion. The general public's perception is that the nationalist right has been far more effective than the socialist left in its construction of an enemy against which it is then able to frame disparate demands, fears and grievances. In *Whiteshift*, Eric Kaufmann asks, 'Why are right-wing populists doing better than left-wing ones?' and 'Why did the migration crisis boost populist-right numbers sharply while the economic crisis had no overall effect?'[63] Indeed, given the depth of the economic crisis and the skyrocketing of inequality, the fact that the economic populism of the socialist left, with its sharp critique of the rich, seems to have been less effective that the right's cultural populism raises serious questions of both rhetoric and strategy. For Kaufmann, as well as for Roger Eatwell and Matthew Goodwin, the explanation is simple: the left is not taking seriously the issue of immigration.[64] But the reasons for socialists' inability to prevail discursively over their right-wing rivals run far deeper.

Under neoliberalism, citizens have been trained to admire the

63  Eric Kaufmann, *Whiteshift: Populism, Immigration and the Future of White Majorities* (London: Penguin, 2018), p. 21.
64  Roger Eatwell and Matthew Goodwin, *National Populism: The Revolt Against Liberal Democracy* (London: Penguin, 2018), pp. 162–3.

economically successful elite above them while despising those below. Xenophobia grounded in contempt for the weak has become the natural accompaniment of possessive individualism. Furthermore, neoliberal common sense has taught us that being rich is good – that we should imitate celebrities and overachievers and envy their unique lifestyles, while detesting the poor. This situation is reminiscent of the plot of the 2019 film *The Platform*, in which prisoners admire those living above them and treat those living on lower floors as undeserving takers, over-looking the fact that they may soon find themselves condemned to those lower floors. Moreover, immigrants – and ethnic minorities – make for an effective enemy because they can often be easily identified by the colour of their skin, their dress, or their accent. They are visible on the streets, on public transport and in surgeries, hospitals and workplaces; people living in working-class neighbourhoods have daily encounters with them, sometimes fractious.

Conversely, rich people are not a part of most people's everyday life experience. They are mostly encountered in an indirect, medi-ated form, because of both their numerical scarcity and the fact that they live in wealthy, often gated neighbourhoods, while jetting around the world using their own private means of transport. This means that the popular image of the rich is heavily shaped by TV and the press, which often present them in a highly favourable light. This makes for a radically different scenario compared to the one preva-lent at the height of the workers' movement in the West. Industrial capitalists were directly experienced on the shop floor by workers, and the hostility towards them could be more easily personalised. In the dispersed and externalised workplace – especially in the manu-facturing sector – the boss is either invisible or not perceived as the person in control, but rather as a mere relay of global forces – and sometimes even as a victim of the system. By globalising production and dislocating the economy from society, neoliberal externalisation has also displaced the visceral antagonisms that developed around the workplace.

In response to these challenges, the left needs to consider its targets carefully in order to work out how to make its representation of social conflict more compelling and better grounded in everyday experience. It needs to find ways in which the enmity now being directed at specific individuals among the super-rich can be rendered more structural

– aimed at the system stacked in favour of the corporations that support them. Furthermore, it needs to realise that workers often suspect intellectuals as much as entrepreneurs and fear that socialism, rather than bringing liberation, will merely mean a shift from the dominance of the latter to control by the former. Only by constructing a discourse in which the fight against the economic oligarchy yields both greater economic protection and more democratic control will it be possible to overcome these suspicions.

# 8

# The Post-pandemic State

We live in a time in which the return of big government is invoked as the means to deal with multiple crises – from the 'state of exception' and emergency decrees during the Covid lockdowns to gigantic stimulus plans to resuscitate an ailing economy, from the successful management of the pandemic by the Chinese government and other East Asian countries that have historically embraced developmental statism to discussions about the need for an activist state to deal with climate change, state interventionism is coming back with a vengeance. As *Foreign Policy* declared in March 2020: 'We are all statists now.'[1] Similarly, in the *Financial Times* Janan Ganesh wrote: 'The terms of political discourse have moved unmistakably in favour of government over just a few weeks. We are living through a reputational comeback for what conservatives have disdained as the "administrative state".'[2] While, at the height of the neoliberal era, the consensus view was that the state was wasteful, and that government intervention should be minimal, today even free market centrists are forced to make ideological concessions on the issue. This trend crucially affects the relationship between the state and the economy. As argued by

---

1  James Crabtree, Robert D. Kaplan, Robert Muggah et al., 'The Future of the State', *Foreign Policy*, 16 May 2020.

2  Janan Ganesh, 'Coronavirus and the Comeback of the Administrative State', *Financial Times*, 11 March 2020.

Grace Blakeley, the present scenario increasingly resembles the condition described by Lenin as 'state monopoly capitalism', a regime under
which government and corporations, far from being independent, are
increasingly fused together.[3] In a time of Bidenomics and resurgent
keynesianism, 'the challenge we face is not agitating for more state
intervention'; rather 'we must concern ourselves with how state power
is being used – and who is wielding it'.[4] While post-neoliberal neo-
statism seems to offer an opening for socialist politics, the present
condition is best conceived as a new political and ideological battle-
ground over which the nationalist right and socialist left are fighting to
define the post-neoliberal world.

Radically diverging narratives describing the direction and purpose
of the post-pandemic state are emerging at opposite ends of the political spectrum. The national populism of the 2010s already had a statist
component. Most notably, the statist turn on the right has taken the
form of a new 'authoritarian statism', to use Poulantzas's phrase, which
emphasises the state's coercive and disciplinary function and the
repression of popular struggles.[5] This authoritarian statism is exemplified by the way the nationalist right has used the state to attack minorities, migrants and dissidents – something that became vividly apparent in the US with the 2020 Black Lives Matter protests, when heavily
armed police were deployed in many cities to break the demonstrations. In Italy, Matteo Salvini often wore shirts sporting police force
insignia in public to express his support for law enforcement officers
and vowed in his brief period as minister of the interior to restore
security to Italy by any means. In June 2018, for example, he stopped
an NGO ship rescuing migrants at sea, proclaiming: 'The state is going
back to being the state.'[6]

On the economic front, the nationalist right has done away selectively with some of the anti-statist tenets that were prevalent in the
neoliberal era. It has embraced a 'proprietarian protectionism',
focused on defending local capital from international competition,
so as to buttress the existing system of property. Besides partly

---

3   Blakeley, *The Corona Crash*, p. 33.
4   Ibid., p. 35
5   Nicos Poulantzas, *State, Power, Socialism* (London: Verso, 2000).
6   'Migranti, Salvini: '"Finita la pacchia. Non saranno Ong straniere a decidere chi
sbarca in Italia" ', YouTube.

abandoning fiscal conservatism, it has turned its back on the neoliberal free-trade consensus that, until recently, overwhelmingly dominated the conservative camp. Starting in 2018, Donald Trump has pursued a fierce trade war with China, accusing its main trading partner of unfair commercial practices. In the UK, Boris Johnson stressed that Brexit offered the opportunity for a new era of state economic interventionism.

The left's vision of the interventionist state is informed by a social protectivism advocating a rejuvenation of Keynesian ideas and social-democratic priorities. Progressives have demanded a recuperation and extension of the welfare state, a revision of trade treaties, and greater latitude in state aid for strategic firms, to avoid a repetition of the humiliating scene of countries scrambling for scarce medical supplies and vaccines on the international market. Furthermore, the left has viewed the pandemic as an opportunity to shift the balance of the economy towards public ownership and revive a more proactive industrial policy, along the lines of the 'entrepreneurial state' discussed by Mariana Mazzucato, and to expand access to health and education, while giving workers a say in how their companies are run.[7] This progressive protectivist vision projects an egalitarian state shielding society from economic exposure and discrimination; it combines a reassertion of effective state action with a strengthening of democratic control over its decisions.

This change in discourse cutting across the political spectrum reflects a radical transformation in the popular perception of politics. In a world ensnared by geopolitical chaos and economic decline, citizens are looking to the state as a possible source of stability and security. Resurrecting the power of the state appears as the necessary answer to the political dilemmas of the Great Recoil: the neoliberal rollback of the state is now seen as the root cause of our societal crises. To return to the Platonic metaphor of the ship of state, many leaders have come to see the neoliberal state as a rudderless vessel, incapable of weathering coming global storms. The issue that divides them is what new course should be set by the ship of state.

---

7    Mariana Mazzucato, *The Entrepreneurial State: Debunking Public vs. Private Sector Myths* (London: Anthem, 2013).

## The State Is Back

The current transformation in perceptions of the state stems from a moment of collective realisation. A number of recent events have produced a 'demonstration effect' illustrating the continuing power and necessity of government. The 2020 coronavirus emergency called for a level of state mobilisation not seen in most countries since the end of World War II. Political leaders the world over have passed emergency measures, often by decree and through the partial suspension of parliamentary prerogatives. Police forces, and sometimes the army, have been mobilised to guarantee observance of quarantines and to transport medical materials, and even coffins containing the bodies of victims of Covid-19. Governments have had to build emergency hospitals, taking inspiration from those built at lightning speed in China to treat the ill, to roll out mass testing programmes to identify those infected, including asymptomatic patients, and to initiate massive vaccination campaigns, while hiring thousands of extra doctors and nurses.

Nevertheless, the coronavirus pandemic is only the culmination of a series of crises that have contributed to a reassertion of the role of the state as a pillar of collective welfare and survival. The 2008 financial crisis already highlighted the dishonest ideological view that markets are capable of solving every societal problem unhindered by government. The pretence that the market was independent from the state ground to a halt on the day the Wall Street banks had to be bailed out by tax payers. Financial companies, such as Royal Bank of Scotland, HSBC and Lloyds in the UK, and AIG, Fannie Mae and Freddie Mac in the United States were exposed as giants with feet of clay whose life or death depended on the decisions of government. This demonstration of the state's role in guaranteeing the conditions for market survival exposed the fact that markets can only be efficient when shielded by active patronage of the state.[8] Furthermore, it indirectly revealed the state's complicity in corporate power and a distribution of wealth and income skewed in favour of the rich, putting the phrase 'socialism for the rich' back into circulation.

---

8   Tooze, *Crashed*. See also Chapter 2, above.

The coronavirus crisis and its disastrous management in many Western countries has only reinforced these lessons, emphasising the need for effective government action. The sudden halt to economic activity pushed many companies to the brink of bankruptcy, and unemployment hit the double digits almost immediately. Governments offered lines of credit to companies and benefits to workers in order to prevent the economy from collapsing, in the largest coordinated government stimulus since the Great Depression. While, in 2008, states devoted their resources to saving banks, in 2020 they were forced to bail out the entire economic system. As Julian Borger noted in the *Guardian*, the neoliberal suspicion of the state, expressed in Ronald Reagan's famous assertion, 'The nine most terrifying words in the English language are: I'm from the government and I'm here to help', seemed to have come into head-on conflict with contemporary reality.[9]

Emergency statism has also been partly accepted by the neoliberal centre. Policy-makers in the US, and to a lesser extent in the EU, have shelved the fiscal conservatism of the neoliberal era, approving massive stimulus programmes that strongly increase public investment and social transfers. Nevertheless, even in such circumstances, the main recipients of government largesse have continued to be private corporations, to which generous subsidies and financial arrangements have been offered. In fact, the return of statism does not guarantee a turn towards progressive social policies. As argued by Grace Blakeley, stimulus programmes were used first and foremost to protect big firms and to give handouts to the capitalist class in a repetition of what happened in 2008.[10] At a symbolic level, the positive effect of the state's response to the pandemic has been that many have come to realise that much of people's livelihood is based on the provision of public services including healthcare, state education and social welfare, and that ultimately without good public services the national economy and private companies suffer.

Massive state intervention is also required to deal with the titanic environmental challenges that lie ahead. Some activists have discussed

---

9    Julian Borger, 'The State We're In: Will the Pandemic Revolutionize Government', *Guardian*, 26 April 2020.
10    Blakeley, *Corona Crash*, pp. 16–17

the need for a 'climate Leviathan' to hasten a post-carbon transition.[11] The rapid cuts in emissions, massive climate change adaptation and transformations of energy infrastructure that are needed in order to avoid the most catastrophic climate change scenarios can be achieved only under the aegis of a daring interventionist state. The domino effect involving overlapping economic, environmental and health crises is making citizens aware of the central role of government in shaping our individual and collective destinies, for both good or ill, as well as high-lighting how some of the injustices of the present system are taking place on the watch of the nation-states. A reality that was difficult to acknowledge in the 1990s and 2000s, in a time of economic growth and rampant consumerism, has become incontrovertible after a decade of austerity that has resulted in economic chaos and geopolitical turmoil. Post-war social-democratic statism strove to overcome fascist and communist statism while keeping inequality at bay. Protective statism is needed today in order to defeat the threat from the nationalist right and restore security in society.

While moving away from neoliberal laissez-faire, we should be careful not to fall into the opposite trap of statolatry – the worship of the state as an infallible actor. Hard-earned lessons from the twentieth century about the possible totalitarian tendencies of stat-ist regimes should not be overlooked. The history of the states of the former Soviet Bloc provides a reminder of the risk of wholly subordinating society to the state. Furthermore, statism was as much an attribute of fascism as of communism. Fascists accompa-nied strong state intervention and industrial policy with a strenu-ous defence of private financial interests and major capitalist firms; meanwhile, workers saw their wages stagnate and democracy and civil rights were stolen away from citizens. Dictators such as Hitler and Mussolini built a 'corporatist state' in which the interests of economic classes and occupational groups would supposedly be reconciled, once all forms of social conflict had been silenced. Hence, the return of the state does not necessarily herald a more democratic world and indeed might usher in new forms of oppres-sion and exploitation.

---

11   Joel Wainwright and Geoff Mann, *Climate Leviathan: A Political Theory of Our Planetary Future* (London: Verso, 2018).

The theory of the state has long been recognised as an Achilles' heel of Marxist thinking. While Marx was not blind to the question of the state and the practical management of power, he did not develop a positive theory of what a socialist state would look like. In *The Communist Manifesto*, Marx and Engels famously depicted government as a 'committee for managing the common affairs of the whole bourgeoisie'.[12] Lenin took a similarly reductive viewpoint when he wrote of 'a special apparatus for compulsion which is called the state'.[13] In this view, the state was essentially the capitalist state – the weapon protecting the rapacious hand of capital.

In his political writings, such as *The Civil War in France* and *The Critique of the Gotha Programme*, Marx showed a more practical engagement with the question of the state. Discussing the Paris Commune in the first draft of *The Civil War in France*, he talked about the need for a 'social republic': 'that is a Republic which disowns the capital and land-owner class of the State machinery to supersede it by the Commune, that frankly avows "social emancipation" as the great goal of the Republic and guarantees thus that social transformation by the Communal organisation'.[14] Furthermore, in *The Critique of the Gotha Programme*, he argued: 'Freedom consists in the conversion of the state from an organ superimposed on society, into one completely subordinated to it'.[15] Nevertheless, compared with Marx's economic analysis, these remarks were provisional at best, offering little guidance on how to deal concretely with state power.

A more fully drawn Marxian theory of the state did not emerge until Antonio Gramsci addressed the subject. Writing in the aftermath of Bolshevism and fascism, Gramsci reminded readers of the 'autonomy of the political', acknowledging the role of state institutions in processes of social coordination, reproduction and legitimation. His was a

12    Karl Marx and Friedrich Engels, *The Communist Manifesto* (London: Penguin, 2002), p. 37.

13    Vladimir Lenin, *State and Revolution*, annotated with an introduction by Todd Chretien (Chicago, IL: Haymarket, 2015), p. 73.

14    Karl Marx, 'The Civil War in France', in Bruno Leipold, 'Marx's Social Republic', in Bruno Leipold, Karma Nabulsi and Stuart White, eds, *Radical Republicanism: Recovering the Tradition's Popular Heritage* (Oxford: Oxford University Press, 2020), p. 174.

15    Karl Marx, 'Critique of the Gotha Programme' in his *The first international and after*, ed. D. Fernbach vol. 3 (London: Verso, 2010).

watered-down version of the Hegelian view of the necessity of the state, which Hegel famously expressed in *The Philosophy of Right* when he affirmed that the state is the 'ethical whole, the actualisation of freedom' or even 'the march of God in the world'.[16] As Gramsci stressed, the state performed a crucial structural function, holding together the dominant power bloc within society. This unifying function was not limited to the state's apparatus of coercion, but also encompassed its ideological functions the education system, the church, and all those structures through which hegemony was exercised.[17] Borrowing a Machiavellian metaphor, Gramsci argued that the state was similar to the centaur – a half-man, half-horse creature, combining the brute force of repression with the soft power of persuasion.[18] Following in Gramsci's footsteps, Nicos Poulantzas would affirm that the state was 'the factor of *cohesion* of a social formation and the factor of *reproduction* of the conditions of production of a system'.[19] In this sense, society and the state are not opposed, as the capitalist distinction between civil society and political society leads us to assume. Rather, society can only exist by virtue of a state apparatus holding it together as a social formation, thus guaranteeing its continued existence.

## State and *Stabilitas*

The association of the state with order, security and stability is alluded to in the word itself. It is derived from the Latin *status* (condition, circumstances, position), appearing in the early Middle Ages in various European languages and popularised by its use in the work of Machiavelli. The preoccupation with the *status rei publicae*, going back to Cicero, stems from the fact that the state is seen as a stable, if not altogether permanent, structure, which also provides an anchoring point in the event of major crises. Parties, movements, symbols and leaders will

---

16   G. W. F. Hegel, *Hegel's Philosophy of Right.*, transl. Thomas Malcolm Knox (London: Oxford University Press, 1975), p. 279.

17   Antonio Gramsci, *Selection from Prison Notebooks*, ed. Quintin Hoare; Geoffrey Nowell-Smith (New York : International Publishers, 2008), pp. 262–6.

18   Ibid., p. 170

19   Nicos Poulantzas, 'The problem of the capitalist state', *New Left Review* 58: 1 (1969), 67–78.

come and go, but the state can usually be expected to outlast them all, providing an institutional framework through which a society reproduces itself. Nation-states – with their definition of a fixed territory considered to be the home of a political community – have demonstrated remarkable stability. An example of this tendency is provided by the many formerly colonised lands in Africa, Asia and Latin America, whose borders have changed very little since decolonisation, despite the fact that they were created by European imperialists in blatant disregard for local ethnic and cultural divisions.

As post-Keynesian economist Hyman Minsky – the author of the prescient work *Stabilizing an Unstable Economy* – noted, the stabilising function of the state also applies in the economic realm – as, for example, in the role of 'automatic stabilisers' within the fiscal system.[20] This term is used to describe the way in which, in phases of economic stagnation, citizens' tax liabilities fall due to a drop in their income, while state transfers increase in the form of unemployment benefits and other social welfare provisions. These mechanisms provide a means of evening out the fluctuations in the business cycle without any active intervention by policymakers, thus resulting in economic stimulus that can prevent the deepening of economic recessions. This is why the dismantling of the welfare state pursued during the neoliberal era is not only socially unfair, but also systemically dangerous. Many countries learned this lesson the hard way during the coronavirus crisis, when they were obliged to scramble to create ad hoc forms of social provision.

Obviously, the ostensible stability or even 'harmony' offered by the state – celebrated by Menenius Agrippa in his famous Mons Sacer speech during the first secession of the Roman plebs and by Confucius in *The Analects* – is often simply a coded justification for class domination.[21] But the left, if it is sincere in its determination to supplant the existing regime with a new one, cannot evade the question of order. The strong appeal of the state's promise of security and stability among large sections of the popular classes who are particularly vulnerable to

---

20   Hyman Minsky, *Stabilizing an Unstable Economy*, 3 volumes (New York: McGraw-Hill, 2008).
21   Confucius, *The Analects of Confucius*, ed. and transl. Simon Leys (New York: W. W. Norton, 1997).

hardship, and sensitive to social disruption and lack of security, should never be underestimated. This demand for social security is particularly resonant in the current circumstances, when patterns of life are marked by extreme economic uncertainty due to the generalised exposure to global market forces and disruptive, if not outright destructive, techno- logical innovation. While, until recently, prevailing common sense was pervaded by an acceptance of the neoliberal emphasis on flexibility, adaptiveness and individual autonomy, the experience of repeated crises has given new appeal to demands for stability at many levels, starting with secure employment. In the neoliberal worldview, a lifelong career as a humble state employee was perhaps the least appealing prospect; today, however, many people would grasp at such an opportunity.

What the socialist left and nationalist right share is a criticism of the neoliberal centre, whose gutting of the state has affected key stabilising functions that allow society to achieve cohesion and navigate social transformation. However, their views of the state diverge in relation to the parameters of the *security* they demand from it. Like other keywords of the post-neoliberal lexicon – such as sovereignty, protection and control – security is a highly polysemic term. It can mean security against immigrants and other 'undesirables', delivered at the point of a truncheon or the barrel of a gun; but it can also mean social security – the provision of a safety net to protect people from economic hardship, and women and minorities from violence and harassment. In line with the timeless motto 'No justice, no peace!' the left should argue that the only form of security that can guarantee durable stability is social secu- rity: protecting citizens from poverty and exclusion, and guaranteeing that everyone's basic needs for a decent life will be met. It is from this standpoint of social security as the product of ongoing redistributive conflicts that a progressive view of protective statism can be developed.

As Chapter 4 discussed, protection is a constitutive element of all political communities: there is no political community without protec- tion. The state is implicated in a number of protective operations of the most disparate kinds – defence against possible military attack; mainte- nance of public order; protection of local industry against banks and the exigencies of the global market; protection of the environment; various forms of social protection and insurance (benefits, pensions, and so on); and the provision of public healthcare. These various forms of protec- tion are all routine functions of the state that guarantee the reproduction of society and its ability to withstand internal and external pressures. But each has a different genesis, and different political biases. In Nicos Poulantzas's words, state institutions are 'the material condensation of a class relationship of forces' – the historically sedimented results of class struggles.[22] For example, the law and order sort of protection has traditionally been a signature policy of the right, while social protection – in the form of public services, welfare provisions and strong unions – has traditionally been identified with the socialist left.

If these protective functions of the state, long taken for granted, are now becoming the object of political contention, it is because the neoliberal dismantling of the state has eroded many of them – in particular macro-economic protective functions. From trade tariffs, progressively eliminated due to global trade integration, to the weakening of labour regulations in the name of flexibility, societies and governments have been deprived of key means of protection. Particularly affected has been the state's ability to control monetary, fiscal and industrial policy and to withstand the pressure of markets and multinational corporations. As a result of this sustained attack, the neoliberal state resembles a lame beast. This is dangerous for democracy, given that, as observed by Nicos Poulantzas, 'it should indeed be remembered that wild animals are most dangerous when they are wounded'.[23] In fact, under neoliberalism, the erosion of state economic interventionism was accompanied by a progressive strengthening of the repressive apparatus of the state in many countries. Precisely because the state was no longer attending to the mission of guaranteeing full employment, social security and stability, it had to strengthen the coercive means at its disposal for keeping in line the growing numbers of those on the losing end of the new order. The rapid growth in incarceration rates in the US in the aftermath of Clinton's social welfare reforms is a sad case in point.[24]

The coercive face of the state can project an impression of decisiveness and effectiveness that economic intervention has, by and large, lost due to a pervasive global interdependency that leaves little room for manoeuvre on macroeconomic policy. It is not by chance that, in the

22   Nicos Poulantzas, *State, Power, Socialism* (London: Verso, 2000), p. 192.
23   Ibid., 205.
24   Thomas Frank, 'Bill Clinton's Crime Bill Destroyed Lives, and There's No Point Denying It', *Guardian*, 15 April 2016.

present era, in many countries the ministry of the interior has come to be more coveted than the ministry of industry or finance. A minister of the interior can easily refuse entry to a rescue ship at a national port, or order a raid against squatters occupying a building, as Salvini has repeatedly done. But an economic minister cannot so easily stop a company from moving jobs overseas, or prevent digital corporations from avoiding taxes, without bringing into question the accepted norms of neoliberal globalisation. This situation is a boon for the right, which has traditionally appealed to voters concerned about crime and interested in law-and-order policies. Therefore, a key question is establishing the degree to which it is possible to overcome this imbalance and revive forms of state economic interventionism that have long been abandoned. To explore these issues in the continuation of the chapter we will examine the new economic and trade policies pursued by the right and the left.

## The Right's Corsair State

The proprietarian protectionism at the heart of the right's post-neoliberal vision is only partly neo-statist. It shares with neoliberalism precisely its orientation towards the defence of private property and low taxation; what sets it apart from neoliberalism is, first and foremost, its embrace of trade protectionism. The nationalist right's distancing from neoliberal orthodoxy on free trade has been one of the most remarkable ideological transformations of the Great Recoil. Leaders of various nationalist parties have radicalised a criticism of globalisation and free trade that was already present *in nuce* in the New Right during the 1980s and 1990s, and brought it into the political mainstream in the wake of their electoral success. Trade protectionism has become the key component of the national-populist vision of a 'corsair state', in which the state is conceived as something akin to a pirate ship prowling the seas of the world looking for spoils, while fighting aggressively against the vessels of other nations.

This turn towards protectionism has been most clearly manifested in Donald Trump's four years as US president. Trump's stated objective at the beginning of his presidency was re-shoring US manufacturing jobs that had moved overseas, for which he blamed unfair competition from

China and Europe. Before becoming president, Trump had accused Beijing of profiting from an artificially undervalued currency; during the 2016 election campaign, he repeatedly criticised China and Germany of unfair competition allowing them to reap enormous trade surpluses. After becoming president, he began imposing tariffs on goods such as solar panels, washing machines, as well as steel and aluminium, sparking tensions with trade partners including Canada, Mexico and the European Union. In 2018 he turned against China, setting tariffs on Chinese goods totalling US$500 billion. China retaliated, levying tariffs of US$185 billion on US imports. This tit-for-tat process sparked intense commercial tensions and uncertainty about future economic prospects. The trade war was eventually halted with the signing of the Phase One Trade Deal in January 2020, in which China committed to increasing its purchase of US products by US$200 billion by the end of 2021, as well as making commitments on intellectual property, forced technology transfers and currency manipulation.

Trump celebrated the deal as a victory; but, according to many analysts, it was at best Pyrrhic. The trade war had negative effects on the US economy, including a slowdown in growth, amounting to between 0.3 per cent and 0.7 per cent in 2019, and the loss of up to 300,000 jobs as a consequence of falling demand from China and a redirection of trade flows away from the United States, causing hundreds of farms and freight companies to go bankrupt.[25] Furthermore, many commentators have raised doubts over whether China will ever honour the trade deal. Imports from the United States have stagnated partly as a consequence of trade disruption caused by the Covid-19 pandemic while exports from China to the US grew by 46 per cent.

The confrontation between the United States and China has increasingly focused on the tech sector. The US government has taken measures against the dominant role played by Chinese telecommunications giant Huawei in the 5G mobile technology infrastructure, arguing that its persistence would lead to Chinese control over strategic communication networks, with nefarious implications for national security. This development was compounded by Trump's threat to ban popular video-sharing app TikTok in the summer of 2020,

---

25   Ryan Hass and Abraham Denmark, 'More Pain than Gain: How the US-China Trade War Hurt America', *Brookings Institution*, 7 August 2020.

eventually forcing the company to sell its US operation. During the longstanding trading dispute of 2018–20, the United States has used its control over the microchip sector, on which Chinese industry remains dependent, as a stranglehold to force the Chinese into submission. For their part, Chinese authorities have frequently threatened bans on the export to the United States of rare-earth materials, 80 per cent of which are mined in China, and which are essential for the production of all sorts of technological products, from smartphones to wind turbines. This dispute is a reflection of how digital technology – a key tool of control in contemporary societies – has come to be perceived as a decisive area for the exercise of sovereignty. In the present world, political sovereignty cannot exist without some degree of technological sovereignty.

A similar protectionist stance has been articulated by other leaders on the nationalist right, such as Matteo Salvini, Marine Le Pen and Boris Johnson, who have often blamed deindustrialisation and the loss of manufacturing jobs in their countries on free trade. However, this discourse is strongly contradicted in practice. Despite their fiery denunciation of the European Union, leaders like Salvini and Viktor Orbán have strong interests in the maintenance of European trade, since they enjoy support from companies that build semi-finished products for German industry. In fact, in the course of 2020 Salvini reneged on much of his anti-EU discourse when he came under pressure from members of the party who are close to the export industry. Similarly, while Brexit was often presented by its populist advocates as a protectionist move to defend against foreign competition for jobs, especially in the manufacturing and fishing industries, in practice it embodies an aggressive, mercantilist conception of free trade. The driving motivation behind changes in trade policy was to overcome what were perceived to be excessively restrictive EU trade, labour and environmental regulations, including on the importing of goods banned within the EU and on foreign investment in the healthcare sector – as revealed by a document leaked during the 2019 election campaign according to which the NHS was 'on the table' in negotiations between the United States and the UK.[26]

---

26   Peter Walker and Rowena Mason, 'Jeremy Corbyn on the Offensive over Donald Trump's Plans for NHS', *Guardian*, 3 December 2019.

This intermixing of protectionist and free-trade impulses is not altogether surprising. Free trade, rather than being completely 'free', is always framed and regulated by numerous measures that guarantee extensive protection to multinational corporations, including 'patents, copyrights, licenses, business secrets, trade tariffs, the police [. . .], insurance, the entire veil of property law, the courts, the might of the state when needed here and abroad, and now, of course, the World Trade Organization', as US labour activist Kim Moody argues.[27] In this context, private corporations are not to be understood simply as independent private entities, but rather as strategic extensions of nation-states, much like the chartered colonial companies of previous centuries. This attitude is revealed, for example, in Boris Johnson's bellicose rhetoric describing the UK as 'world beating' – a development of the view of a 'buccaneering capitalism' as articulated by former prime minister David Cameron. Similar in spirit is the reference made by right-wing politicians to a US or British 'exceptionalism', supposedly allowing them to do what other countries are barred from.

What this ambiguous stance reveals is that – rather than doing away with globalisation, as their public discourse suggests – the real agenda of nationalist-populist leaders entails digging trenches from which the global trade war can be more conveniently fought. The protectionist measures they espouse have no connection to supposed goals of social or environmental improvement. The right's application of tariffs is disconnected from any industrial policy that might lead to future breakthroughs in technology and overall well-being. It is the typical 'beggar-thy-neighbour' policy, intended to put other nations and their industries at a disadvantage. Ultimately, as Moody notes, 'Competition and protection are the two means to maximizing profits in the world market place. The more vicious the global competition, the more barbed the wire of protection that capital seeks.'[28] Rather than providing a cure for the sense of exposure engendered by neoliberal globalisation, the right's mercantilist instincts risk opening such wounds further – especially for workers who will need to pay more for basic goods, and will find fewer employment opportunities because of escalating trade wars.

---

27   Kim Moody, 'Protectionism or Solidarity? (Part I)', *Against the Current* 87: 3 (2000).
28   Ibid.

The class bias of proprietarian protectionism is all the more apparent when we move from trade policies to examine fiscal and labour policies, which remain very much in line with those of the neoliberal era. While the right has often adopted a 'workerist' rhetoric, it has directly attacked workers' rights and their ability to organise, demonstrating a profoundly individualistic economic ethos bordering on social Darwinism. The most infamous case of such legislation is Viktor Orbán's 'slave law' – a reform in labour regulation that allows companies to demand workers work 250 to 400 extra hours per year.[29] Many other nationalist leaders have pursued similar moves to curtail workers' rights. Donald Trump launched a 'Pledge to American Workers' programme designed to 'expand programs that educate, train, and reskill American workers'. In the 2020 State of the Union address, Trump claimed: 'Our agenda is relentlessly pro-worker'. Despite these inklings of state corporatism, his actions in government strongly undermined collective bargaining, repealing modest labour regulations that had been introduced by Barack Obama. While unemployment fell during the initial part of his term, wages continued to stagnate.

This pro-business bias is even clearer in the right's tax policies, the policy area that is most in continuity with the neoliberal agenda. Trump's flagship 2017 tax reform, worth US$1.5 trillion, overwhelmingly bene-fited the rich. Top marginal tax rates were significantly reduced. As Emmanuel Saez and Gabriel Zucman argue in *The Triumph of Injustice*, Trump's tax cuts have exacerbated social inequality. The richest families now pay an effective tax rate of 23 per cent – lower than the bottom half of US households, which pay 24.2 per cent.[30] In fact, Trump's initial coronavirus stimulus bill worth $2.2trillion (the CARES act) also contained $135 billion in tax breaks for the rich – four times the amount provided to house and feed citizens.[31] As the Economic Policy Institute noted, Donald Trump 'systematically rolled back workers' rights to form unions and engage in collective bargaining with their employers, to the

---

29    Shaun Walker, 'Hungary Passes "Slave Law" Prompting Fury among Opposition MPs. Hungary President Signs Controversial "Slave Law"', *Guardian*, 12 December 2018.

30    Emmanuel Saez and Gabriel Zucman, *The Triumph of Injustice: How the Rich Dodge Taxes and How to Make Them Pay* (New York: W. W. Norton, 2019).

31    Rosa DeLauro, 'Rep. Rosa DeLauro: We Must Repeal Trump's $135 Billion Hidden Tax Giveaway for Wealthy Real Estate Investors', *Fortune*, 3 May 2020.

detriment of workers, their communities, and the economy'.[32] The taxation proposals of the European nationalist right are even more extreme. Matteo Salvini and Viktor Orbán have toyed with the idea of a flat-rate income tax – a policy that would only magnify existing inequalities. The right's promise of a departure from neoliberal globalisation thus heralds the combination of mercantilist trade policies with a Social Darwinist attitude to labour and taxation. If anything, it offers an even worse prospect than neoliberal capitalism: a nationalist state monopoly capitalism in which monopoly capital is protected by the full force of the corporatist state, while workers are even more ruthlessly exploited.

## The Left's Social Protectionism

The view of the state as a means of economic protection takes radically different forms on the left from those deployed by the right. The left focuses on the goal of social protection rather than the defence of property, and it seeks to pursue a more pacific trade protectionism based on regulations and measures against social and environmental dumping, rather than indiscriminate tariffs designed to punish economic competitors. This position is well represented by the declarations of some leftist leaders who have espoused what Jean-Luc Mélenchon has termed 'solidarity protectionism'.[33] In 2019, Labour shadow chancellor John McDonnell remarked: 'We reject the whole principle of free trade';[34] and in 2020, Bernie Sanders commented: 'We need a trade policy that benefits American workers and creates living-wage jobs, not unfair trade agreements written by multi-national corporations.'[35]

Opposition to new trade treaties proposed in the late 2010s, such as the botched Transatlantic Trade and Investment Partnership (TTIP),

32   Celine McNicholas, Margaret Poydock, and Lynn Rhinehart, 'Unprecedented: The Trump NLRB's Attack on Workers' Rights', Economic Policy Institute, 16 October 2019, at epi.org.

33   See, for example, Jacques Généreux, 'Entretien Pour un "protectionnisme solidaire"', Alternatives Economiques, 21 April 2017, at alternatives-economiques.fr.

34   Jim Pickard and Robert Shrimsley, 'Jeremy Corbyn's Plan to Rewrite the Rules of the UK Economy', Financial Times, 1 September 2019, at ft.com.

35   Bernie Sanders' Fair Trade Policy, at berniesanders.com.

are a further indication of the growing protectionist sentiment on the left. This proposed bilateral trade treaty between the US and the EU was roundly criticised by trade unions, NGOs and environmental activists, who decried its likely impact on food safety, jobs and national sovereignty. Furthermore, questions were raised about its implications for democracy given the secrecy surrounding its negotiation – the records of which were classified. The new US president, Joe Biden, rather than departing from Trump's protectionism, has pursued his own protectionist course, continuing the aggressive stance towards China of his predecessor, and dictating 'Buy American' rules redirecting public procurement towards national products and services.

Trade protectionism is certainly not new to the left. Many socialist governments have embraced protectionist measures as necessary instruments to defend fledgling industries. The import-substitution policies pursued by emerging countries in the post-war era to reduce their reliance on core capitalist nations are an example of this. But the main components of the economic course proposed by the likes of Sanders and Mélenchon draw attention because they mark a discursive rupture with left discourse in recent decades; while isolated figures, such as anti-trade campaigner Walden Bello, have long stressed the need for de-globalisation, many centre-left politicians accepted global integration as a *fait accompli*.[36]

Marxists like to emphasise the internationalism of Marx and Engels, who supported free trade against protectionism. But their opinion was strongly qualified. In his 1848 speech, 'On the Question of Free Trade', delivered at the Democratic Association of Brussels shortly before *The Communist Manifesto* was published, Marx argued: 'When you have overthrown the few national barriers which still restrict the progress of capital, you will merely have given it complete freedom of action', and asserted that '[a]ll the destructive phenomena which unlimited competition gives rise to within one country are reproduced in more gigantic proportions on the world market'. Only in the conclusion to his speech did he express tactical support for free trade, saying that, 'in general, the protective system of our day is conservative, while the free trade system is destructive', and therefore 'the free trade system hastens the social

---

36  Walden Bello, *Deglobalization: Ideas for a New World Economy* (London: Zed, 2008).

revolution. It is in this revolutionary sense alone, gentlemen, that I vote in favour of free trade.'[37]

In our current circumstances, in which the arrival of a proletarian revolution seems quite a remote eventuality, few activists on the socialist left would be ready to accept such an argument in defence of free trade. While it has allowed access to consumer goods at very low prices, unregulated global trade has been used as a means to suppress workers' wages and rights, while chain retailers and e-commerce have pushed local businesses out of the market. Ha-Joon Chang, the bestselling Korean economist who was part of Labour's New Economics initiative, argues that 'free trade' is a myth that has been peddled by the most powerful economic states to emerging economies, in order to turn the latter into hunting grounds for the multinational corporations originating in the former.[38] Today's hegemonic free trader was yesterday's laggard trying to catch up by protecting domestic industry. Accepting the gospel of free trade at face value entails a self-inflicted subservience to the rapacious logic of international capitalism.

The left's dominant attitude to trade policy is different from that exhibited by Donald Trump and other nationalist leaders in a number of respects. First, it is framed not in terms of a competition between national economies, or of the pursuit of mercantilist policies, but in terms of fostering socially just and environmentally sustainable development within and among nations. Second, its aim is to set moderate tariffs as a means of introducing some level of friction in global trade that might act as a guardrail against the most obnoxious forms of social dumping, while emphasising the need for stricter social and environmental standards. Besides tariffs, other available measures that have recently been discussed include bans on imports that are environmentally destructive, such as goods with excessive plastic packaging; certifications of compliance with minimum social and environmental standards; greater leeway in infringing intellectual property when faced with medical need or the necessity of catching up technologically with competitors. Furthermore, socialists argue that

---

37   Karl Marx and Friedrich Engels, *Collected Works, Volume 6: Marx and Engels, 1845–1848* (London: Lawrence & Wishart, 1976), p. 450.

38   H. J. Chang, *Kicking Away the Ladder: Development Strategy in Historical Perspective* (London: Anthem, 2002).

governments should make more liberal use of state subsidies to support strategic industries and firms, allowing countries to reduce economic dependency in certain areas – for example, computing and communication.

This difference in approach is important, given the strong suspicion towards trade protectionism on the left. It is often argued that protectionism damages workers. Countries on the receiving end of protectionist measures will usually reciprocate, with the consequence that many products and services become more expensive for the final customers. This does much to explain why large sections of the labour movement have, throughout history, had more sympathy for free trade than for protectionism. However, protectionism is always a matter of degrees. It is one thing to engage in an outright trade war, such as the one waged by Donald Trump against China; but quite another to introduce more limited rules and moderate tariffs in areas particularly exposed to social and environmental dumping. An effective overhaul of international trade will also entail the drafting of new international trade agreements enshrining minimum labour and environmental standards. Fair-trade activists have long demanded that the International Labour Organization be strengthened and that its core labour standards, identified in the *Declaration of the Fundamental Principles and Rights at Work*, become an integral part of the regulation of global trade.[39]

Opposition to global economic integration is often accompanied by demands for a re-localisation of the economy. Environmental activists have long emphasised the need for a local re-anchoring of the economy, as a means to increase sustainability and empower local communities. Socialists are increasingly embracing this view. An example of this trend can be found in the public contracting practices of local authorities as in the so-called 'Preston model', that was a signature proposal of Jeremy Corbyn's economic vision. The term refers to the economic model pioneered in the Lancashire city, where the Labour council implemented new rules on public contracting that committed local authorities to only using local suppliers.[40] The experiment was hailed as a successful

---

39   International Labour Organization and Asian Development Bank, 'CORE Labour Standards Handbook' (ILO/ADB: Manila, 2006).

40   Martin O'Neill, 'The Road to Socialism is the A59: The Preston Model', *Renewal: A Journal of Labour Politics* 24: 2 (June 2016), p. 69.

example of 'civic socialism'; unemployment fell below the national average. This logic of relocalisation is very relevant to the battle against climate change, given that the carbon footprint of global trade, including for example the carbon dioxide emissions produced by merchant ships, is a notable enemy of ecological sustainability.[41]

Many commentators on the left have also stressed the need to re-impose controls on capital accounts, and this issue has also been discussed in US and EU policy circles.[42] Some rightly caution that, due to the current degree of integration in international capital markets, the unilateral introduction of capital controls may come at a very high cost. Rather than dreaming of 'magic switches' that can reinstate capital controls immediately, a realistic approach to this question would proceed incrementally, concentrating on establishing the technical and political conditions for such a policy to be viable. A tax on financial transactions, such as the famous 'Tobin Tax', or financial residency regulations limiting capital mobility, would be useful not only to generate tax revenues, but also to chart the movements of private capital, thus improving the 'legibility' of financial transactions from the state's perspective, as a necessary step towards introducing a degree of friction into capital flows.

In coming years, the demand for growing protectionism, and the move from globalisation to 'regionalisation' (in the sense of world regions), may led to a sea change in trade and investment policies. While it is true that global integration can be a force for prosperity for some, it must not continue to be a source of economic insecurity and social dislocation for most.

## Monetary Autonomy

Monetary policy is a fundamental lever of political control over the economy; throughout history, the state's right to issue currency has been one of its main prerogatives. Hobbes famously described money as the

41   Henrik Selin and Rebecca Cowing, 'Cargo Ships Are Emitting Boatloads of Carbon, and Nobody Wants to Take the Blame', *The Conversation*, 18 December 2018.
42   Michael A. McCarthy, 'How a President Bernie Sanders Could Take on Wall Street', *Jacobin*, 8 August 2019.

Leviathan's blood, coursing through its economic veins. But this key element of sovereignty has been severely weakened during recent decades. Globalisation has wrested away state control over the currency and the money supply through the internationalisation of global finance. At the same time, the growing emphasis on central bank independence under neoliberalism has facilitated the oligarchic drift in economic policy-making. The debate about monetary policy has been particularly intense in the European Union, given the many unpopular decisions taken by the European Central Bank in the aftermath of the 2008 crisis. Both moderate left economists like Joseph Stiglitz and radical ones like Costas Lapavitsas have harshly criticised the behaviour of the European Central Bank and the painful social consequences of adoption of the euro, especially for southern European countries such as Italy, Spain and Greece.[43]

One manifestation of a renewed interest in post-Keynesian economics is the popularity acquired by Modern Monetary Theory (MMT). MMT postulates a new 'general theory of money', which is, broadly speaking, the opposite of conservative monetarism. Initially formulated in the United States by former broker Warren Mosler and scholar L. Randall Wray, MMT holds not only that deficits and debt are not such significant problems as neoliberals suggest, but that the state has no real financial constraints on its spending.[44] According to proponents of MMT, any state that controls its own currency can always pay for its goods, services and debts by using 'monetary financing' – in other words, governments can pay for their spending by printing more money. MMT economists such as Stephanie Kelton have voiced criticism of the 'deficit myth' – namely, the idea that deficit spending is wasteful and a threat to solvency.[45] This is tantamount to heresy among neoclassical economists, who traditionally recommend that all public spending be fully funded, either through taxation or cuts in other departments, and that central banks should

---

43   Joseph Stiglitz, *The Euro: And Its Threat to the Future of Europe* (London: Penguin, 2016); Costas Lapavitsas, *The Left Case Against the EU* (Oxford: John Wiley, 2018).

44   Thomas I. Palley, 'Money, Fiscal Policy, and Interest Rates: A Critique of Modern Monetary Theory', *Review of Political Economy* 27: 1 (2015).

45   Stephanie Kelton, *The Deficit Myth: Modern Monetary Theory and How to Build a Better Economy* (London: John Murrary, 2020).

not engage in discretionary monetary policy, focusing instead on maintaining price stability.

Embraced by the likes of Bernie Sanders and Alexandria Ocasio-Cortez, MMT is useful in revealing the inconsistencies of neoliberal policies while reviving Keynesian thinking on public investment and social spending as multipliers of economic activity, thanks to their capacity to increase effective demand. Furthermore, it has the merit of undermining monetarist orthodoxy mandating fixed growth in the money supply. The suggestion that spending deficits are no big problem, appears like a welcome antidote to a decade of merciless austerity and insistence on the impotence of the state. However, MMT also generates serious conundrums. In a floating exchange rate system, no state, except perhaps the global hegemon, is in complete control of its currency. While it is true that inflation is not necessarily the devastating threat neoliberals argue it is, advocates of MMT can be guilty of overlooking inflation altogether – a risk that has notably been a key reason for the repeated failure of populist projects in Latin America.

MMT comes close to a 'solutionism' – as Grace Blakeley has argued.[46] It entails the naive belief that firm popular control over the central bank, combined with a few keystrokes to issue more currency when required, can suffice to redress deeply entrenched economic imbalances. An example of such banal thinking is MMT's sophistical argument that taxation is not necessary to fund public spending, merely because of an accounting technicality – namely, the fact that tax receipts are generated after state spending has taken place. MMT may thus be read as an intellectual reflection of the pervasive financialisation of the economy, at a time when central banks – and in particular the Fed and the ECB, whose financial 'bazookas' are often invoked in times of crisis – have acquired immense power. Furthermore, MMT focus on the money supply over other economic processes diverts attention from questions of industrial policy and public ownership, which are crucial to economic protection and democratic control, and building a public economy focused on socially desirable ends.[47]

---

46   Grace Blakeley, *Stolen: How to Save the World from Financialisation* (London: Repeater, 2019), p. 252.

47   Milton Friedman, 'Monetary Policy: Theory and Practice', *Journal of Money, Credit and Banking* 14: 1 (1982).

## A New Public Economy

After years of rampant privatisation and cuts to public services, it is essential to invert the direction of travel. The coronavirus crisis has brutally revealed the consequences of decades of cuts to public services – starting with health, which has been ravaged by successive waves of privatisation. Self-described 'First World' countries discovered they did not have enough hospital beds to accommodate growing numbers of patients, or the necessary social welfare measures to cope with the burgeoning unemployed. This crisis also illuminated the nefarious social consequences of poorly funded education and childcare services – especially for women, many of whom must carry most of the burden of family care on top of their daily work.

A post-pandemic socialist platform needs to refocus attention on essential, bread-and-butter issues that have for too long been over-looked, starting with public services. The left's long-standing defence of public services has been dramatically vindicated by recent events, and current circumstances offer an opening for an expansion of the social arm of the state. In recent years activists have proposed an extension of 'free at the point of use' or subsidised services in the field of transportation, medicine and even food. These policies, which are in fact the revival of time-honoured socialist proposals, could prove electorally rewarding; many surveys have pointed to large majorities supporting an extension of government intervention, public services and welfare.[48]

A particularly pressing question is that of social-welfare measures to deal with ballooning unemployment amid the economic aftershock of the coronavirus crisis and the major social emergency that we are likely to see during the 2020s. While countries led by right-wing governments such as the UK adopted emergency social measures, such as the furloughing of employees, which covered 8.5 million workers, in many cases these measures will elapse after the end of the coronavirus emergency with the risk of a devastating social aftershock. Other governments have instead established new permanent social-welfare provisions, such as the guaranteed minimum income approved in Spain in May 2020. Surveys showed that it had broad popular backing, to the

---

48   Megan Brenan, 'New High 54% Want Government to Solve More Problems in US', *Gallup*, 28 September 2020 at gallup.com.

point that even the far-right Vox Party was forced to reconsider its opposition. Rebuilding a strong safety net is fundamental when facing an uncertain future. But this needs to be accompanied by the creation of new jobs, especially in the public sector, strong mobilisation for wage increases after years of stagnation and the creation of a 'job guarantee', with government hiring those out of work as an employer of last resort, as proposed by MMT theorists.[49]

The tide is also turning in discussions of industrial policy. In recent years, many scholars have called for the state to pursue a more interventionist role. Mariana Mazzucato's reference to an 'entrepreneurial state' expresses the idea that the government should become more involved in industrial policy, and that it must often be willing to take risks – sometimes financial – in order to facilitate innovation.[50] Debates about the need for higher levels of economic intervention have also unfolded in connection with discussions of climate change policies, and in particular the Green New Deal proposed by progressives in the United States. As popularised by Democratic congresswoman Alexandria Ocasio-Cortez, the Green New Deal was designed to address both environmental collapse and the economic hardship that will flow from it. This policy would create millions of new jobs in manufacturing: an effective selling point for this policy among the working class, including those in peripheral areas, where many green projects would undoubtedly have to be based.[51] Joe Biden has pledged $2 trillion in investments for a green transition; but the risk is that much of this money will end up in the pockets of large corporations disingenuously laying claim to green credentials.

Energy will be another key area of policy-making in coming years. Oil and oil products account for around one fifth of the value of international trade. But a number of signs point to the fact that the oil-based energy system is losing the economic and political battle; meanwhile, renewable energy is becoming more efficient and politically attractive. The expansion of renewables means, among other things, that countries

    49    Annie Lowrey, 'A Promise So Big, Democrats Aren't Sure How to Keep It', *Atlantic*, 11 May 2018.
    50    Mariana Mazzucato, *The Entrepreneurial State: Debunking Public vs. Private Sector Myths* (London: Anthem, 2013).
    51    Kate Aronoff, Alyssa Battistoni, Daniel Aldana Cohen and Thea Riofrancos, *A Planet to Win: Why We Need a Green New Deal* (New York: Verso Books, 2019).

are likely to become more self-reliant in terms of their energy produc-tion, given that wind and solar power are geographically more uniformly distributed than fossil fuel deposits. The replacement of oil-based energy with renewable energy may also help shift economic patterns, acting as a form of indirect import-substitution. Increasing local energy produc-tion would reduce imports, and thus reduce the need for exports to pay for them. This, in turn, would release more resources to be consumed and invested locally in the framework of a more 'circular' and localised economy.

A real recovery of public control over the economy should also involve the nationalisation of all strategic utility companies and the socialisation of credit – an area where private banks have failed, declin-ing to provide finance to crisis-stricken businesses and households. Water, gas, electricity and telecommunications are 'natural monopo-lies' that have been inappropriately privatised during the neoliberal era, depriving the state of control over strategic parts of the economy. Credit should be redirected away from speculative finance and towards productive activities through the creation of public banks and the nationalisation of ailing financial institutions. While, as Engels argued, state ownership does not necessarily do away with capitalism, he added that it is 'the handle to the solution', and indeed nationalisation has been a traditional goal of socialist and social-democratic govern-ments.[52] The blueprint of Chinese state capitalism, the French model of mixed capitalism and the Italian state's ownership of strategic enter-prises are often cited as examples of how countries might build more self-reliant economic systems. Nationalised industry can enable profits to be captured for the public good and facilitates stronger worker control over the management of businesses; it is also, from time to time, a matter of necessity, if strategically important private companies, considered 'too big to fail', are to be prevented from going bankrupt.

A debate has recently opened about the state's role in the manage-ment of companies – such as various UK rail franchisees or the Italian aviation company Alitalia – that had to be temporarily nationalised to avoid bankruptcy. Politicians have debated whether the state should claim its quota, or 'golden share', on company boards. Unsurprisingly,

52   Friedrich Engels, *Socialism: Utopian and Scientific* (Amsterdam: Resistance, 1999).

representatives of the capitalist class strongly opposed government intervention in the governance of companies. But these criticisms seem to go against the prevailing public sentiment. While, in the aftermath of the 2008 crisis, governments offered free money to banks and large businesses without asking for anything in return, this time it will be more difficult to make the public swallow such an arrangement. The massive funds injected by the state into private companies in the aftermath of the coronavirus crisis have to be used as a unique opportunity to reassert public interests in economic decisions, and that includes the possibility of expanding state ownership.

A public economy is by its nature less exposed to attack by capitalists, including relocation. One cannot easily offshore a schoolteacher, nor can foreign investors conclude a takeover of a company in which the state holds a golden share. The reconstruction of an economy with strong state participation could provide countries with heavier ballast to weather economic storms and reduce economic dependency. Some fear that expanding public ownership of firms will lead to uncontrolled proliferation of technocracy. To avoid the bureaucratisation characteristic of the social-democratic past, an expansion of the public economy should be combined with new forms of democratic control, including the participation of workers in the governance of firms and a democratic transformation of economic planning.[53]

An economy directed towards the public good will also need to rein in of the power of multinational companies. Besides companies such as Nike, McDonald's and Benetton, whose rapacity has already been denounced by the anti-globalisation movement, the 2010s have been marked by the triumph of digital corporations – including Google, Facebook, Amazon, Airbnb and Uber – that have used the virtual nature of their activities as an excuse for all sorts of unfair practices. These companies' disruptive business model has so far been predicated on the cannibalisation of existing local markets in services; hence its description as an 'extractivist capitalism'.[54] Online retailers have destroyed high streets all over the world; Amazon alone has condemned to closure food

---

53   See above, Chapter 5.
54   Henry Veltmeyer and James F. Petras, *The New Extractivism: A Post-neoliberal Development Model or Imperialism of the Twenty-First Century?* (London: Zed Books, 2014).

retailers and bookshops that were important pillars of local communities. Meanwhile, Uber has driven thousands of local taxi companies out of business. Protecting the local economy, including small and medium businesses and the self-employed, from the ravages of these multinational entities is an essential prerequisite in fostering a more self-reliant economic ecosystem. This is especially important in the wake of the Covid crisis, which has severely damaged the petty bourgeoisie of shopkeepers, artisans and bar and restaurant owners, rendering them even more receptive to the blandishments of the nationalist right. Furthermore, the slow rollout of vaccines, especially in Continental Europe, and the profiteering behaviour of companies such as AstraZeneca and Pfizer, has sparked outrage and led to calls for waiving vaccine patents and nationalising vaccine production. To forestall widespread social despair in the aftermath of the coronavirus emergency, it is necessary to construct a social protective state, one that takes strategic industries under national ownership and ensures that important decisions affecting jobs and people's livelihoods are brought back under the control of the public. A key condition for the success of this mission is the reconstruction of a sense of community and citizenship, starting from the national level, as we will see in the next chapter.

# 9

# Democratic Patriotism

A key question for socialists amid the present crisis of globalisation is how to resolve the conflict between nation-states and the global market, at a time when the former have been weakened by the latter, leading to a widespread sense of agoraphobia. One of the most surprising social effects of the pandemic was the way it was initially accompanied by a swelling of patriotic sentiment in most countries. From China to Italy and Spain, citizens hung signs and national flags from their balconies, coming out at set times to applaud nurses, doctors, cleaners and other key workers on the front line of the pandemic, and sang popular local songs by way of encouragement, such as the Spanish song 'Resistiré' ('I Shall Resist'). Politicians often called on citizens to demonstrate their unity and behave responsibly; and, in surprising numbers, citizens showed that they would observe their civic duties. The old notion of republican virtue, premised on a sense of community, seemed to resurface above the egotistical urges of neoliberal possessive individualism.

This return of national and republican sentiment amid the Covid-19 emergency – what some people have described as 'isolation patriotism' – is yet another manifestation of the resurfacing of modernist notions long overlooked under neoliberalism. Not only is the crisis of globalisation putting key links in the global trade chain in danger, thus undermining physical interconnectedness; it is also highlighting the weakness of the forms of social identity that were prevalent during neoliberalism's heyday. The cosmopolitan consumerism that for three decades fuelled the rise of the global middle class is now in disarray, as world tourism and business travel have ground to a halt and have no short-term prospect of returning to previous levels. It is thus time to consider what kind of master identity might substitute for the vapid cosmopolitanism of the global era, and in what ways we might reconcile socialists' commitment to internationalism and the fraternity of all peoples with the reality of the nation and nationhood, and their stubbornness in the face of the forces of global market integration.

This revival of nationhood is most apparent on the right, which, true to form, has eagerly beaten the drum of national chauvinism. In November 2016, the cover of the *Economist* portrayed the arrival of a 'New Nationalism', signalled by the figures of Vladimir Putin, Donald Trump and Nigel Farage playing eighteenth-century war drums, while Marine Le Pen guided them, dressed in the robes of the French Revolution's mythical figure Marianne. Putin is considered to be the mastermind of this nationalist wave. Since the 2010s, he has embraced an aggressive nationalist rhetoric arguing that globalisation was an enemy of the world's peoples. Trump has also adopted an aggressive nationalist stance, launching attacks on Iran's top military brass and stoking trade disputes and geopolitical confrontation with China. In France, Le Pen, whose propaganda choreography invariably involves the tricolour, has repeatedly signalled her Europhobic nationalism. In September 2018, she delivered a speech baldly titled 'Nations Will Save Europe'. Meanwhile, Jair Bolsonaro adopted the nationalist, and anti-secular, slogan 'Brazil above everything, God above everyone!' in his victorious 2018 campaign. The popularity of Matteo Salvini since his ascent to leadership of the Lega, which he reshaped into a national party, was largely predicated on his jettisoning of Lombard regionalism and embrace of nationalism.

On the left, denunciations of the aggressive nationalism of figures such as Trump and Le Pen have gone hand in hand with a progressive reclaiming of patriotism. In Spain, Pablo Iglesias has most clearly expressed a commitment to civic patriotism, seeking to reappropriate national pride from Francoist bigotry, reframing it in terms of a sense of duty towards the national community and its constitution. He has often accused the right of wanting to claim exclusive ownership of the nation, insisting that patriotism means not the waving of flags but commitment to the country's social values. In August 2019, Congresswoman Ilhan

Omar responded to racist attacks from Trump and his followers by stat-
ing that she and Alexandria Ocasio-Cortez represented 'true patriotism',
a patriotism that was 'not about blindly supporting a single
Administration' but about 'fighting for our country and its dignity' and
'making sure people of our country and our Constitution are uplifted
and protected'.[1] During the UK general election campaign of 2019,
Jeremy Corbyn declared that he considered himself a patriot, while his
successor, Keir Starmer, has celebrated the idea of a 'progressive patriotism'. This revival of the celebration of nationhood has also been manifested in many social movements – most recently the French Gilets
Jaunes, who have often adopted national symbols and a rhetoric of
national solidarity.

     In order to develop a winning strategy in the present conjuncture, it
is necessary to take account of the identity crisis that has been caused
by the failures of globalisation. Rather than seeing locality and nationality as the manifestations of an antediluvian particularism, it is time
to adopt a more sympathetic attitude towards people's sense of belonging and national identity. It must be acknowledged that democracy is
by definition place-bound, the demos being largely defined by its
topos, the physical location where it is established, and that actually
existing democracies are still identified with the space of the nation-
state, while solidarity is by and large defined by local allegiances and
attachments to place. The solution to the false opposition between
nationalism and globalism should be a democratic patriotism that
articulates democratic and socialist goals in accordance with the
culture, practices and customs of specific polities, with their established common sense traditions and values. At the local level, this
recuperation of place-bound identities could be described as 'provincial socialism' – to expand on the municipal socialism developing in
many urban areas with strong left movements.[2] This term designates a
strategy aimed at tailoring political discourse to the concrete conditions of local communities and their needs. Only by adopting the
vantage point of nation and locality will it be possible to develop a

     1    Mark Sumner, 'Rep. Ilhan Omar Explains True Patriotism in the Face of Trump's
Racist Nationalism', *Daily Kos*, 18 July 2019, at dailykos.com.
     2    Owen Hatherley, *Red Metropolis: Socialism and the Government of London*
(London: Watkins Media Limited, 2020).

progressive politics responding to the crises of identity that the era of neoliberal globalisation has left in its wake.

## The Nation's Homecoming

The current reframing of politics along national lines is a cultural shock for many people, because it seems to go against the grain of the promise of an ever-more interconnected globalisation culminating in a global *œcumene*.[3] As the opening chapters made clear, neoliberal globalisation proclaimed the imminent demise of the nation-state and its substitution by supranational organisations and regional free trade areas along the lines of the European Union. It was expected that intensifying economic and cultural integration would structurally weaken nation-states. Global flows cutting across borders would create strong planetary interdependence, leading to a re-mixing of people, products and cultures, in something of a global melting pot. The international system of nation-states, in force since the Westphalian treaty of 1648, would eventually be replaced by a world governed under a single banner – either a common empire or a federation of liberal democracies.[4]

Bold predictions of the coming of a post-national world seemed grossly mistimed in the aftermath of the 2008 financial crash, and even more so since the beginning of the coronavirus pandemic. Prophets of the demise of the nation-state have underestimated how deeply ingrained nations are in political history and people's consciousness, as well as their centrality in organising mass democracy. Even during the heyday of globalisation, nations never really went away. As US sociologist Craig Calhoun showed in his emphatically titled *Nations Matter*, liberals 'underestimate the work done by nationalism and national identities in organising human life as well as politics in the contemporary world', and overlook 'how central nationalist categories are to . . . democracy, political legitimacy, and the nature of society itself'.[5] The

---

3   Ulf Hannerz, 'Notes on the Global Ecumene', *Public Culture* 1: 2 (1989), 66–75.

4   Michael Hardt and Antonio Negri, *Empire* (Cambridge, MA: Harvard University Press, 2016).

5   Craig J. Calhoun, *Nations Matter: Culture, History, and the Cosmopolitan Dream* (London: Routledge, 2011), pp. 7, 8.

importance of the nation is only becoming more apparent, as the retreat of globalisation appears to have rekindled national identifications.

Questions of nationhood are resurfacing with a vengeance at all levels in the Great Recoil: in international negotiations, in trade policy, in debates about the recovery fund in the EU and the public-health response to the pandemic and in the race for coronavirus vaccines. This trend reflects the crisis of globalisation and the geopolitical realignments engendered by it. Unrivalled US hegemony – the central pillar on which the entire edifice of real-world globalisation rested – is now faltering. Donald Trump's disastrous handling of the pandemic, the pressure of domestic revolts against institutional racism and the increasing prominence of China are upsetting long-held geopolitical certainties and reopening the grand game of international relations. Existing loyalties and alignments having been thrown into disarray; numerous countries are seeking new positions in a changing landscape, while bilateral relations and a greater focus on regional integration steal the stage from global multilateralism.

The national question invoked here is specific to present historical conditions and very different from the familiar pattern of struggles for national liberation. Except for a few well-known cases – such as those of the Scots, the Quebecois, the Catalans, the Kurds and the Palestinians – what is at stake is not the demand for the independence of stateless nations. Rather, the crux of the matter is the viability of well-established nations in a context in which much of their power seems to have been lost due to the exposure and dislocations created by neoliberal globalisation; not the formal independence of nations, but rather their substantive, practical autonomy. This perception of a 'lost nation' that had to be taken back was central to the narrative of Brexit, like that of many European sovereigntyists clamouring for an exit from the EU, or the national-populist sentiment that propelled Donald Trump into the White House. Yet, a similar impression also infuses many progressive movements that denounce how globalisation has denied power to ordinary people.

Nations and nationhood are famously divisive topics on the left, where 'flag-waving patriot' is tantamount to an insult. The nation is customarily associated with right-wing ideas, and the crude nationalism espoused today by figures like Trump and Le Pen with wars, fascist movements, racism and oppression. Nationalism has been wielded since the nineteenth century by conservative and fascist forces as a means of subduing class conflict and crushing the left. Socialists and communists have been branded as foreign agents and their internationalism painted as a betrayal of fundamental patriotic commitments. Nonetheless, by brushing off the national question and equating patriotism with nationalism, the left fails to do justice to the historical meaning of these words, and how they have been mobilised in the service of political revolution and social reform.

The struggles for national independence and unification in Greece, Italy, Hungary, Poland and Germany in the nineteenth century; the 'patriotic wars' conducted by Soviet Russia and other nations against Nazi domination; wars of national liberation in Algeria, Cameroon, Angola, Vietnam and tens of other countries – all such struggles for national liberation have been high on the list of the left's most cherished causes. Many central figures in the pantheon of socialism, including Marx and Engels themselves, were involved in such upheavals, and saw national independence as a legitimate democratic objective. To this day, many left activists eagerly support national struggles for independence. Moreover, Latin American socialist populism in Bolivia, Brazil, Argentina and Venezuela has been deeply infused with patriotism. It is true that making concessions to national identity is always a risk – during the 2010s some leftist renegades have joined nationalist causes in an opportunistic bid to reconnect with the working class. But branding anyone who does not subscribe to a liberal, cosmopolitan worldview as 'left nationalist' is manifestly deluded.

Rather than considering the nation as a monopoly of the right, it is necessary to understand it as a crucial political battlefield, as Otto Bauer proposed.[6] Nations have been the protagonists of history, for both good and ill. As liberal theorist Isaiah Berlin pointed out, they have been responsible for both history's greatest achievements and its most appalling disasters.[7] It would be impossible to understand the two world wars of the twentieth century, or any other bloody conflicts in recent history, without appreciating how they resulted from excesses of

6   Otto Bauer, *The Question of Nationalities and Social Democracy* (Minneapolis, MN: University of Minnesota Press, 2000).

7   Isaiah Berlin, *Concepts and Categories: Philosophical Essays* (Princeton, NJ: Princeton University Press, 2013).

nationalism, and their translation of those excesses into imperialist ambition and aggression, as Michael Mann has noted.[8] However, it would be equally impossible to imagine democracy, public services, the arts, culture and scientific research without reference to the nation. National belonging is a reality whose persistence has made a mockery of many predictions of its imminent demise. Rather than snobbish disdain, this reality requires sober consideration.

The nation is central to the doctrine of political legitimacy. Its durability derives from the fact that, to this day, national institutions are perceived as more legitimate, and therefore more democratic, than supranational ones.[9] At the most basic level, the nation is a group of people who share some ascriptive characteristics to do with common descent, territory, history and culture. The idea of a nation fundamentally implies the existence of a 'homeland' – the territory or 'seat' of the nation, whose borders are seen as natural and permanent – and of a people living on that land, claiming common descent. Finally, it entails a common history and culture, a common language, and a common set of representative institutions. All these different characteristics are packaged together in the idea of the nation.

Different understandings of the nation entail different and often contradictory political meanings and implications. From Johann Gottfried Herder onwards, the Romantic tradition of ethno-nationalism has placed emphasis on the ethnic, linguistic and cultural elements of common descent. From the moderate version of German nationalism that appeared in 1848, this kind of cultural nationalism evolved into a more explicit ethnic nationalism after German unification. The invocation of 'blood and soil' (*Blut und Boden*) popularised by Nazi functionary Richard Walther Darré, and informed by racial theory and agrarian ideology, would inspire the murderously racist nationalism of the Third Reich.[10] The other major tradition of European nationalism originates from the French Revolution, and is more republican and explicitly political in nature. Nations, in this model, can comprise people of a variety of

---

8   Michael Mann, 'A Political Theory of Nationalism and Its Excesses', in Sukumar Periwal, ed., *Notions of Nationalism* (Budapest: Central European University Press, 1995), p. 44.

9   Ernest Gellner, *Nations and Nationalism* (Malden, MA: Blackwell, 2013).

10   Anna Bramwell, *Blood and Soil: Richard Walther Darré and Hitler's Green Party* (Bourne End: Kensal Press, 1985).

races as long as they accept and respect the country's constitution. French Jacobinism embraced the notion famously articulated by the Abbé Sieyès that the people were the nation – the community of all citizens represented by the same institutions and obeying the same laws.[11]

Regardless of the basis on which the nation is defined, what seems to disturb cosmopolitan intellectuals is the nation's built-in particularism: the fact that it implies a division of humanity by arbitrary borders. Hegel viewed the nation as a space of universalism that transcended local differences, and dreaded the arrival of a post-national space which, instead of universalism, would unleash chaos.[12] But it is clear that, in the public imagination, the nation is today perceived as embodying the particular rather than the universal. The world of nations is no doubt a world of sometimes manifestly absurd fragmentation. The borders dividing the 193 United Nations member-states appear to many as irrational – something to be overcome in order to move towards a truly planetary society. But what cosmopolitans often miss is the strength of belonging and identification, and the sediments of history in which they germinate, which render the overcoming of the principle of nationality very unlikely even in the long term.

While the division of humanity into nations may indeed seem an atavistic phenomenon, the particularism and pluralism of nations stems from the basic reality of geography, and from the way in which physical distance and separation have bred historical and cultural differences. In *The Spirit of the Laws*, Montesquieu argued that it was ultimately the very extent of the planet and the distance between different populations that led different societies to develop in parallel.[13] Societies are organised concentrically around specific places – their capital cities, their monuments and markets – which act as cultural, administrative and commercial centres of the nation. Even our highly interconnected world, dominated by instant communication and fast, cheap air travel

---

11    Emmanuel-Joseph Sieyès, 'What Is the Third Estate?', *Sieyès, Political Writings: Including the Debate between Sieyès and Tom Paine in 1791*, ed. and transl. Michael Sonenscher (Indianapolis, IN: Hackett, 2003), p. 134.

12    G. W. F. Hegel, *Hegel's Philosophy of Right*, transl. S. W. Dyde (London: Dover, 2005).

13    Charles De Montesquieu, *Montesquieu: The Spirit of the Laws*, ed. Anne M. Cohler, Basia Carolyn Miller and Harold Samuel Stone (Cambridge: Cambridge University Press, 1989), p. 243.

(suspended for months during the pandemic), has not done away with this basic principle. The power of location, of distance, proximity and place continues to organise human communities. This has become all the more apparent in periods of lockdown during the pandemic, when we have come to realise the extent to which we remain prisoners of place; of our homes, our neighbourhoods, and our nations.

## Mazzini's Dream

To respond to the problem of nationality is not to deny the existence of humanity as a whole, nor to say – as Carl Schmitt implies – that any form of humanitarianism is a fraud and a cover for imperialist interests.[14] Rather, it means accepting that the universal of humanity appears in history through the particular form of different peoples and their histories. Following the dialectical thinking of Hegel, the seeds of universalism are found in particularity. What makes us human, hence universal, beginning from language, is what in turn makes us distinct, what divides us into numerous linguistic and cultural communities, and distinct nations. This diversity is something to celebrate for its own sake – a legacy of the rich history and complex challenges of our ancestors – and should not be seen as an obstacle to the development of a universalist politics. The universal cannot be achieved simply by a leap of faith beyond the parameters of existing reality. Rather, it should be the product of an exhaustive quest through particularism.

The view of the nation as anti-universalist was already criticised by Giuseppe Mazzini, the republican intellectual and activist who campaigned tirelessly for Italian unification and inspired the national liberation struggles of the nineteenth century. Mazzini sought to reconcile the humanitarianism of early socialist movements with the demand for national self-determination that emerged in revolutionary Europe from the 1820s. His view of the nation was infused with the romantic conception of the people as the protagonist of history. But he was adamant that national struggles were not in contradiction with the goal of uniting what, with an idealism typical of his era, he described as the

---

14   Carl Schmitt, *The Concept of the Political* (Chicago: University of Chicago Press, 2008), pp. 53–4.

'family of humanity that has only one altar, one thought, one poem as its hymn, and one language to sing'.[15] The first duty of all citizens, according to Mazzini, was 'to humanity'. No other principle, including the national principle, could override the 'law of human life'.[16]

For Mazzini, the nation was not a fixed and permanent entity. It was historical, and therefore mutable. He wrote memorably: 'We do not believe in the timelessness of races. We do not believe in the timelessness of language. We do not believe in the timeless and powerful influence of climate in the development of human activity'.[17] Moreover, Mazzini was strongly critical of 'narrow and mean Nationalism . . . jealous of everything that surrounded it'. He identified nationalism with the expansionist spirit of despotic rulers, and defended a patriotism informed by people's sense of civic duty to their communities. Only by overcoming dynastic nationalism and breeding a sentiment of belonging and attachment in each country would people cast off their chains and transform international relations into peaceful cooperation between countries.

Rather than viewing the nation as a 'manifestation of the past, a medieval concept that has caused much bloodshed, and that continues to fractionalize God's thinking on earth', as cosmopolitans would do, he argued that revolutionaries should face up to the reality of the nation.[18] They should approach the nation as a necessary step in the construction of a human community based on mutual understanding and solidarity. 'For us, the end is humanity; the pivot, the point of support, is the country', he argued, while retorting that, for cosmopolitans, the individual rather than the collectivity of the nation provided such a pivot. This view inspired Giuseppe Garibaldi, the hero of Italy's unification, who, besides being a patriot, was a strong advocate of socialism, founding many worker's associations around Italy. Garibaldi was also committed to racial equality, as he demonstrated in his fraternal comradeship with Andrea Aguyar, a black former slave from Uruguay, nicknamed 'Andrea il Moro', who died defending the revolutionary Roman Republic in 1848.

---

15   Giuseppe Mazzini, *A Cosmopolitanism of Nations: Giuseppe Mazzini's Writings on Democracy, Nation Building, and International Relations*, ed. Stefano Recchia and Nadia Urbinati (Princeton, NJ: Princeton University Press, 2009), p. 56.

16   Ibid.

17   Ibid., p. 55.

18   Ibid.

Mazzini's republican approach reveals the fallacy of the opposition between sovereigntyism and globalism invoked by the nationalist right and widely accepted in current political discourse. Sovereigntyism posits the idea that the nation-state can and must have complete control over the national territory, because it constitutes the only level at which politics is legitimate. Globalism instead asserts that control can only be achieved at the global level, because it is only at that scale that they can hope to confront the major problems facing humanity. In other words, while nationalism or sovereigntyism are absolute particularisms, globalism wears the robes of abstract universalism. Sovereigntyism and globalism are in reality what Hegel would describe as false absolutes: concepts with no bearing on actually-existing political reality, which is never completely national or completely global. Only the most fanatical supporter of sovereignty would want to live in an autarchic country, cut off from the world. Equally, no one would want to live in a world at the absolute mercy of global forces, where all decisions were taken at the international level, stripping citizens of nation-states of any form of local control.

To overcome this false opposition, a way forward lies in embracing what could be termed 'democratic patriotism': a commitment to one's local political community and its democratic institutions and customs as a stepping stone towards a universalist politics. This concept is a reference to Jürgen Habermas's 'constitutional patriotism'. For Habermas, constitutional patriotism is 'a consensus on the procedure for the legitimate enactment of laws and the legitimate exercise of power' enshrined in the country's law.[19] Democratic patriotism goes beyond this minimalist notion of a patriotism limited to this acceptance of the constitutional state as a necessary framework. Rather, it operates on the assumption that democracy is always patriotic, because, by definition, it is the power of a particular demos inhabiting a specific territory and implies a place-specific sense of belonging and pride on the part of its members. Sentiments of belonging are not an obstacle to democracy; rather they are its pre-conditions.

Certainly, patriotism is a singularly loaded term that does not have good press on the left. 'Social patriotism' was the term used by Lenin to

19    Jürgen Habermas, *Inclusion of the Other: Studies in Political Theory*, ed. Ciaran Cronin and Pablo De Greiff (Hoboken, NJ: John Wiley, 2015), p. 117.

attack the chauvinism of the German Social-Democratic Party, and in particular its vote in favour of Imperial Germany's entry into war.[20] However, Lenin himself was not deaf to the question of national self-determination. He famously locked horns with Rosa Luxemburg in defence of demands for Polish independence and argued that communists had to fight resolutely against national oppression.[21] Ultimately, Marx and Engels, despite their criticism of the nation as a bourgeois construct, had a more nuanced perspective on the issue than is generally acknowledged, favouring nationalisms of the oppressed.[22] Cosmopolitan leftists like to quote the famous passage in *The Communist Manifesto* affirming that 'working men have no country'; but they skip over the ensuing sentences, where Marx argues: 'Since the proletariat must first of all acquire political supremacy, must rise to be the leading class of the nation, must constitute itself *the* nation, it is, so far, itself national, though not in the bourgeois sense of the word.' This generalisation of the class into the nation was precisely what Antonio Gramsci meant when he said that workers had to become the hegemonic class in national politics.

In order to make patriotism a conduit for democratic politics to distinguish it from nationalism, and to clarify what ethical imperatives it entails. As George Orwell noted in his famous essay 'Notes on Nationalism', while nationalism is aggressive and power-hungry, patriotism is 'defensive, both militarily and culturally'. Nationalism 'is inseparable from the desire for power', whereby 'the abiding purpose of every nationalist is to secure more power and more prestige'.[23] The national sentiment of inhabitants of great imperialist powers is always bound to lean more towards these forms of aggressive nationalism than the sentiment of nationhood in countries that are weaker, or subordinate to others. By contrast, patriotism indicates 'devotion to a particular place and a particular way of life, which one believes to be the best in the world but has no wish to force on other people'[24] In terms of the dialectical relationship between the interior and

---

20   Vladimir Lenin, 'Dead Chauvinism and Living Socialism', in Vladimir Lenin, *Collected Works Volume 21* (New York: International Publishers, 1932), pp. 94–8

21   Vladimir Lenin, *The Right of Nations to Self Determination* (Westport, CT: Greenwood Press, 1977).

22   Erica Benner, *Really Existing Nationalisms* (London: Verso, 2018).

23   George Orwell, *Notes on Nationalism* (London: Penguin, 2018), p. 21.

24   Ibid.

exterior, nationalism's focus is always external; it constitutes itself in opposition to other nations. Patriotism, on the other hand, is directed inward – towards the search for the soul of the nation. On the right, references to the nation are invariably antagonistic and exclusive. The identity of the nation is premised on the exclusion of immigrants and foreigners – those originating from other nations – symbolised as germs infecting the body of the demos. On the left, the adoption of patriotic motives instead betokens the affirmation of republican values of community and solidarity binding internally all members of a given polity. This has important implications for socialist politics. Patriotic duty, in the sense used by leftist populists like Podemos's leader Pablo Iglesias, does not entail merely living up to the principles of the country's constitution, but also recognising the principles of social justice, solidarity and unity, as well as the ambition for self-improvement displayed in the best pages of a nation's history.

The urgency of patriotism has to do with a struggle for re-internalisation and re-localisation that is central to the logic of the Great Recoil. As Orwell noted, patriotism involves a 'devotion to place' – the celebration of one's place of birth and/or residence; acknowledgement of the struggle and suffering of previous generations; and commitment to constructing a better society. This 'return to place' is fundamental to democracy, especially in the present times of 'revenge of geography'.[25] Democracy is always emplaced. It is around places, from the Athenian agora and Jean-Jacques Rousseau's Geneva to contemporary nations, with their extensive communities and territories often encompassing millions of citizens and thousands of square kilometres, that politics is constituted. Nations may well be 'imagined communities' too extensive for citizens to know each other, but they are communities based on location nonetheless.[26] Furthermore, it is true, as Gramsci already noticed, that the modern world is marked by an apparent mismatch between the cosmopolitanism of the economy and the nationalism of politics.[27] Business is global, but all politics is local: democracy is rooted in place, and thus

25   Robert D. Kaplan, *The Revenge of Geography: What the Map Tells Us about Coming Conflicts and the Battle against Fate* (New York: Random House Trade Paperbacks, 2013).

26   Benedict Anderson, *Imagined Communities: Reflections on the Origin and Spread of Nationalism*. (London: Verso, 2006).

27   Antonio Gramsci, *Further Selections from the Prison Notebooks*, ed. and transl. Derek Boothman (Mineapolis, MN: University of Minnesota Press, 1995), p. 353.

tied to the particularities of settings and identities. This contradiction has to be reconciled, 'domesticating' the genius of the economy, re-embedding economic activities within territories and their networks of common responsibility.

The reclaiming of patriotism and a commitment to community concretely manifested in projects of regional development for depressed areas may do much to address the rebellion of the peripheries that has to date been a boon to the right. As we have seen when discussing the relationship between class structure and contemporary politics, the left is heavily reliant on the urban middle-class electorate which, tends to view globalisation positively and to look at the anger of non-urban voters as backward-looking. This is a long-standing problem for the left, which, as already argued by sociologist Teodor Shanin, has a problem understanding and mobilising constituencies outside of urban areas.[28] Yet, if progressives want to be in government rather than in opposition, they need to come to terms with the grudges of those in the rural peripheries, rather than simply branding all provincial voters as chauvinistic and parochial. The very promise of the 'nation' as equality and community among all citizens, regardless of their circumstances and location, provides an entry point to develop a political proposal to appeal not only to cities but also to small and medium-sized towns. The municipal patriotism pursued by many recent leftist mayors around Europe, such as Ada Colau in Barcelona and Luigi De Magistris in Naples, comes more easily to urban classes than national patriotism. But a nation socially divided between city and hinterland is neither viable nor desirable. In fact, the 'ghettoisation' of the left in urban centres has in the past itself precipitated turns towards reaction. Municipalism, or municipal socialism, thus needs to be accompanied by a provincial socialism that attends to the needs of the hinterland and informs the development of policies capable of reducing the sense of exposure to the effects of uncontrolled competition in the global market. This will entail rising to the challenge of building organisations in non-urban areas which the left has for too long seen as impossible to win over, but which will be decisive in overcoming the toxic polarisation of city and countryside.

---

28  Teodor Shanin, *The Awkward Class: Political Sociology of Peasantry in a Developing Society: Russia 1910–1925* (Oxford: Clarendon Press, 1972).

## The Nation as Protective Structure

The contrast between the protection-orientated character of today's new socialism and the aggressive nature of nationalism is crucial. The patriotism advocated by the socialist left sees the nation's merit in its protective nature – in the forms of community and solidarity embedded in it, and its ability to provide a shield against the ravages of imperial powers and global capital. This protective role is particularly important for weaker nation-states that are under pressure from regional and global hegemons. Advocacy of the protective role of the nation can be found in unlikely places within liberal and Marxist thought. For example, Hannah Arendt and Franz Neumann, two German Jews who were the earliest scholars to produce a political analysis of the ideology and organisation of Nazism, did not subscribe to liberal cosmopolitanism. Many would probably expect Arendt and Neumann, who had to flee their own country because of Nazi persecution, to be fervent critics of the nation. But their argument runs precisely in the opposite direction. Arendt and Neumann viewed Nazism not as a nationalist phenomenon, but as a supra-national and imperialist movement that, far from conceiving the nation as the supreme value, saw it as an intolerable fetter to its unquenchable thirst for aggression and expansion.

*Nationalsozialismus*, of course, espoused nationalist propaganda; but, as Arendt explains, its racism and imperialism, rather than reinforcing it, aimed at 'destroy[ing] the pattern of the nation-state'.[29] As she famously puts it in the opening page of *The Origins of Totalitarianism*, 'The Nazis had a genuine and never revoked contempt of the narrowness of nationalism, the provincialism of the nation-state, and they repeated time and again that their "movement", international in scope like the Bolshevik movement, was more important to them than any state, which would be necessarily bound to a specific territory'.[30] While the Nazis indulged in 'hypernationalistic talk', they were nonetheless 'prepared to destroy the body politic of their own nation, because tribal nationalism, with its immoderate lust for conquest, was one of the

---

29    Hannah Arendt, *The Origins of Totalitarianism* (Boston, MA: Houghton Mifflin Harcourt, 1973), p. 39.
30    Ibid.

principal powers to force open the narrow and modest limits of the nation-state and its sovereignty'.[31]

Antisemitism, a key component of Nazism, was not nationalistic, but rather 'supranationalist', curiously mirroring the supra-national 'Jewry' it antagonised. In this context, the 'supranationalism of the antisemites' harboured the aim of constructing a 'dominating superstructure which would destroy all home-grown national structures alike'.[32] This supranational character of antisemitism resonates with contemporary extremist cultures such as the so-called alt-right. The white supremacism espoused by the alt-right is racist rather than nationalist. The objective of figures like US neo-Nazi Richard Spencer is the establishment of a 'white ethnostate', with the banishment of minorities to Bantustans. Furthermore, some alt-rightists see the secessionist Confederate states, rather than the United States that defeated them, as their fatherland. Rioters who stormed the Capitol on 6 January 2021 carried Confederate flags, and took down a United States flag in the hall of the Senate to substitute it with a Trump flag. Despite their pretences, they are not actual 'patriots', but simply racists.

Arendt's defence of the nation-state derived from her understanding of how the horrors of World War II, and particularly the genocide of Eastern European Jews, were facilitated by the disintegration of nation-states. Millions of Jewish people were transformed into stateless citizens deprived of any protection enshrined in national laws, thus becoming easy victims of the Nazi killing machine. Loss of national rights meant the loss of human rights. In line with Mazzini's argument, for Arendt, the universal rights of humans were not incompatible with the national rights of citizens; indeed, the latter constituted the practical line of defence for the principles embodied in the former.

Like Arendt, Neumann – the influential first historian of Nazism with his *Behemoth* – was convinced that Nazism was not nationalism, but a racial imperialism based on the affirmation of a superior race and its right to determine life and death. As Neumann puts it, the focus of Nazi ideology was 'the sovereignty of the Germanic race'.[33] This racial

---

31   Ibid., p. 41.
32   Ibid.
33   Franz Leopold Neumann, *Behemoth: The Structure and Practice of National Socialism, 1933–1944* (Lanham, MD: Rowman & Littlefield, 2009), p. 168.

sovereignty was very different from the sovereignty of the nation, because, unlike the nation, race has no territorial limits, and thus knows no barriers to its power. The project of a *Grossdeutsches Reich* pursued by Hitler centred on a community of racial descent and its right of conquest, prefigured by the Germanic invasions and the Teutonic knights who colonised the east, rather than on a bounded historical nation. This boundless ambition is the element which made Nazi ideology so aggressive.

Neumann was so adamant about the dissociation between Nazism and the nation-state that, in a central passage of *Behemoth*, he urged 'a defence of state sovereignty'.[34] He argued that the notion of sovereignty in the present was 'progressive' for two reasons. First, this was because it enshrined 'the juristic equality of all states and the consequent rationality of international relations . . . If every state is sovereign all states are equal.' Sovereignty thus created 'rationality in an anarchic world' and 'a clear-cut delineation of the spheres of power, [subjecting] to the power of the state only those who live within its territory and a select few (citizens) outside'.[35] The nation is understood as part of a community of nations, much in the same way as the individual is understood as part of the community of society, thus protecting its autonomy and independence in its internal affairs. The doctrine of national sovereignty views interference and encroachment by foreign powers as contrary to the principles of self-determination and democracy.

The second reason why sovereignty deserved praise was that the boundedness of the nation-state 'creates a barrier' which 'limits the extent of state power at the same time'.[36] Borders are structures that not only protect the state from external enemies and dangers, real or perceived, but also 'contain' the state, preventing it from overstepping its power. In other words, the advantage of the nation-state is found precisely in its weakness: the bordered character of the state, its self-contained territoriality, poses a limit to an otherwise boundless power. All sincere democrats should therefore defend national sovereignty as a protective mechanism against the assaults by expansionist states and their corporations. This is the protective or defensive sense in which

---

34   Ibid.
35   Ibid.
36   Ibid., pp. 167–8.

patriotism should be reclaimed. But the reconstruction of national democracies also entails a reimagining of the international order such that the sovereignty of each nation may be effectively reconciled with that of others.

## World Government and European Chaos

Far from being hermetically sealed territories, nations always exist within an international system, a 'community of nations'. Diplomatic relationships, embassies, bilateral and multilateral treaties, wars, military and economic alliances, trade cartels, migration, religious and cultural relationships are some examples of phenomena that by defintion criss-cross and transcend national borders. Only the most obtuse sovereigntyist can pretend that any issue is resolved by a straightforward resort to the iron principle of national sovereignty. For thoughtful socialists, the question should be what new framework of international relations is desirable and realistic as a means of achieving the recovery of a greater scope of popular sovereignty without sparking conflict between nations.

The classic problem of international relations is how the divergent interests of different nation-states may be managed and resolved peacefully. From arguments about primary resources and fishing rights to industrial competition, territorial disputes, and religious and ethnic strife, the reasons for conflict between nations are many. Moreover, economic protectionism has been widely criticised as a 'beggar-thy-neighbour' exercise that often leads to retaliation, and ultimately trade wars. These issues raise the question of how a system marrying international peace and national democracy might be achieved. Various solutions have been proposed to this dilemma, and supranational institutions such as the World Trade Organization and the International Monetary Fund, as well as regional federations like the European Union, include as part of their founding mission the prevention of escalating conflict and war. Rather than leading to the pacification of conflict and the ushering in of a unified world, however, supranational governance has often contributed to the deepening of national rivalries. What is therefore required is a new approach to international relations that might actually resolve conflicts rather than exacerbate them.

The problem of international conflict was famously the topic of Kant's essay 'Perpetual Peace'.[37] Few essays are so often cited by liberal cosmopolitans; indeed, Kant is considered a spiritual father of the European Union. But few texts have been so flagrantly misread and misunderstood. In the essay, Kant famously proposed a blueprint for an international federation of states – one that has gone on to inspire European federalists like Altiero Spinelli.[38] Kant cautioned against the destructive power of international war, stressing the necessity of dialogue between nations. But Kant was far from a radical cosmopolitan and did not entertain the idea that nations might disappear. He carefully cautioned against the risks of what he described as a 'world government' – a form of executive power superseding national governments. World government would ultimately produce results in direct opposition to those intended: instead of delivering perpetual peace, it would result in perpetual war.

Kant offered two arguments as to why world government posed a threat. First, by dint of its dimensions, its threat to peace would be significantly greater than that of a nation-state. If left unchecked, it would acquire the size of an unbeatable Leviathan with more access to finance, a larger repressive apparatus and more military firepower at its disposal than a conventional state. Second, the establishment of a world government, far from ensuring stability and peace, would inevitably foster conflicts at the periphery. People from marginalised nations in border regions would naturally be prone to rebellion. Thus, the integrative pull of world government would be matched by a contrary impulse at the margins, resulting in bloody conflict. Like Mazzini, Kant did not see the self-determination of national communities as contradicting universalism and reason. Rather, he proposed a system by means of which diverging interests could be negotiated and reconciled.

These considerations can help us better understand the dilemmas posed by European integration, which in recent years has become a tinderbox for confrontations between nationalists and globalists. Rather than a Kantian federation, the 'neo-functionalist' model of Jean

---

37   Immanuel Kant, *Perpetual Peace: A Philosophical Sketch*, transl. Lewis White Beck (Cambridge: Cambridge University Press, 1970).
38   Thilo Zimmermann, *European Republicanism: Combining Political Theory with Economic Rationale* (London: Palgrave Macmillan, 2019), pp. 25–53.

Monnet, one of the chief architects of European unity, resembles the project spelled out in Friedrich Hayek's 1939 essay, 'The Economic Conditions of Interstate Federalism', in which he argued that such a federation between states would have to impose restrictions that would be 'even greater than we have hitherto assumed and that their power of independent action would have to be limited still further'.[39] While this text had little direct, practical influence over the founding of the European Community, its notion of 'negative integration' closely articulates the logic of European integration following the Maastricht Treaty, with the creation of a single market and then a single currency.[40]

The European Union has become a sort of non-state, whose power is mostly negative, consisting in the regulation and administrative coercion of member-states. While dismantling much of the power and sovereignty of participating countries, the EU has not moved on to the construction of a higher-order sovereignty. It has created a 'sovereign void' that it is either unable or unwilling to fill. As Adam Tooze has noted, the European Commission remains a weak institution with very limited staffing, and is therefore incapable of compensating for the loss of power of member-states.[41] In other words, European integration has stopped at the *pars destruens*, ripping apart the sovereign structures of protection and control formerly operated by member-states. The four freedoms articulated in the 1992 Maastricht Treaty – free movement of goods, capital, services, and labour – have deprived nation-states of the ability to restrain capital flows and protect their industries from fierce international competitions; thus, rather than driving economic 'convergence', the effect has been to polarise continental economies even further. Similarly, the budgetary rules enshrined in the Maastricht Treaty, and their strict spending limits (reinforced by the 'expenditure benchmark' introduced since 2001), have forced countries, especially in the South of Europe, into prolonged recession.

---

39   Friedrich Hayek, 'The Economic Conditions of Interstate Federalism', *New Commonwealth Quarterly* 5: 2 (1939), 131–49.

40   Fritz Scharpf, 'Negative Integration: States and the Loss of Boundary Control', in Christopher Pierson, Francis G. Castles and Ingela K. Naumann, eds, *The Welfare State Reader*, 2nd edn (Cambridge: Polity, 2006), pp. 223–5.

41   Adam Tooze, *Crashed: How a Decade of Financial Crises Changed the World* (London: Penguin, 2018).

A similar logic applies to the prohibition of state support for strategic industries in EU member-states, which has deprived governments of control over industrial policy on the basis that this would offend against the sacred principle of capitalist competition. Needless to say, this move has not been accompanied by any effective industrial policy at the continental level. While countries have lost the power to manage their industrial strategy, the European Union has made no significant progress in compensating for the resulting policy vacuum. This fact does much to explain why Europe is so far behind in terms of its development of strategic technology, compared to countries like the United States, China and South Korea. The European Central Bank, which controls the currency used by 340 million Europeans, is guided only by the imperative of limiting inflation, while other goals – such as reducing unemployment – remain 'discretionary'. Meanwhile, fiscal havens such as the Netherlands, Luxembourg and Ireland coax businesses and their tax revenues away from other member-states by offering corporate tax-residency programmes. Thus, rather than leading to greater comity between the nations of the European continent, the EU has deepened national enmities, leading to a rekindling of suspicions and rivalries of a kind that have not been seen for many decades.

The European Recovery Fund approved in July 2020, however, demonstrates that the EU is not completely impermeable to the political transformations now taking place. While the fund is widely seen as insufficient considering the scale of the crisis, especially when compared to the responses of other countries (€750 billion in the EU versus $2trillion in the first stimulus package in the United States), it points to a partial repudiation of the logic of austerity, as also seen in the suspension of the Stability Pact at the outset of the pandemic. It is significant that if, after 2008, the European Union responded with demands for austerity, it is now responding with a stimulus, however inadequately. These developments also suggest that the European Union may be moving away from a federalist model and towards a more confederal and inter-governmental one, in which countries maintain greater executive power and have to face fewer constraints; an EU closer to the thinking of Charles de Gaulle than of Jean Monnet. Given the enduring controversies over nationhood and state authority that this chapter has explored, this seems like a more realistic direction for the managers of European integration to adopt. Still, the neoliberal dogmas crystallised in the Maastricht Treaty and the Stability Pact hang like the sword of Damocles over any long-term prospect of a reorientation of economic policy within the EU. Due to the action of the so-called Frugal Four (Austria, Denmark, the Netherlands and Sweden) in pursuit of austerity, and pressure from the Bundesbank hawks and the German government, that intends to soon reintroduce the 'debt brake' limiting its own spending, the momentary relaxation of budgetary rules may soon be followed by a return to the austerity orthodoxy. This risks plunging Europe once again into the chaos seen during the sovereign debt crisis of the early 2010s, forcing member-states to undergo 'reforms' consisting of new privatisations and cuts to public spending that would devastate the economic and social fabric of European societies and may spark new populist revolts.

## Integrationists and Exiters

Two main responses have so far been seen to the crisis of globalisation and the resurfacing of the question of nationality. On the one hand, there are globalists, who propose that the global system be maintained and expanded; on the other there are 'exiters', who argue that leaving the system of international agreements is the only way forward. For advocates of European integration, and of global integration more generally, today's political problems derive from the fact that integration has not gone far enough. They decry nationalism as an obstacle to 'deeper integration', in the jargon often used by the European Commission. Moreover, they argue that the scale of global problems – such as climate change, or the successful efforts of digital companies to avoid tax – makes the construction of institutions operating on a global scale particularly urgent.

Exiters have been at the forefront of the battle against EU integration. Besides Brexit, a number of other 'exits' have been widely discussed in recent years – from Grexit, especially during the 2015 crisis, to, more recently, Frexit and Italexit. Sociologist Albert Hirschman famously discussed voice, protest and exit as ways for voters and consumers to express their opinion.[42] His theory mostly referred to the relationship

---

42   Albert O. Hirschman, 'Exit, Voice, and the State', *World Politics* 31: 1 (1978).

between consumers and businesses. According to this theory, if people do not find a way to have a 'voice' – in other words, a channel through which to express their dissent – they will tend to 'exit', abandoning a system or organisation altogether.[43] The term exit denotes a moment of 'withdrawal' – a backward movement, much like that of the Great Recoil, away from a given situation. But it also alludes to a homecoming, or return to self. This was apparent in the nostalgic nationalism ventilated during the pro-Brexit mobilisations conveying the promised recovery of a lost 'British exceptionalism' on the world scene.

Exit should always be an option – from a romantic partnership as much as from a political group or international treaty; but there is clearly a facile element in the political imaginary associated with this idea. The term presupposes a sharp dividing line between the nation and the supranational space of which it is a part, suggesting that the solution is for the former to leave the latter, but without specifying the destination. Ultimately, exit is never a self-contained event, but represents movement: exiting one arrangement entails entering another. There is no 'outside' of the international system of nations; every exit is just a repositioning. In the case of Brexit, this has proved clear in the way in which, on the point of exiting the EU, the UK has sought a stronger relationship with the United States, reinforcing a long-standing Anglo-American compact. It should be borne in mind that, for any country that is not the United States, China, and perhaps soon India, exiting does not guarantee freedom and independence, but often leads to new forms of subordination in place of the old.

Regardless of the problems with the imaginary of exit, it is clear that the momentum behind such movements reflects the failure of prevailing forms of supranational integration, which are too often perceived as involving a curtailment of democracy. A new, progressive approach to foreign relations should not condition the resolution of international disputes on the muting of popular sovereignty. No true international entente, no benevolent participation in larger identities, can develop by merely negating national identities and interests. A large measure of

---

43   According to Nick Couldry, one of the features of neoliberalism has been limiting the possibility for voice, due to the post-democratic turn of political systems. One may say that in this situation it is as if there were no other choice for citizens but to exit if they are to express their dissent. Nick Couldry, *Why Voice Matters: Culture and Politics After Neoliberalism* (London: Sage, 2010).

national autonomy – itself a function of material self-sufficiency – is a necessary condition for a peaceful international order and fruitful transnational collaboration, rather than an obstacle to them. Too often in the past, encroachment on national sovereignty – most obviously in the many recent wars in the Middle East – has proved disastrous, however much it might supposedly have been animated by the benign intention of exporting democracy and securing international peace. This does not mean that international cooperation is not necessary. There are many examples of successful transnational collaborations that allow countries to coordinate their effort and mediate their conflicts. Think about joint international initiatives such as the European Space Agency and CERN, among other collective scientific bodies, which allow nations to pool their resources to achieve things they would be unable to do in isolation. Future challenges will call for new efforts of bilateral and multilateral cooperation, the resolution of disputes massive and for investment in transnational infrastructures. But they will also call for an extension of democracy at all levels.

The basic condition for any international treaty should be that it is democratic in a double sense. First, all treaties should be supported by a majority of the electorate in each member country, and entering into them should be validated by ample discussion and, where necessary, popular referenda. Citizens have had their fill of international agreements passed over the heads of the electorate without proper consultation. International treaties should never be used as a political crowbar to limit democratic control by citizens over their economy, environmental protections and labour rights. These problems have afflicted many international treaties signed under neoliberalism, which aimed to muzzle popular sovereignty and provide legal protections for corporations from national governments. Such mechanisms are inimical to democratic control and social protection; they are the deplorable emblems of a failed neoliberal globalisation.

The kind of patriotism I propose is thus strongly internationalist in its posture. While affirming the primacy of the nation as the space of democratic intervention, it acknowledges the need for close international cooperation, mutual tolerance and authentic openness grounded in autonomy. There are many signs that we are heading towards a Balkanised globalisation – or, to put it more positively, to a situation in which unrivalled US hegemony is going to give way to a greater role for

China and more autonomy for other countries and world regions. International tensions are likely to grow, as has already been seen in Donald Trump's escalating rhetoric against China, as well as in the developing conflict between India and China. Furthermore, imperial powers, starting with the US and China, are likely to battle to secure their spheres of influence at the expense of the autonomy of nation-states. Amid this reshuffling of international relations, the left should fight against undemocratic forms of international integration and imperial interference, while advocating for forms of international cooperation that are fair and workable – cognisant of the fact that only by satisfying the legitimate desires of national communities to recoup some degree of self-determination can an authentic and realistic internationalism be effectively pursued.

# Conclusion

The Great Recoil may seem to offer a dire outlook for progressive politics. But this moment of 'turning back to itself' of politics has its silver lining. The present era offers precious opportunities for social introspection about the dangers of uncontrolled capitalism. At the same time, the pandemic has made it self-evident that we all rely on the actions of other people and on a collective structure of care for our individual and shared survival. Furthermore, following Hegel's view of *Erinnerung*, the Great Recoil is not simply the coda of a dying epoch, but also the prelude to a moment of *Aufhebung*, or sublation – an overcoming of the present order of things and the emergence of a new world.[1] In recapitulating the fallacies of thirty years of rampant neoliberalism and the grievances of those left behind by the forward drive of capitalist innovation, we are presented with a moment of necessary retreat before moving forward, as expressed in the French phrase '*reculer pour mieux sauter*' ('going backward to better jump forward'). Now is the moment when scores can be settled and justice can eventually be won; but also the time when a transformative project for a future society beyond the failures of neoliberalism can finally be imagined.

In the course of this book, we have seen how the chronic crisis of the 2010s has come to its terminal stage, as neoliberal lies were exposed, revealing the contours of a new world with markedly different forms of

---

1  Hegel, *Phenomenology of Spirit*, 492–3.

social regulation and economic governance. The decline of neoliberalism and its vicious confrontation with populism, compounded by the change in common sense produced by the shock of the pandemic, have spawned the emergence of a protective neo-statism that seems bent on replacing neoliberalism as the dominant ideological framework. Lockdowns, quarantines, pandemic controls, mass vaccination campaigns, furlough programmes and massive public investment plans all reflect the return to an activist state. Meanwhile, the public has increased its acceptance of the need for greater government interventionism beyond what was already considered necessary in light of the coming climate emergency. In the midst of this radical shift in perspectives, foundational neoliberal notions – individualism, the free market, deregulation, shareholder capitalism – which have been broadly hegemonic for a generation, have become increasingly indefensible, leading to a radical reordering of the ideological horizon.

## The Political New Normal

Contemporary ideology is not only defined negatively, in opposition to neoliberalism. It also carries its own distinctive content, manifested by the emergence of new political keywords that evoke a radically different imaginary from that of the roaring 1990s and early 2000s. Most representative of this change in the political lexicon is the neo-statist trinity: sovereignty–protection–control. These muscular signifiers, which occupy the centre of the political 'new normal' of the post-pandemic era, conjure a vision of contemporary political challenges as revolving around a healing of the body politic – a restoration of social cohesion and of state capacity in the face of the disruption ushered in by economic globalisation, and a cure for the sense of dislocation and exposure it has engendered. They express a desire for stability, security and safety that is at loggerheads with the pursuit of disruptive modernisation that was dominant in the neoliberal era. In fact, in many respects, they project a reversal of neoliberal discourse and the triad – openness–opportunity–entrepreneurialism – that insisted on the need to unlock the bolts of all social systems, institutions and organisations so as to unleash the full power of individual creativity and private initiative.

If these seductive neoliberal terms are now giving way to their neo-statist alternatives, it is because the political project of which they have been the flagbearers has produced disastrous results. Openness has turned into exposure, opportunity into downward social mobility and entrepreneurialism into a byword for rapacity. In this sense, the neo-statist political lexicon is a rational attempt to make sense of radically changed social conditions and to redress social preoccupations that can no longer be ignored regardless of one's political persuasion. If, during the neoliberal boom years, dreams of growth and enrichment seduced many voters, particularly in the middle class, they seem to have no bearing on contemporary reality, in circumstances of economic retrenchment. Political discussion today focuses on restorative goals of re-establishing essential, minimum conditions for society's existence – on issues of sustainability, reconstruction and repair rather than growth.

The promises of protection, stability, security and sovereignty that occupy centre stage in the endopolitics of post-neoliberal neo-statism are more attuned to the bitter realities of the early twenty-first century. In the present moment of economic and social involution, ideological representations dwell on visceral aspects of politics that have to do with survival, stability and reproduction, with the desire to re-establish a sense of order in a world gripped by anxiety about the future. Sovereignty, protection and control are the ground zero of politics after a decade of economic crisis and political instability. They highlight the degree of uncertainty that has been engendered by forty years of neoliberal dominance, and the need to find a different point of equilibrium for society, for the relationship between politics and economics, and for the system of international relations.

The fact that the post-neoliberal left and right share a common jargon does not mean that the present moment of neo-statism is a phase of complicity between the radical right and the radical left – as some neoliberals, including Tony Blair, have suggested. If anything, as we have seen in the course of the book, the populist moment of the 2010s and the statist turn of the early 2020s point to precisely the opposite of the horseshoe, whereby the ideological extremes meet one another. These are years of profound polarisation in which radically alternative solutions to the neoliberal impasse are being spawned, and antagonistic social blocs formed. The populist moment has led to the resurgence of strong left and right identities, to a revival of nationalism on the one hand and socialism on the other. While both nationalist right and

socialist left appeal to the people against the elites, they have very different elites in mind; and while they both speak about the need for a
stronger state, their visions of the state are at loggerheads.

Terms such as 'sovereignty', 'protection', 'control', 'security' and 'stability' – that organise contemporary political discourse – are thus best
understood as pliable *social demands* to which radically different *political responses* can be given. The right's response is focused on a proprietarian protectionism that marries nationalist communitarianism to
hyper-individualism. Its aggressive assertion of sovereignty ('America
First!') revolves around affirming the supremacy of 'full citizens' over
mere residents, or 'inhabitants', and of 'owners' over 'workers', combining a defence of property with a Darwinian supremacism of the strong
over the weak. On the left, the neo-statist discourse instead takes the
form of a social protectivism, in which the demand for protection is
addressed through the promise of greater social, health and environmental protections; through a politics of care that strengthens social
support systems to respond to people's sense of vulnerability while reinforcing social reciprocity and solidarity.

History will decide whether the left, the right or the centre will claim
hegemony in this new ideological landscape. In fact, while the nationalist right was until recently expected to win the battle for post-neoliberal
hegemony, the difficulties it has experienced in the course of the
pandemic because of its embrace of anti-science scepticism show that
the contest remains undecided, and the ideological transition is still in
flux. The temporary retreat of the nationalist right may usher in a temporary return of the neoliberal centre; but now is also the moment for the
socialist left to be ready to seize its chance.

## A Socialism That Protects

The neo-statist turn of the Great Recoil calls for a revival of long-aban-
doned social-democratic ideas. Extension of health provision and
welfare coverage, Keynesian easy money and demand management,
even nationalisation and planning, all taboos during the 1990s when
neoliberalism made inroads into European social democracies, are now
once again on the table as people try to work out alternatives to a failing
economic system. The revival of democratic socialism associated with

Bernie Sanders and Jeremy Corbyn, and the ascendance of the 'millennial socialism' epitomised by Alexandria Ocasio-Cortez, are certainly focuses of great interest, and potential nightmares for the business oligarchy.[2] But the risk of resurrecting socialism is that it might appear a nostalgic move with no bearing on contemporary reality. As I have argued throughout this book, a revival of socialism in the current circumstances should develop along the lines of a social protectivism – a 'socialism that protects', with questions of social protection and democratic control at its heart.

Social protectivism entails the marrying of the traditional socialist commitment to equality to the pursuit of social and environmental security, in an era when citizens feel threatened by existential risks that put their livelihoods, if not their very survival, at stake. It means responding to the all-too-rational fear that is harboured by large sections of the population about the chaos of the present, and imagining new public institutions and provisions to deal with these times of deep uncertainty. As we have seen, there are currently many social grievances that call for a revival of the protective function of politics already raised by classical philosophy. Confronting the skyrocketing unemployment that is throwing millions into destitution requires the repair of social safety nets and the establishment of universalist provisions and of a job guarantee for the unemployed. Similarly, runaway globalisation has created the need for protectionist measures to recover national control of strategic industries, which need to be safeguarded against disruptive digital oligopolies, and to safeguard local economies against the ravages of global finance. Finally, environmental disasters provoked by climate change and biodiversity loss require extensive measures of climate mitigation and adaptation, safety enhancement and land protection.

This focus on protection implies a radical reframing of the left's priorities away from the vanities of the neoliberal era. The fact that protection sounds today like an unfamiliar notion on the left is due to the fact that, for a long time, the policies of capitalist democracies have been informed by different notions – by the neoliberal politics of social aspiration, concerned more with upward mobility, competition and innovation. As we have seen, embracing the neoliberal gospel in the 1990s, centre-left

2  Jeremy Gilbert, *Twenty-First-Century Socialism* (Hoboken, NJ: John Wiley, 2020).

leaders like Bill Clinton, Tony Blair and Gerhard Schröder were complicit in the weakening of welfare and labour provisions, and embraced a possessive, individualistic framework. They looked upon social safety nets and workers' organisations as fetters hindering private initiative and individual freedom, and became suspicious of government protection seen as paternalistic and anti-entrepreneurial. In the imaginary of Third Way supporters, protection came to be equated with a backward-looking attitude at odds with free trade commitments and the openness and the enterprising spirit of the 'New Times'.

Given the current decay of neoliberalism, it is necessary to recover some of the spirit of post-war social democracy, what in the UK is called 'the spirit of 1945', which in the early post-war period led to the creation of the NHS and the welfare state. We need to build on this tradition of social protection in the present, expanding on it to meet the egalitarian demands of emerging causes ranging from environmentalism to feminism. In the course of its history, the left has pursued its own notion of protection. It has fought for class solidarity and social care, and the defence of the livelihoods of the most underprivileged sectors of society. It has promoted measures to make sure that the gains of technological improvements would be equally shared, instead of resulting in job losses and economic dislocation. In the era of digital oligopoly, the left must fight for egalitarian taxation and boost the power of organised labour, so that productivity gains finally translate into wage increases and progress in living standards.

The adoption of the framework of a 'socialism that protects' implies a rethinking of the left's attitude towards modernisation and technological transformation. In recent years, various voices on the left have argued that the dizzying pace of technological innovation may hasten the end of capitalism and the beginning of a more just order. This is the position associated with the proponents of the post-capitalist 'accelerationism' articulated by authors such as Nick Srnicek, Paul Mason and Aaron Bastani.[3] The return to an emphasis on the development of productive forces found in Marx and Lenin, where technical progress was seen as a

3   Paul Mason, *Postcapitalism: A Guide to Our Future* (London: Macmillan, 2016); Nick Srnicek and Alex Williams, *Inventing the Future: Postcapitalism and a World without Work* (London: Verso, 2015); Aaron Bastani, *Fully Automated Luxury Communism* (London: Verso, 2019).

precondition of communist revolution, betrays a Promethean optimism at odds with the current historical predicament. If accelerationism in the mid-2010s represented a welcome antidote to the failure of imagination of the left in recent decades, and its consequent inability to look beyond the impoverished landscape of the present, today it risks having little to offer those who find themselves displaced by technology or environmental crisis.

The present historical conjuncture requires a different political imaginary – one that calls for the reassertion of the primacy of 'inhabitation' over 'improvement', in Karl Polanyi's terms. From a structural standpoint, the current landscape is defined by deceleration and the re-territorialisation of capitalist accumulation, which in turn brings into question the idea that capitalism is reaching some sort of escape velocity. This condition does not necessarily bode ill for the left. In many circumstances, socialist possibilities have emerged precisely in conditions of capitalist crisis and depression, in moments of inertia, and of rebellion against forced modernisation. Revolutions are not necessarily products of the acceleration of capitalism's productive forces, as Gramsci noted in his famous description of the Russian Revolution as a 'revolution against *Capital*.'[4] Walter Benjamin famously pursued this line even further, saying that, while Marx saw revolutions as the 'locomotive of world history', they often resembled something else: 'the act by which the human race traveling in the train applies the emergency brake.'[5] This perspective is made particularly relevant by the nature of contemporary 'externalised' capitalism, resistance to which involves creating frictions to check the speed of global flows.

Today, it is not only technology and the threat of automation that are seen as dangers that call for social resistance and protection by a new state Leviathan, but also the global forces of international commerce, finance and tourism. New technologies have created exposure without

---

4    Antonio Gramsci, *Gramsci: Pre-Prison Writings*, ed. Richard Bellamy, transl. Virginia Cox (Cambridge: Cambridge University Press, 1994), p. 41.

5    W. Benjamin, *Walter Benjamin: Selected Writings*, 4 vols, ed. Michael W. Jennings (Cambridge, MA: Belknap/Harvard University Press, 2003), Volume 4, p. 402. On this question it is relevant to read the critical work of Benjamin Noys on accelerationism. Benjamin Noys, *Malign Velocities: Accelerationism and Capitalism* (Winchester, UK: Zero Books, 2014).

producing significant social improvements, and productivity growth.[6] A protective socialism should depart from the idea of modernisation for modernisation's sake dear to neoliberals. Technological transformation and modernisation must be 'domesticated', and can be beneficial only insofar as they are embedded in social institutions and accompanied by protective mechanisms that can make societies capable of absorbing change.

The primacy of protection in contemporary politics does not foreclose the possibility of an open society, in the general sense of a society that prizes diversity, tolerance and international dialogue. In fact, it is only by guaranteeing social protection – by fostering a minimum sense of security and constructing a shield against the great variety of threats that have become ever more apparent – that authentic openness can be fostered. If people are left wholly exposed to dangers, given no defence against the intrasiveness of open markets, and not provided with the necessary means of sustenance to engage with the condition of an ever more complex society, it is obvious that one of their responses will be in the form of retreat offered by the nationalist right. This is certainly an age of fear; but, in the fight against common threats, we may also find the root of a new sense of unity, and a credible hope grounded in unblinking realism.

## Building the Socialist Republic

The reassertion of the primacy of politics over economics calls for a reconstruction of state capacity and the connected extension of democratic control. As this book has shown, the baptism of fire of the neoliberal era consisted in the demolition of the social-democratic consensus, and of the Keynesian institutions exerting control over capital movement and fluctuations in exchange rates and wages that stabilised capitalism after World War II, reducing public authorities to mere facilitators and guardians of the market economy. From the perspective of the current health and climate crises, these positions appear in retrospect to have been shockingly reckless. Neoliberalism has proved ineffective during the pandemic – the global market manifestly unable to provide

6   Aaron Benanav, *Automation and the Future of Work* (London: Verso, 2020).

people with ventilators and face masks when their supply was a matter of life and death – and governments have had to step in to solve collective problems that could not be addressed by private initiative. The challenges ahead call for a renewal of the state's ability to mobilise vast resources in order to address societal challenges and threats; for investment in public housing, welfare support, educational facilities, and neighbourhood-based initiatives for enabling social cohesion and reducing inequality.

This is particularly true in the case of climate change policies, where generational upheaval has combined with the catastrophic wildfires in Australia and California in 2020 to give a new urgency to the priority of environmental protection. Major coastal defences, massive projects to decarbonise energy production, the overhauling of transportation and food systems, and the development and distribution of vaccines are all likely in the coming years to demand unprecedented levels of collective mobilisation and government intervention.

The emergence of post-neoliberal protective statism is bound to raise new political dilemmas and antagonisms. It should always be remembered that the return of state interventionism and developmentalism is not necessarily a path towards progress. Elitist forces will no doubt seek to use it merely to buttress an unequal social system. As we have seen, many governments have pumped billions of dollars into capitalist companies during the Covid crisis, in a farcical recapitulation of the 'socialism for the bankers' that emerged in 2008. Even when governments must rescue failing companies, liberal pundits insist that the state should be kept off company boards, so as to allow the mystical processes of the market to unfold unmolested. The 2020s may see the emergence of a type of state-backed monopoly capitalism in which the power of government is used as a lifejacket enabling large corporations and private interests to escape the imperative of redistribution. What is certain is that the pandemic has increased the stability of authoritarian governments that have succeeded in providing for the needs of their people. What is more, it would be a mistake to think that neoliberalism in any form will disappear. In fact, we are likely to see growing resistance from neoliberals to rising statism and pressure to implement austerity measures as soon as the worst of the pandemic ends, which would have disastrous consequences for workers and citizens.

To forestall the risk of a regressive and authoritarian statism as well as the cyclical return of the neoliberal demand for austerity, the left should direct an activist state towards the goal of the reconstruction of a truly mixed economy, in which a strong government sector and indicative planning might enable a robust welfare state that attends to the needs of disadvantaged sectors in society – including people living in depressed non-urban areas, those faced with wage inequality, and anyone struggling with precarity and unemployment (in particular women, minorities and youth). The current liberal realignment seen in the US, and to a lesser extent in the EU (for example, as exemplified by Mario Draghi's 'good debt' in the context of the European recovery plan), calls for a rethinking of the left's strategy. Bidenomics acknowledges the magnitude of present social and environmental threats. But like FDR and Keynes a century before him, he fundamentally aims to mend the capitalist system and restore its credibility. The challenge ahead lies in moving beyond the left's criticism of neoliberal austerity to create a new focus on socialist demands for public ownership, workplace democracy and the redistribution of private wealth. The disbursement of vast public resources should be accompanied by real control over decisions about spending. An activist state cannot merely be the saviour of private enterprise, making up for yet another market failure, saddling the public with more debt and no power in return. The new protectivist state must take back control over strategic assets in such a way as to meet the requirements of the ecological transition. Large corporations, whose power now often exceeds that of nation-states themselves, must be broken up and, where feasible, nationalised, and wealthy estates must once again be made subject to punitive taxation. No economy, no society, should ever again be subjected so helplessly to the whims of ideological proprietarianism and its lingering institutions.

One of the most remarkable phenomena of our era is the return of long-discredited state planning. As we have seen, planning in any form was seen by neoliberals as heretical, since it strove to impose a direction upon the free market, which was axiomatically assumed to embody superior wisdom in the allocation of resources. But justified criticism of mandatory planning in a command economy also ended up discrediting more moderate forms of indicative planning, which involve the setting of targets and strict regulations, and until the 1980s were often used in mixed economies. State planning is of paramount importance in the ecological transition, in which market mechanisms such as carbon trading have failed to limit emissions, while most industrial corporations have proved themselves incapable of strategic and long-term thinking. The coronavirus crisis has made clear the indispensable role of the state in marshalling resources in times of emergency. What has proved necessary during this crisis will become permanent – namely, swift government intervention to protect society from pervasive risk. Ultimately, no true democracy worthy of the name can exist without the recovery by the state of its capacity to plot an economic course.

Progressives should also guard against the reinvigoration of state power leading to a redoubled technocratic society. The bureaucratic turn of socialism, and the concomitant evolution of Western social-democracy into technocracy, ultimately conspired to discredit both ideological tendencies, in particular among the working class. To avoid the trap represented by experts and technocrats ruling over a population kept in ignorance, new democratic institutions and procedures have to be implemented; all important economic decisions have to become once again the product of collective deliberation and democratic debate. Tools that might assist in reasserting both state and popular sovereignty range from legislation favourable to trade unions – whose decline has led to wage stagnation and a contraction of labour's share of economic output – to the participation of employees on company boards and the fostering of co-operatives for small and medium-sized businesses. Only a move beyond the neoliberal view of the economy and society as open-ended, of history as solely a product of chance and the invisible hand of the market, and of the state as impermeable to the popular will can ensure the establishment of a democratic socialism that delivers protection to citizens while also granting them a meaningful degree of control.

## Re-shoring Politics

A key theme of this book has been the need to come to terms with the emplaced and territorial nature of political communities, and to take heed of the sense of dislocation that has been generated by neoliberal globalisation. One realisation that has accompanied the Great Recoil is that geography matters, and that political identity can only be ignored at one's peril. For too long, cosmopolitan liberals and radical leftists dabbled in fantasies of a de-territorialised global democracy – a world without borders. It is essential to accept that there is such a thing as the power of place, and to accommodate the related right of territorially defined communities to exercise control over their destiny. Neoliberal externalisation has led to a wrenching away of power from the levels of immediate social identification, starting at the local and national scales. The physical distancing of political decisions from citizens' direct experience and technocratic domination are the source of the widespread perception of lack of democratic control. This dislocation constitutes the wound in which the nationalist right festers, proposing narratives of betrayal and resentment, often informed by conspiracy theories in which a global new world order is working tirelessly against the rights and desires of nations.

By framing itself as being on the side of the nation, the right has often managed to manoeuvre the left into the trap of appearing to be in favour of globalisation – an increasingly losing proposition and an absurd one given that it was the left that first developed a critique of globalisation. Any opposition to nationalism that hopes to be electorally competitive must come to terms with the existence of national identity and its role in defining membership of a polity. This is the spirit of the democratic patriotism I advocate. In contrast to Habermas's constitutional patriotism, what this implies is not abstract adherence to a common institutional framework, but a recognition that democracy is always grounded in specific sites of identification – the nation, one of the most important innovations of modernity, still constituting the preeminent site. In accordance with Giuseppe Mazzini's insights, democratic patriotism means the anchoring of socialist goals of equality and freedom in specific locations, customs and idioms, cognisant of the fact that an authentic universalism can only be attained by means of a voyage through particularism.

This approach also provides a framework to rethink the left's electoral strategy and the battle for consensus. In recent years socialists have been strongly undermined by overidentification with metropolitan centres and the progressive urban middle class. An inability to reach beyond progressive urban electorates and middle-class bubbles has been a major factor in recent left defeats. Some narratives of left *embourgeoisement* are exaggerated, and, as we have seen, the left's social bloc also comprises the service precariat, which faces some of the most intolerable working conditions and particularly poor pay. However, it is clear that progressives have significant difficulty in taking the grievances of non-urban voters seriously – particularly those of industrial workers in provincial areas. It is essential that the socialist left develops policies addressing the concerns of peri-urban and ex-urban communities that have found themselves most sharply subject to the destructive effects of globalisation. But achieving this goal will entail more than rhetorical appeals. It will require major investments in regional development in depressed areas, as well as vigorous organisational efforts in peripheral areas, too long considered unwinnable for the left.

While a progressive reclaiming of patriotism is necessary to deal with the crisis of globalisation, it should never be used as a means to justify a conservative turn, as it has with Labour under Keir Starmer. As I have argued, the much-debated 'cultural backlash' mobilised by the nationalist right, and the wave of racism, bigotry and outright fascism infecting the public sphere, can only be read through the prism of the global economic downturn.[7] It is the loss of sovereignty, protection and control, the shrinking of employment opportunities and the cuts to public services suffered after the Great Recession that have made declining cities and communities more amenable to the message of national populism, which breeds a culture of aggressive white nativism that scapegoats immigrants for the crisis of Western identity. The only way to win over this electorate is by attacking the core of the problem: the vulnerability and precariousness that have been engendered by rapid and uncontrolled globalisation and technological change. This means restoring jobs and dignity, investing in public housing and education, and refocusing government spending so as to boost the recovery of deprived communities.

Democratic patriotism and provincial socialism are the translation in the realm of political strategy for what Karl Polanyi described as a process of re-internalisation pursued by societies attacked by capitalist rapacity. Under present circumstances, re-internalisation means the 're-shoring' of politics and the recovery of democratic power, bringing back under public control a range of economic activities that are now

---

7   P. Norris and R. Inglehart, *Cultural Backlash: Trump, Brexit, and Authoritarian Populism* (Cambridge: Cambridge University Press, 2019).

left to the whims of the global market. This may seem like a voluntarist dream – or worse, a nostalgic yearning for the sense of authenticity conferred by notions such as 'the local', or 'the national'. But it is justified by the dynamics of social identity, and it has the potential to leverage vigorous economic and geopolitical tendencies emerging amid the crisis of globalisation. The energy transition will require a re-localisation of many activities, from food production to the supply of energy, whose current operation around the planet is a major contributor to unsustainability. Capitalism itself is increasingly turning towards re-localisation in the name of 'resilience'. Many among the capitalist class have become aware that the model of neoliberal externalisation poses serious risks to their operations, and that long and complex supply chains are vulnerable to disruption. This realisation is reflected in the currently fashionable talk within business circles of re-shoring, on-shoring and farm-shoring. The trend towards re-localisation, and regional rather than global integration, constitutes a historic opportunity to reassert political control over economic processes for the benefit of the social majority.

The social republic we should work towards should not be imagined as an autarchic island. We should not dabble in isolationist fantasies, which all too often translate into either a new imperialism or a subservience to global hegemons, as the case of post-Brexit Britain, which henceforward will be more dependent on the fitful goodwill of the US, clearly illustrates. A restoration of the primacy of popular sovereignty and democracy does not imply an imaginary exit from international relations. No 'populism in one country' can last for long, and no nation can square up on its own either to the power of multinational corporations or to that of the great powers among modern nations. Furthermore, it should always be borne in mind that the recovery of popular sovereignty means first and foremost an internal recovery and redistribution of power, challenging national capitalist elites that constitute the main obstacle to real democracy and the local relays of the global market. Too often, international conflict and chauvinism has been used as a means to defuse internal class conflicts. 'Turning back to itself', in accordance with the direction of travel of the Great Recoil, society is forced to look at itself in the mirror, accepting responsibility for its own problems, rather than looking for an external Other to blame for its ills.

In the coming years, these themes are likely to reverberate in political debates. We are by now aware that no real return to pre-Covid-19 normality will ever be possible and we should also abandon the misguided hope for the infinite growth of neoliberal globalisation. The hazards that may lie ahead include a Greater Depression engulfing the world economy and producing mass despair; an environmental catastrophe such as the rapid thawing of the Siberian permafrost; a serious social strife escalating into political violence; and possibly even geopolitical confrontation escalating into a new cold war between the United States and China. Fears of ecological collapse compounded by the reality of economic decline, geopolitical chaos and social uncertainty are likely to further exacerbate social conflicts, triggering ideological and geopolitical confrontation. Given the magnitude of impending dangers – some of which have truly catastrophic implications – the demand for security and safety, and the imperative of returning power to the state in the name of the people, is likely to endure. Only a post-pandemic left informed by a progressive politics of social and environmental protection – a protective socialism that champions popular sovereignty and democratic control – can hope to neutralise the narrative of the nationalist right and channel the social fear and political anxiety of the Great Recoil towards the construction of a safer and more egalitarian future.

# Index

Abbé Sieyès, 231
accelerationism, 117, 254–5
Agamben, Giorgio, 74, 129
agoraphobia, 5, 8, 14, 45, 64–5, 93,
    95, 109, 113, 141,147, 170, 224
    See also exposure, globalisation
al-Qaeda, 178
Amazon, 46, 57, 153, 164
    and tax avoidance, 186
    and trade unions, 164
    effect on local economy, 159, 222
    Turk, 66
    workers, 153, 185, 188
Andic, Isak, 183
anti-intellectualism, 106, 192
    See also experts
anti-semitism, 189, 239
Apple, 46, 55,57
Aquinas, Thomas, 73
Ardern, Jacinda, 34
Arendt, Hannah, 161, 238–9
Aristotle, 3, 71, 126, 136–8
Arnault, Bernard, 182

Arrighi, Giovanni, 45, 53n22
ASEAN Free Trade Agreement
    (AFTA), 47
Asian financial crisis (1997), 59
austerity, 2, 11, 32n25, 44, 51, 159,
    192, 201, 218, 244–5, 257–8
autarchy, 112, 136, 138, 140, 234, 262
autonomy, 10, 33, 48, 66, 70, 77, 92,
    123, 126, 136–8, 143
    individual, 205
    monetary, 216
    national, 140–1, 228, 240, 247–8
    of the political, 202

Bannon, Steve, 24, 107, 190
Bastani, Aaron, 254
Bauer, Otto, 229
Bauman, Zygmunt, 141
Bebel, August, 164–5
Beck, Ulrich, 9, 10n13
Bello, Walden, 213
Benjamin, Walter, 255
Berlinguer, Enrico, 146

Bezos, Jeff, 51, 182–3, 185–6

Biden, Joe, 3, 6, 33, 104, 107, 149, 164, 220

Bidenomics, 33, 197, 213, 258

Black Lives Matter, 86, 104, 172, 197

Blair, Anthony, 19, 30, 88, 251, 254

Blakeley, Grace, 23, 88n69, 135, 184, 197, 200, 218n46

Blum, Léon, 37

Bodin, Jean, 72–3

Bolsonaro, Jair, 13, 22, 26, 93, 225

Boltanski, Luc, 55

Böhm, Franz, 82

bolshevism, 202

borders, 41–3, 72–5, 97, 115, 121, 139–40, 172, 181, 204, 227, 230–1, 240–1

Borger, Julian, 200

Bourdieu, Pierre, 163

Branson, Richard, 182

Braudel, Fernard, 45

Bregman, Rutger, 184

Breitbart, 110

Bretton Woods Agreement, 46–8, 51, 57

Brexit, 41, 120, 131–2, 148, 198, 209, 228, 246, 262

Brexiteers, 9, 120, 155

See also Leave campaign.

Brexit Party, 97

Brown, Gordon, 89

Brown, Wendy, 181

bureaucracy, 80, 121–4, 135

See also technocracy

Bush, Jeb, 191

Calhoun, Craig, 227

Camus, Renaud, 180

capitalism, 1, 5, 7, 10, 14, 31, 38, 50, 52–55, 58–9, 65–6, 79, 88, 112–3, 159, 210, 254–6, 262

and escapism, 141, 255

anti-capitalism, 189–90

digital, 10, 12, 188

extractivist, 99, 222

global, 167, 214

state capitalism, 221

state monopoly capitalism, 197, 212

uncontrolled, 117–9, 249

See also neoliberalism

Capitol Hill riots (6 January 2021), 25, 28, 239

care, 96, 119, 251, 254

childcare, 107, 219

healthcare, 12, 16, 43, 107, 168, 200, 205, 209

politics of, 105–7, 109

workers, 97, 152, 178

caste (political elite), 170, 190–1

CasaPound, 29

Chang, Ha-Joon, 214

Chávez, Hugo, 23

Chiapello, Eve, 55

China, 47, 51, 53–4, 91, 105, 111, 116, 122, 140, 167, 198, 208–9, 213, 215, 225, 228, 244, 246, 248, 263

Cicero, Marcus Tullius, 71, 101, 203

class, 22, 25, 27, 38–40, 60, 118–9, 142, 144–7, 161–3,165–6, 170, 180–2, 188, 192, 200–1, 204, 206, 212, 235–7, 241, 251, 253–4, 259, 262

blocs, 146–7

déclassement, 25, 158

fragmentation, 164
*See also* middle class, trade unions, working class
climate change, 10, 44, 52, 64, 97, 103, 105 107–10, 134, 196, 201, 216, 220, 245, 253, 257, 263
Clinton, Bill, 19, 33, 48, 88, 254
Clinton, Hillary, 31, 162
Colau Ada, 70, 237
complex systems theory, 139–40
Confucius, 116, 204
Conservative Party, 31, 149
conservatism, 19, 27, 39
    cultural, 63, 166
    fiscal, 198
conspiracy theories, 28–9, 98, 106, 121, 129, 131, 142, 180, 191, 260
Conte, Antonio, 132
control, 10–11, 13–5, 21, 38, 40–3, 72, 120–1, 123–5, 156, 209, 217, 234, 243
    and protection, 101, 110, 114, 117
    and sovereignty, 72, 74–5, 78–81, 84, 90, 92, 94
    as autonomy, 135–8
    as domination, 126–9
    as direction, 130–4
    democratic, 129, 141, 170, 180, 193–4, 218, 221–3, 244, 247, 253, 256–61
    etymology of, 124–5
    lack of, 163, 187 190
    loss of control due to globalisation, 57–9, 62, 65–6, 206
    mania, 142
    technological dimension of,

132–3
Corbyn, Jeremy, 2, 6, 13, 20, 24, 30–1, 98, 145, 162, 182, 184, 191, 226, 253
coronavirus,
    *See* Covid-19
corruption, 171, 182, 192–3
cosmopolitanism, 12, 16, 224–5, 233, 236
Covid-19, 2, 4, 8, 10, 26, 29, 34, 38, 43, 44, 81, 106–7, 118, 125, 134, 176, 183, 196, 199
    economic crisis, 19, 29, 34, 51
    masks, 9–10, 82, 106
    vaccine, 125, 199, 223, 228
Crouch, Colin, 91, 133
Cummings, Dominic, 69
cybernetics, 123, 130
Dante Alighieri, 132
Darré, Richard Walther, 230
Da Silva, Luis Iñacio Lula, 23
Debray, Régis, 139
De Benoist, Alain, 179
Deleuze, Gilles, 102, 125
Deliveroo, 153
De Magistris, Luigi, 237
democracy, 11, 23, 28, 41, 59, 88, 120–4, 129, 169, 206, 213, 226–7, 230, 233–4, 246–7, 258–62
    and control, 120–2, 124, 126, 133–5, 141, 187, 201
    and sovereignty, 76–78, 89–93
    and the populist right, 28, 33
    illiberal, 28–9
    participatory, 163
    post-democracy, 91
    territorial, 9, 40, 74

Democratic Party (US), 23, 33, 88,
    104, 191
Deneen, Patrick, 35
developmentalism, 196
Di Battista, Alessandro, 69
digital economy, 61, 66, 161
    oligopolies, 170, 222
    See also specific companies,
        extractivism, gig economy
Donne, John, 138
Draghi, Mario, 258

Eatwell, Roger, 148, 193
elite, 7, 23, 70, 135, 142, 252
    anti-elitism, 20–2, 29, 39, 170, 182,
        191
    economic, 57, 135, 157, 178, 182,
        184, 189, 194, 262
    cultural, 15, 170, 192, 192
    metropolitan, 63
    political, 182, 190, 193
    See also experts
endopolitics, 4, 7, 66–8, 93, 122, 144, 251
    See also re-internalisation
Engels, Friedrich, 202, 213, 22,
        229, 235
    Erinnerung, 5–6, 67, 249
    Eucken, Walter, 82
    European Central Bank (ECB),
        138, 217, 244
    European Union (EU), 47, 52, 54, 69,
        90, 98, 112, 167, 179, 242–3, 258
    Evola, Julius, 75
    exit (as political strategy), 245–6
    exopolitics, 4, 7, 54
    experts, 29, 59, 91, 131–2, 143,
        161, 182, 191, 259
    See also elite

exposure, 12–3, 45, 58, 64–6, 91, 99,
        113–4, 147, 156, 167, 198, 205,
        210, 228, 237, 250–1, 255
externalisation, 5, 8, 13, 45, 54–9,
        60–3, 65–6, 93, 99, 141, 194,
        260, 262
    offshoring, 54–6, 58–6, 154, 207
    outsourcing, 13, 55–8
    See also exopolitics
Extinction Rebellion, 109
extractivism, 12, 99, 222

Facebook, 46, 57, 222
Farage, Nigel, 97, 172, 225
fascism, 18, 38, 114, 161, 180, 201–2,
        261
    right-wing populism as, 27–28
fear, 8, 13, 15, 41, 48, 65, 100–5, 110,
        145, 180, 192, 253, 256, 263
    common, 103
    mutual, 104
    of decline, 163, 179
    of migrants, 118
Fidesz, 171
finance, 48, 88, 121, 199–200, 205,
        217–8, 221–2
    and externalisation, 57–8
Five Star Movement, 32, 69, 153, 170,
        190–1, 193
flat tax, 212
Floyd, George, 104
Fordism, 153, 155
Forza Nuova, 28
Foucault, Michel, 74, 82–3, 125, 133
Frank, Thomas, 24, 63
Fraser, Nancy, 36, 86
free trade, 19, 27, 33, 36, 46–7, 83, 92,
        111, 198, 207–9, 212–4, 227

*See also* globalisation

French revolution, 72, 76, 230

Friedman, Milton, 18, 38, 50, 71, 79, 82, 84–7, 89–90, 134, 218n47

Friedman, Thomas L., 50

Front National, 149–50, 173, 179

Fukuyama, Francis, 49

Fusaro, Diego, 179

Galston, William A., 61

Ganesh, Janan, 196

Garibaldi, Giuseppe, 233

Gates, Bill, 183

Gellner, Ernest, 230n9

Giddens, Anthony, 88, 159n37

gig economy, 153, 164, 188–9

Gilets Jaunes, 6, 20, 24, 62, 70, 116

Glass-Steagall act, 47–8

globalisation, 4–9, 12–3, 16, 19, 25, 34–5, 42–4, 49–54, 57, 62–8, 76, 88, 93, 97, 120–1, 136, 139–40, 171, 207–9, 211–7, 224–7, 247, 253, 259, 260–3

de-globalisation, 44, 52, 213

global supply chains, 58, 262

global trade, 44–7, 58, 66, 85, 90, 112, 121, 139, 200, 206, 210, 214–6, 224

Goodhart, David, 63–4

Goodwin, Matthew, 148, 193

Google, 57, 222

Gramsci, Antonio, 2, 3, 18, 165, 202–3, 235–6, 255

Great Barrington Declaration, 129

Great Depression (1930s), 19, 47, 51, 165, 200

Great Recession (2008–11), 2, 19, 51, 62, 158, 175, 261

2008 financial crisis, 19, 30, 44, 51, 91, 185, 199, 200, 217, 227

Green New Deal, 220

Greenspan, Alan, 91

Grillo, Beppe, 31–2, 193

Guilly, Cristophe, 62

Habermas, Jürgen, 128, 234, 260

Habitation, 112–3, 117

*See also* Polanyi, Karl

Haider, Jörg, 173

Harberger, Arnold, 90

Hartz IV labour reforms, 48

Harvey, David, 50

Hayek, Friedrich, 14, 18, 38, 71, 77–80, 84, 86–90, 243n39

Hegel, Georg Wilhelm Friedrich, 67, 84, 127, 133, 203, 231–2, 249

Herder, Johann Gottfried, 230

hinterland, 60–1, 237

*See also* periphery, revenge of geography

Hitler, Adolf, 78, 173, 201, 240

Hobbes, Thomas, 9, 14, 73, 80, 92, 98–100, 102–3, 115–7, 132, 216

Hobsbawm, Eric, 81

Huawei, 208

Icke, David, 142

ideology, 3, 13, 18–9, 21–2, 32, 81, 93, 160, 167, 173, 230, 239, 250

ideological eras, 37–9

Iglesias, Pablo, 69–70, 96–8, 182–4, 225, 236

illiberalism, 28–9

immigration, 26, 36, 64, 75, 106, 109, 129, 166, 171–5

as unifying threat, 170, 175–7,
    179–81, 193
opposition to, 36, 171–8
Indignados (movement), 32, 70
individualism, 10–1, 80–1, 84, 94,
    112, 157, 194, 224, 250, 252
industrial policy, 7, 16, 83, 130, 198,
    201, 206, 210, 218, 220, 244
Inglehart, Ronald, 63
International Labour Organization
    (ILO), 151, 215
International Monetary Fund (IMF),
    32n25, 138, 241
Islamic State of Iraq and the Levant
    (ISIL/ISIS), 97, 178

Jaurés, Jean, 164
John of Salisbury, 73
Johnson, Boris, 92, 120, 179, 191–2,
    198, 209–10
    See also Conservative Party, Brexit
The Joker (film), 184
Jones, Owen, 191

Kaczyński, Jaroslaw, 174
Kaczyński, Lech, 174
Kant, Immanuel, 75, 105, 169, 242
Kaufmann, Eric, 180, 193
Kelton, Stephanie, 217
Keynes, John Maynard, 47, 57, 137–9,
    198, 258
Keynesianism, 6, 19, 27, 51
Kondratieff, Nikolai, 37
Kriesi, Hanspeter, 159
Kuper, Simon, 161

Labour Party (UK), 30, 153, 162,
    261

Laclau, Ernesto, 22n5, 25n15, 39n32,
    40, 144
Laffer curve, 185
La France Insoumise, 6, 30, 111, 162
Lapavitsas, Costas, 217
Leave campaign, 10, 22, 68, 120, 131,
    154, 191
Lega Nord, 32, 97, 146, 148–9, 172–3,
    181, 225
Lenin, Vladimir, 165, 197, 202,
    234–5, 254
Le Pen, Jean-Marie, 173
Le Pen, Marine, 10, 26, 69, 121, 149,
    155–6, 167, 171–2, 176, 209, 225
    See also Front National
Leviathan, 9, 46n4, 73, 100, 102–3,
    115, 201, 217, 255
Levitt, Theodore, 45
libertarianism, 25, 41, 53, 81–2, 94,
    129
Lincoln, Abraham, 174
Lind, Michael, 36, 60
Linera, Álvaro García, 49
Loach, Ken, 152, 189
Luce, Edward, 35
Luhman, Niklas, 139
Luxemburg, Rosa, 235
Lyotard, François, 102

Machiavelli, Niccolò, 14, 81, 98,
    100–1, 110, 117, 126–7, 142, 203
Macron, Emmanuel, 24, 98, 111–2,
    149
Madison, James, 86
Mair, Peter, 144
Mann, Michael, 230
manufacturing, 8, 12, 46, 49, 53–5,
    60–2, 150–4, 207–9, 220

ruralisation of 154–6
*See also* globalisation
Mao, Zedong, 131, 169
Marcuse, Herbert, 5
Marx, Karl, 76n25, 84, 202, 213, 229,
    235, 255
Marxism, 93, 148, 187, 192, 202, 213
Mason, Paul, 162, 254
Mazzini, Giuseppe, 232–4, 242
Mazzucato, Mariana, 198, 220
McDonnell, John, 212
McInnes, Gavin, 28
McLuhan, Marshall, 50
Mélenchon, Jean-Luc, 6, 30, 69, 111,
    212
Menenius Agrippa, 204
mercantilism, 209, 212, 214
meritocracy, 133
    *See also* elite
Merkel, Angela, 34
Michels, Robert, 164
middle class, 12, 156–9, 185, 188–9,
    237, 251, 260
    alliance with working class,
        164–6
    fragility, 156, 158
    global, 225
    old and new, 160, 162
    *See also* socio-cultural
        professionals
Milburn, Keir, 145
Minsky, Hyman, 204
Mirowski, Philip, 87
Modern Monetary Theory (MMT),
    36, 217–8
Molyneux, Stefan, 171
Momentum, 121
monetarism, 19, 27, 36, 48, 217

Monnet, Jean, 242
Montesquieu, 230
Mont Pelerin Society, 87
Moody, Kim, 210
Mosler, Warren, 217
Mouffe, Chantal, 22–3, 144, 169
Mounk, Yascha, 24
Mudde, Cas, 22, 177n23
multinational corporations, 46, 206,
    210, 214, 222, 262
Musk, Elon, 53, 182
Mussolini, Benito, 201

NAFTA (trade treaty), 47, 88, 111
Nagle, Angela, 139
nation, 27, 30–1, 119, 180–1, 193,
    197–9, 227–9, 230, 233
    national liberation, 228–9
    nation-state, 72–4, 76–9
    protective function of, 242–3
nationalisation, 3, 16, 33, 130, 221
nationalism, 24, 28, 36, 83, 167, 213,
    225–8, 230, 233, 252, 260
nationalist right, 42, 118, 121, 252
Nazism, 161, 238, 240
Neel, Phil A., 61
Negri, Antonio, 102
neoliberal centre, 25, 34–6, 158, 161,
    191, 200
neoliberalism, 2–4, 18–21, 24, 35–6,
    63, 81–7, 92–3, 144–5, 186, 193,
    206–7, 249, 256
    progressive, 36, 86
    *See also* globalisation
neo-statism, 2–3, 11, 14, 20–1, 36, 67,
    250–1
    *See also* state, statism
Neumann, Franz, 238–40

New Deal, 37, 65, 154
New Right, 150, 179, 207
Nixon, Richard, 53
Norris, Pippa, 63
North Korea, 140
Norqist, Grover, 82
Nozick, Robert, 82

Obama, Barack, 33, 211
Ocasio-Cortez, Alexandria, 98, 171,
    182–3, 218, 220, 226, 253
Occupy Wall Street, 20, 24, 70, 157,
    188
Oesch, Daniel, 159
Omar, Ilhan, 171, 225
openness, 36–8, 83–7, 138–9, 141,
    247, 250, 254, 256
Orbán, Viktor, 22, 28–9, 75, 171, 176,
    178, 209, 211–2
organic intellectuals, 164–6
Ortega, Amancio, 182–3
Orwell, George, 128, 165, 235–6

Pappas, Takis, 28
Parasite (film), 184, 188
Partido Socialista Obrero Español
    (PSOE), 32–3
Partito Democratico (PD), 23, 25, 32,
    191, 235
patriotism, 192, 224–6, 233–8, 241,
    260–1
    constitutional, 234, 260
    democratic, 234, 269
    difference from nationalism, 235
People's Party (US), 23
periphery, 45, 60–3, 242
    See also hinterland
Peterson, Jordan, 118

Piketty, Thomas, 51n17, 150, 160,
    164, 167
Pim Fortuyn List, 174
Pinochet, Augusto, 90
planning, 77, 78, 85, 101, 121, 222,
    252
    democratic, 133
    indicative, 134, 258
    mandatory, 134
The Platform (film), 194
Plato, 84, 98–101, 105, 115, 117, 131,
    134, 198
    ship of state, 198–9
Podemos, 13, 24–5, 30, 32, 40, 94, 96,
    162, 182, 188, 191, 236
Polanyi, Karl, 3, 5, 7, 65–7, 112–4,
    117, 255, 261
Popper, Karl, 77, 84–6
populism, 2–3, 13, 20–30, 35–6,
    39–49, 67, 133, 144–6, 169, 193
    cultural, 24, 29, 32, 182
    economic, 24, 182, 190
    left-wing, 30–2, 190
    pluto-populism, 190
    right-wing, 29, 171–2, 177–8, 190
post-neoliberalism, 20, 197, 205, 207,
    222, 251, 259
Poujade, Pierre, 160–1
Poulantzas, Nicos, 3, 28, 146n6,
    158–9, 161, 189, 197, 203, 206
precariat, 146, 150–2, 157–8, 178
    See also class
Presley, Ayanna, 171
Preston model, 215
Prodi, Romano, 19, 88
protection, 9–10, 92, 94–5, 97–101,
    147, 159, 243
    and obedience, 115–7

border, 97, 181
economic, 111–2, 150, 195, 212–3,
    218
environmental, 107–9
health, 100, 106
nation as protective structure,
    238–41
social, 114, 167, 205–9, 219
See also protectionism
protectionism, 11, 33, 44, 98–9, 112,
    114, 214
and import-subtitution, 213
and relocatisation, 215
proprietarian, 119, 197, 207, 252
social protectivism, 3, 11, 16, 33,
    96, 112, 118–9, 198, 212, 252
trade, 14, 79, 111, 150, 208–10,
    214
see also mercantilism
public economy, 218, 219, 222
See also state ownership
public services, 51, 90, 112, 150, 167,
    170, 176, 200, 206
See also care
Putin, Vladimir, 29, 225

QAnon, 28, 98, 142, 191

racism, 24, 28, 64, 86, 107, 172–3,
    174, 194, 228, 238
and welfare chauvinism, 178–9
islamophobia, 178
Rand, Ayn, 82, 84
Reagan, Ronald, 19, 27, 38, 48, 87,
    149, 200
Recovery Fund (EU), 134, 186, 228,
    244, 258
Reeves, Richard, 157

regional development, 12, 237, 261
re-internalisation, 5, 7–8, 13, 65, 67,
    143, 236, 261
See also Erinnerung
re-localisation, 156, 262
re-shoring, 59, 207, 262
Remain campaign, 138
republicanism, 3, 69, 76, 80–1, 87,
    136, 193, 224, 234–6
Republican Party (US), 145, 174,
    190–1
revenge of geography, 60, 236, 259,
    260
Riffle, Dan, 183
Rodden, Jonathan A., 154
Rodrik, Dani, 24, 47n7
Romney, Mitt, 149
Roosevelt, Franklin Delano, 37, 65,
    154, 258
Rouban, Luc, 162
Rousseau, Jean-Jacques, 3, 74, 76, 78,
    80–1, 94, 102, 187, 236

Saez, Emmanuel, 211
Salvini, Matteo, 10, 13, 22–3, 26–8,
    32, 93, 97, 121, 131, 146, 155–7,
    172, 175–7, 180, 207, 209, 212,
    225
Sánchez, Pedro, 117
Sanders, Bernie, 31–2, 69, 94, 98, 111,
    153, 162, 182, 187, 191, 212–3,
    218, 253
Sassen, Saskia, 60n36, 89
Scaramucci, Anthony, 145
Schmitt, Carl, 74–6, 127, 145, 169,
    232
Schröder, Gerhard, 19, 30, 88, 254
Schumpeter, Joseph Alois, 159

security, 8–9, 33, 41, 58–9, 69, 82,
    112–6, 118–9, 125, 163, 169–70,
    178, 205, 250–6
  national, 91, 197
  social, 21, 88, 96–8
  state, 198, 203–5
Slobodian, Quinn, 77, 82–3
Smith, Adam, 81
Snyder, Timothy, 29
social democracy, 19, 37, 48, 65, 88,
    229, 254
socialism, 2, 18, 20, 31–3, 37–8, 80,
    85, 114, 129, 221, 229, 251, 259
  conservative, 166
  protective, 12, 252–3, 263
  provincial, 226, 237, 261
socialist left, 30–2, 36, 42, 118–9, 121,
    129, 167, 182, 187, 193, 252, 261
socio-cultural professionals, 161
Socrates, 84
Sorel, George, 164,
Soros, George, 85, 189
Sorry We Missed You (film), 189
sovereignty, 9, 40, 46, 68–71, 94, 128,
    239–42, 247, 252, 262
  energy, 220–1
  food, 40, 58
  monetary, 206, 217
  national, 57, 59, 67, 177, 181, 234,
    240
  neoliberal stance on, 77–83
  popular, 92–4, 241
  technological, 208–9
  territorial, 74–5, 93, 181
  theory of, 71–7
  See also sovereigntyism
sovereigntyism, 70, 77, 93, 94, 140,
    142, 228

Spencer, Richard, 171, 239
Spinelli, Altiero, 242
Stability Pact (EU), 244–5
stagnation, 8, 19, 26, 87, 184
Starmer, Keir, 226, 261
state, 2, 8–10, 35–7, 40–2, 72–4,
    76–8, 84–5, 87–90, 92–4, 101–2,
    98–9, 105, 111–2, 122, 125,
    220–3
  and stability, 204–5
  corporatist, 201
  European Union as a non-state,
    243–4
  in Marxist theory, 202–3
  neoliberal, 81–3
  ownership, 129, 221, 258
  statolatry, 201–2
  statophobia, 128–9
statism, 2–4, 6–9, 38, 67, 112, 196–7,
    200
  authoritarian, 197, 206
  emergency, 200
  protective, 205, 223, 250, 257–8
Stephens, Philip, 68
Stiglitz, Joseph, 217
Stirbois, Jean-Pierre, 178
Streeck, Wolfgang, 89
Suez Canal obstruction (March
    2021), 58

Tawney, R. H., 113
taxation, 16, 27, 30, 34, 36, 45, 185–6,
    254, 258
  tax havens, 57–8, 188
technocracy, 33, 133, 134–6, 222, 259
  see also meritocracy, experts
Thatcher, Margaret, 78, 92
Thiel, Peter, 53, 187

Thompson, E. P., 113
Thucydides trap, 54
TikTok, 208
Tlaib, Rashida, 171
Tobin Tax, 216
Tooze, Adam, 242
trade unions, 48, 114, 155, 164, 213,
    254
Transatlantic Trade and Investment
    Partnership (TTIP), 212
Trans-Pacific Partnership (TPP), 111
Treaty of Westphalia, 73
Trudeau, Justin, 34
Trump, Donald, 54, 60, 63, 69, 75,
    92–3, 97, 102, 104–7, 111,
    115–6, 121, 145–6, 149, 167,
    171–2, 174–6, 190–2, 198,
    207–9, 211–4, 228, 239
Tsipras, Alexis, 31

Uber, 130, 153, 184, 188, 222–3
UK Uncut, 186
United States, 122, 149, 154, 162, 180,
    208, 215
Urry, John, 59

Vico, Giambattista, 75
von der Leyen, Ursula, 98
von Mises, Ludwig, 14, 71, 80–1, 90

Wallerstein, Immanuel, 45
Washington consensus, 19
Weber, Max, 128
Wilders, Geert, 174, 206
working class, 25, 38, 56, 60, 139,
    145–54, 165–7, 178, 192, 229
World Economic Forum (WEF), 5,
    158
World Health Organisation (WHO),
    93
World Trade Organisation (WTO),
    47, 90
Wray, Randall, 217

xenophobia
    See racism
Xiaoping, Deng, 53

Young, Michael, 133

Žižek, Slavoj, 4n5, 34
Zuckerberg, Mark, 182
Zucman, Gabriel, 211